"I first met Chuc[ ] [ ]Ie immediately impressed me, an[ ] [ ]lest and wisest Christians I know. In *Frequently Avoided Questions*, he teams up with Matt Whitlock, and together they offer a unique and invaluable gift: an honest conversation among committed Christian leaders. The content of the book is rich and thoughtful, and its tone exemplifies the kind of honest, direct, and respectful conversations that are so needed—and too rare—in the church today. I highly recommend this book to younger and older leaders alike, and to parents who need to better engage with their sons and daughters as well."

Brian McLaren, author of
A Generous Orthodoxy and *A New Kind of Christian*

"The authors perform a toccata and fugue or, better yet, raga and salsa, on some of the most difficult questions of our day."

Leonard Sweet, Drew Theological School,
George Fox University, preachingplus.com

"Reading *Frequently Avoided Questions* was a necessary spiritual exercise for me. I was surprised at how much of what the authors label 'old school' thinking still resides in my deep places. Their 'new school' probings and challenges point the way to a more vibrant witness to the gospel. I hope this book will be widely read, both by those who have wanted to avoid the questions and by those who have been wounded by many of the older answers."

Richard J. Mouw, president and professor of Christian philosophy,
Fuller Theological Seminary

"There are lots of people asking questions these days; all of life seems to be 'up for grabs,' and answers once convincing no longer satisfy. Nowhere is this more true than in the realm of Christian faith, where a rapidly changing culture seems to be moving farther and farther away from any interest in or connection with Christianity as it has been generally presented. Chuck and Matt do a brilliant job of addressing some provocative questions that seem to be on the lips of society and also many Christians today; the authors break it all down into very basic and manageable issues and address them with solid theological reflection and true missional desire. This is no easy-answer book. In fact, answers aren't necessarily the point; rather the authors wish to challenge the status quo, question the current approaches, and offer some other ways of engaging both Scripture and culture. This book is challenging, provocative, and immensely hopeful. In tackling tricky subjects head-on, the authors demonstrate the continued vitality of Christian faith and the danger of anchoring one's faith in generic prescriptions and knee-jerk reactions."

Barry Taylor, adjunct professor of popular culture and theology,
Fuller Theological Seminary

AN UNCENSORED
DIALOGUE ON FAITH

FREQUENTLY
AVOIDED
QUESTIONS

CHUCK SMITH JR.
MATT WHITLOCK

BakerBooks
Grand Rapids, Michigan

© 2005 by Chuck Smith Jr. and Matt Whitlock

Published by Baker Books
a division of Baker Publishing Group
P.O. Box 6287, Grand Rapids, MI 49516-6287
www.bakerbooks.com

Printed in the United States of America

Library of Congress Cataloging-in-Publication Data
Smith, Chuck, 1951–
    Frequently avoided questions : an uncensored dialogue on faith / Chuck Smith Jr., Matt Whitlock.
        p.   cm.
    Includes bibliographical references.
    ISBN 0-8010-6543-7 (pbk.)
    1. Generation X—Religious life. 2. Christian life. I. Whitlock, Matt, 1978– II. Title.
BV4529.2.S65 2005
230—dc22   ·   2005019703

Unless otherwise indicated, Scripture quotations are taken from the HOLY BIBLE, NEW INTERNATIONAL VERSION®. NIV®. Copyright © 1973, 1978, 1984 by International Bible Society. Used by permission of Zondervan. All rights reserved.

Scripture marked KJV is taken from the King James Version of the Bible.

Scripture marked NASB is taken from the New American Standard Bible®, Copyright © 1960, 1962, 1963, 1968, 1971, 1972, 1973, 1975, 1977, 1995 by The Lockman Foundation. Used by permission.

Scripture marked Phillips is taken from The New Testament in Modern English, revised edition—J. B. Phillips, translator. © J. B. Phillips 1958, 1960, 1972. Used by permission of Macmillan Publishing Co., Inc.

Contents

1. New World, New School   7
2. Why the Bible?   15
3. Do I Have to Go to Church?   39
4. Do I Have to Sell God?   59
5. Can Christianity Be Reduced to Steps or Stages?   71
6. Does God Speak outside the Bible?   91
7. Is Forgiveness Real?   105
8. What Makes the Christian Experience Unique?   123
9. Are Christians the Morality Police?   141
10. Do Good People Go to Hell?   151
11. Does the Bible Contradict Evolution?   171
12. Am I Supposed to Hate the World?   185
13. Are There Gay Christians?   205
14. Is It Wrong to Take a Job in a Bar?   217
15. Where Is Your God?   229

Postscript   245
Notes   249

1

New World, New School

The world has changed. During the past two hundred years, Christians have been challenged to answer many difficult questions posed by science and philosophy. Drawing from common sense, human reason, scientific research, and a plethora of biblical quotations, evangelical scholars responded to the hard questions and by the middle of the twentieth century were able to present a solid, rational defense of the Christian faith. Their answers were passed on to lay Christians through apologetic publications and courses that churches and other Christian organizations taught.

The stable certainties of Western society from the time of the Reformation in the sixteenth century to the late twentieth century have given way to relentless skepticism. The optimistic outlook of Western society, which lasted until about forty years ago, was badly damaged by two world wars, atomic bombs, environmental problems, mass genocide, and terrorism. If today's scholars and philosophers have challenged the old worldview, popular culture has abandoned it altogether. The worldview that is emerging in the West is radically different from that of previous generations, leaving evangelicals well equipped to answer questions no one is asking. Do we know the new questions? Perhaps more important, do we know how to talk to people outside the church so that they will listen?

This book is about the new questions being asked in popular culture. We will go into more detail about these questions, but first we would like to introduce ourselves.

M From Matt

I work with Youth With A Mission (YWAM), which was founded in 1960 for the purpose of involving young people in short-term Christian service around the world. Today there are more than 1,200 YWAM centers in more than 150 nations on every continent. The services YWAM provides include schools, orphanages, food relief, and medical supplies. The primary objectives of YWAM are to demonstrate the love of God to all people of the world, to know God, and to make him known. Though my wife, Elissa, and I have traveled extensively (you'll hear about some of our journeys in these pages), I now serve on the faculty of the University of the Nations in Kailua-Kona, Hawaii.

Chuck and I are from different generations; I am in my twenties and Chuck is in his fifties. It is only reasonable to expect the difference in age to yield differences in our perspectives. But when Chuck and I first got to know each other, I was immediately encouraged by his readiness to validate my thinking and intuition. He was interested in what I had to say about my Christian experience and the objections to God and church that my non-Christian friends have raised. He also affirmed my vision regarding changes or modifications I believe the church needs to make in its culture and in its interaction with the world around it.

My early Christian experience was formed in a context that encouraged me to categorize every thought, action, object, and person in terms of right and wrong, black and white. I have learned since that time, however, that life is much more complex than I was led to believe. Some Christian leaders I have followed assume that the alternative to black-and-white thinking is a compromised shade of gray, but I have been learning the importance of seeing the world in color.

The world of the Bible is certainly colorful. Take grace and mercy, for example. God forgives the guilty, embraces the rebellious child, and gives his unfaithful people a second chance. Even holiness and righteousness—two very important biblical themes—are colorful, and if interpreted as black and white, they degenerate necessarily into rigid forms of legalism. When I was a new believer, I appreciated the security of living in a black-and-white world under the authority of my pastor. But more recently my growth in faith and various encounters around the world have taught me that asking questions is sometimes as important as having the answers, sometimes more important, because answers tend to signal the end of our journey, whereas questions signal its beginning.

From Chuck

In 1975 I began a church called Capo Beach Calvary and have served as its pastor for thirty years. My father, Chuck Smith Sr., led Calvary Chapel of Costa Mesa, a burgeoning "hippie church" in the 1960s and 1970s, through the turbulent and exciting years of the Jesus Movement. The Calvary Chapel network of churches planted across the United States and around the world is typical of other Protestant churches within orthodox evangelicalism. My passion and vocation is teaching Scripture.

Matt and I decided to write this book together because Matt thinks and feels the heartbeat of his generation, and I, while having an appreciation for the concerns of the youth, am very familiar with the established religious culture that so desperately needs to change its thinking and redesign its structure to connect with people outside the church today. We both feel churches need to be more community, less corporate; more merciful, less mean-spirited; more meaningful, less manipulative.

We have not attempted to produce a book of answers. Rather, we hope to familiarize you with the new questions, so you can begin thinking about how you will converse with other people about God and their spiritual journey. If you listen carefully to the world around you, we think you'll hear many people talking about their spiritual hunger. Very few, however, are looking for stock answers to their questions. Most are looking instead for another human who is willing to struggle through their riddles with them.

We will suggest ideas or strategies to help you formulate answers to new questions, but we want to stress that in the eyes of popular culture, which we hope to infiltrate and influence, if you answer a question *dogmatically*, you are already wrong. Discussions regarding truth must take the form of dialogue rather than monologue, participation rather than preaching, and listening as well as speaking; otherwise people will automatically resist everything we say. Fifty years ago Christians were given *the right answers* to all sorts of difficult questions. Nowadays answers must be *designed* for the individual who asks the question. In many cases, the best way to begin constructing an answer is to learn from the person why he has asked the question.

The challenge facing Christians in popular culture is to present (or *re*present) Jesus in a way that does not immediately shut off communication but opens doors to conversation, discussion, and meaningful debate. If we learn to express our ideas and beliefs in ways that generate interest and dialogue, perhaps providing tentative solutions to objections rather than dogmatic assertions, and as we listen carefully to the ideas and viewpoints of others, reshaping and enlarging our response accordingly, we are likely to become better communicators of God's truth (not to mention better representatives of Jesus Christ). For reasons we will discuss later, people who come to faith in the next two or three decades will need an open-ended approach to their ongoing questions, concerns, doubts, and objections. In short, the challenge is to shift from the old strategy of telling people what they are supposed to believe to a new strategy of assisting people in the formation of their own faith.

As Matt and I read popular culture today, the spiritual need for discipleship has more to do with relationship than downloading information from one person's mind (or from a manual) into another's. Discipleship has more to do with the transformation of a human life than the transfer of information. If a young Christian is interested in information, there is plenty to be found on the Internet. In fact, in the spirit of democratic consumerism, people can create their own discipleship curriculum from a variety of Christian websites. But within popular culture, people are realizing that life change is the result of relational, communal, and spiritual encounters. Sometimes the person who effects the greatest change in our lives is not the brilliant professor who astounded us with her knowledge, but the penniless orphan in Mexico, Thailand, or Russia who grabbed our leg as if he had found a long-lost parent.

From Both of Us

The format of the book is as follows: Matt introduces the question in each chapter with a real-life story that demonstrates its relevance to contemporary culture. Then Chuck reflects on the question in respect to its theoretical background and current application, highlighting the difference between what we will call the old-school and new-school approaches to popular culture.

An explanation regarding our use of "old school" and "new school" is in order, because we tend to vilify the former and idealize the latter. By "old school" we do not mean liberalism, fundamentalism, or evangelicalism but rather a set of specific attitudes, beliefs, and practices—and the subcultures in which they thrive—that emerged in the modern era and were defined by modern concerns. We use "old school" to refer to a conceptual mode of what is no longer an accurate representation of the biblical God within popular culture and "new school" to refer to the *ideal* solution based on Scripture. Our objective is to emphasize the importance of abandoning old-school errors, which most devout Christians agree needs to be done, and live out the new-school implications.

Based on our experience, we think it is generally true to say new-school thinking is more common among younger people and old-school thinking is more common among older generations. Thus throughout this book we often draw close associations accordingly. For example, we sometimes refer to younger people as representing the new school. But of course life is more complex than that, and we freely admit numerous exceptions. Plenty of baby boomers, for example, subscribe to the new school, and many twentysomethings subscribe to the old school. This is mainly because age is only one among many factors that influence a person's thinking and perspective; others include upbringing, culture, exposure to different cultures, and one's own decisions about what to think and believe.

We intend to test the boundaries of religious subcultures drawn by other generations to see if they still hold today, so we ask for your mercy and patience as you read. If we ask questions that seem outrageous, please bear with us. We do not mean to offend anyone, but we request every reader to think through these issues with us and to look at current Christian assumptions with new and discerning eyes. Rest assured that both of us have the highest regard for the inspiration and authority of the Bible. If we have missed some important fact or overlooked a biblical truth, we would appreciate your comments and corrections—our contact information appears in the last note of the Postscript. The project before us is, in fact, one that the whole church needs to undertake at this critical time in history.

We had a difficult time selecting the questions to include, because the list of possibilities is incredibly long. We hope you find the questions we settled on useful in understanding the emerging worldview of popular culture and in constructing effective responses. As you will notice, questions that were raised two hundred, one hundred, or fifty years ago are asked again today, simply because the old answers have been rejected. The problem does not always lie in the insufficiency of the old answers but in the way they are expressed. We need new answers to deal with some questions, we need new communication skills to deal with others, and above all we need to become great listeners. We may also find that on occasion the best response is to follow Jesus's example of answering a question with a question.

Some of the questions you will find here may sound juvenile or border on sacrilege. You may wonder, *How can they even ask that question when the answer is so obvious?* But we want to stress that though the answer may be obvious to you, it is not obvious to a new generation of Christian young people and is even less obvious to their non-Christian peers. We have been asked these very questions repeatedly over the last five or six years.

If we challenge the way Christians use the Bible in relation to questions or people, it does not mean we lack respect for the Bible but just the opposite. Our love and respect for Scripture is so great that we are willing to correct ourselves (or be corrected) if our use of it is not faithful to its true meaning. In fact, there is a sense in which we violate a text whenever we set out to use it for our own purpose. The Bible does not belong to us as much as it calls us to belong to it, be possessed by it, and submit to its life-forming influence and power.

We hope and pray that this book is helpful to every believer who longs to see popular culture pay greater attention to God and his truth. If older Christians benefit from a close look at new worldview issues and if younger Christians receive affirmation regarding their instincts and vision, we are grateful that God has used us to light the fire.

2

Why the Bible?

The Story of Scripture

When you open the Bible and read the first verse, you are stepping into a story. The introductory words, "In the beginning," hardly prepare you for what follows. You wonder, *Is this a children's book?* But as you read, an exquisite love story unfolds, one that stretches over thousands of years, journeys through sandy deserts, scales desolate mountains, parades through the magnificent capitals of world empires, dips its feet in rivers, and launches ships in the Mediterranean Sea. The story's plot may revolve around human events, but there is still more mystery to it than clear facts. At no point are we told everything that happened in a normal day of a character's life. The story leaves room for wonder, dreaming, and specu-

15

lation. The ancient characters invite you to travel with them, sample their culture, feel their emotions, learn their lessons, and meet their God.

By the time we work our way to the New Testament, we realize that the story of Jesus in the words of theologian N. T. Wright, "presupposes a previous story." Israel's past provides the background for understanding the life and ministry of Jesus. But then the Jesus story in the Gospels "ends with a beginning, as the disciples are sent out to preach to the whole world."[1] The larger story begins with the birth of the universe, includes everyone from Adam and Eve to you and me, and travels all the way to "the end of the age." The story is theirs and mine and yours.

In saying that the story is mine and yours, I mean that God's work in the world did not end with the New Testament but continues on to the present, unfolding in world events, threading itself through all the nations, and somehow working everything into the one grand plot of its divine Author. As we follow the story in time, we discover that God has written his truth into the marrow of every human culture, no matter what their myths, gods, customs, or rituals. I want to tell you about one outrageous example of a people whom God wrote into his story, then relate an experience I had among them.

In 1812 American missionaries Adoniram and Ann Judson landed on the shores of Burma with the hope of introducing many people to the Christian faith. They discovered, however, that the Burman people (the majority ethnic group of the various Burmese nationalities) were very content with their Buddhism and strongly resisted the influence of any other religion. The Judsons lived in Rangoon for six years before they saw one person respond to their message. During those years, they taught themselves the Burmese language, Adoniram wrote a Burmese grammar, and he began translating the New Testament into Burmese.

An impatient member of his mission board in America wrote Judson, criticizing him for his lack of results and asked him what sort of opportunities lay ahead. Judson's response was, "The prospects are *as bright as the promise of God*" (italics added).

Eventually the Judsons discovered a vast ethnic group in Burma, known as the Karen, who stubbornly clung to their animistic belief in evil spirits and had thwarted Burman attempts to convert them to Buddhism. They were very interested, however, in hearing what the white missionaries had to say about God. They had good reason to be interested in the Judsons' message, because of a promise in their own mythology. According to the story, in the beginning, the Karen and their "white brother" were given books. The Karen were negligent and lost their book, so they were plagued by evil spirits whom they were forced to appease. But they were given a promise that one day their white brother would return with his book (in some versions of the story it is a golden book), which would restore them to God, whose name is Y'wa, and free them from the spirits. When white missionaries taught the Karen from the gilded pages of the Bible, whole villages became Christians practically overnight. Within ninety years a quarter of a million people—Karen, Kachin, Lahu, Karenni, and Shan people—entrusted their lives to Jesus Christ.

Fast-forward to World War II

In 1942 and 1943 Japanese and British forces clashed in the Asian nations of Burma and Thailand. Both armies enticed and enlisted the Burmese people to take up arms and join their ranks. The British convinced indigenous people living in the dense, mountainous jungles to use their knowledge and skills to aid their forces against the Japanese invaders. The Karen, Karenni, and Shan proved to be excellent marksmen and had unrivaled abilities to move rapidly through the rough terrain of Southeast Asia.

These people were promised freedom in their own land and under their own government if they agreed to fight against the Japanese. When the war ended, British forces were ordered to return home without having fulfilled their promise to the indigenous soldiers who fought beside them. British soldiers were informed that the locals would have to wage their own war for freedom. But to their credit, many soldiers had come to love the tribesmen who fought alongside them and so left their rifles and other weapons behind to aid them in their battle for independence.

Fast-forward to the Present

Indigenous people suffer today at the merciless hands of a few military generals who have decimated villages, enslaved thousands of men and women, massacred entire communities, and committed countless atrocities. The military government changed Burma's name to Myanmar, but the United States refuses to recognize this name because of the Burmese government's false pretense at democracy and their many human rights violations. The survival of entire people groups in Burma is threatened as army units move through the mountains, raiding one village after another.

Villagers who survive the assaults by running for shelter in the jungle are often permanently separated from their families. Children, who have witnessed the brutal rape of mothers and sisters and the murder of their parents, travel in groups through the mine-infested borders, seeking whatever refuge and food may lie in Thailand. The stories that the tens of thousands of orphans in refugee camps tell are appalling and heartbreaking (estimates of orphans in Thai refugee camps range between 180,000 and 225,000).

Though Thailand is reluctant to admit such refugee camps exist, some compounds provide shelter for as many as 58,000 people. Wedged into small areas of the jungle, there is little hope that anyone now living in the squalor of these camps will ever leave. Burma wants them only as slaves, prostitutes, or corpses. Thailand does not want them coming into their cities and villages, so they are not permitted to leave the camps. The refugees have no citizenship, and no one is fighting for their release. Nongovernmental organizations (NGOs) have provided rations of food for them but offer little help beyond that one necessity. Everyone in the camps, whether child or adult, has spent many nights in forty-degree weather with nothing more than their threadbare clothes or a thin sheet to cover them. They make houses for themselves from bamboo with leaf-thatched roofs, but the feeling of death permeates the camps—not only physical death but the death of pride, the will to live, and joy.

In spite of the great loss, sorrow, and feelings of hopelessness that refugees bring with them to the camps, there are a few bright lights who are committed to improving their situation. One of these undaunted heroes is Reverend Doctor Simon or Pastor Simon, as he is affectionately known to his students. Elissa and I enjoyed the great privilege of staying for two weeks at his seminary campus located in one of the refugee camps. Pastor Simon and his family could have lived in the safety of Baguio, Philippines, where he earned his doctorate from a theological seminary, or in Rangoon, but he chose instead to live among his own displaced people. For several weeks Doctor Simon, with his parents, wife, children, and in-laws, walked through jungles on their way to Thailand. During the day, they used their mosquito nets to catch fish, and at night they slept under the same nets. They built a home for themselves as soon as they arrived in the camp, then went to work ministering to the spiritual needs of the refugees.

When we went to the refugee camp, we adopted Karen-style clothing and names to better identify with the Karen nationals as well as to blend in with their culture. This also helped open the hearts of those in the camp to our presence. Since foreigners are not allowed to stay in the camps for extended periods of time (we were not even permitted to visit some camps), we did not leave the camp until we had completed our two weeks of teaching.

In his camp Doctor Simon works with a Christian seminary that has an enrollment of approximately five hundred students. Some have risked their lives to escape one camp to come and study in his school. Most of the professors fly to Thailand from Nagaland, India, and teach for up to three months at a time. Unlike the rest of the camp, the seminary is a place that vibrates with life, hope, and lots of laughter. During the two weeks we taught in the seminary, we had many unforgettable experiences, but there was one that stands out beyond all the rest.

Our team had the privilege of bonding with students as we enjoyed mealtimes together and slept at night in their huts.

The informal conversations we shared with them had a great impact on us. Not only did the students teach us their songs and the rules of their games but they opened their lives to us in the stories they told.

Perhaps because we lived among them for so many days or because we are the same age as the students or because younger Asians have been greatly influenced by Western culture, when their seniors were not present, they treated us like peers. They became less formal around us than is expected from Asian cultures. The more time we spent with them, the more they opened their hearts to us and revealed their deep hunger for the Bible knowledge we had only recently learned ourselves. They felt free with us to raise questions they might not ask in an ordinary classroom situation.

On the first day of the second week of our course on inductive Bible study methods, I was passing out materials to assist the students in our practical application "lab" time. I asked if anyone had questions before we got underway—I assumed some of them might be curious about the particular method of Bible study that we had covered thus far. Never in my wildest dreams could I have anticipated the first question raised. Nor could I have prepared myself to give an answer.

Like the other female students, the questioner was petite. There was nothing in her appearance to make her stand out, and I cannot remember seeing her again after the day she posed her question. "Is it okay," she asked, "for a pastor to defend his church when the Burmese soldiers come into our village? Does God allow us to kill them like they kill us?" I became stone. Even if I had been working on that question for a year, I would not have had the theological insight to give her a confident answer. She was not asking about "just war" in a theoretical context. She was not describing a hypothetical or unlikely situation. I sat there staring at her for such a long time that she started to repeat the question, but I interrupted her and explained that I had heard her question and was thinking about the best way to answer. Should I tell her to turn the other cheek, to love her enemies? Who knows how many innocent villagers were dying in the jungles while I hesitated during that tense silence?

A young man named Lehtie stood up and politely asked if he could answer the question. I thought, *Hurray! I'm rescued.* Lehtie turned to the young woman and said, "No, we are not to fight."

I was shocked. *Are you kidding me?* I thought. *Those Burman soldiers are going to destroy you and your family. It's not a matter of killing but of defending.* Lehtie continued, "We are not fighting for a kingdom here on earth. We are free. We are free because we fight for a kingdom that is not of this world." He grabbed the flesh of his skinny arm and said, "They can beat, hurt, and kill this. They can hold us in this camp, but they cannot take what is in our hearts. And because of that, we are free."

Around the room, heads were nodding in agreement as Lehtie sat down. They understood what he was saying. They were at peace. No arguments or debates, just peace. From then on I noticed the pervasiveness of peace, that it was everywhere throughout their camp. Peace, when they told their stories of horror. Peace, when they awoke at four in the morning to cook their rations. Peace, when the rain and humidity of the dense forest mildewed their clothes and ruined their homes. Peace, because they were free.

I realize there are different ways for Christians to think about Lehtie's response to the question, and there are situations in which it is immoral for a believer to sit by and do nothing when others are being marched off to death (see Prov. 24:11–12). As a friend of mine says, "Sometimes it's not about *you*. If you are attacked, you have the prerogative to turn the other cheek, but if someone else is being attacked, say, a thirteen-year-old girl by a rapist, then you are bound by the love of Christ to risk your own safety and do something." But my point is that here was Lehtie, a kid with no family, a teenager in a refugee camp, yet he had visions, dreams, and hopes larger than those of most of the comparatively wealthy and free youth I knew back home. He had a depth of understanding, a firm resolve, a radical commitment to the teaching of Christ and the kingdom of God. He had found a place for his people in the story.

For Lehtie the Bible is not a book of theological propositions to help him win debates. Rather, it is a story of hope, a story of rags to riches, where the useless become useful, the weak are made strong, the small become great, and God comes before a person's nationality and even before his own body. Lehtie was convinced God had his people in mind before the world began. I cannot say the Bible has had the same impact on my life. But I learned from Lehtie that the story of the Scriptures embraces all cultures of all time. Our lives are bound together by the story in the text, even though we live on opposite sides of the world and in radically different situations. We have been made family by the power of the story.

Is it possible for us to begin here, with the Bible as story? I have discovered that many people in my own culture are desperate to know the story. They are looking everywhere for it. Some people tell us there is no universal story, and other people tell us that everyone who does not believe their story is deceived. Have people walked away from faith, disappointed because the Bible lived only in our mouths and not in our hearts, souls, and bodies as a vital story? If people have been looking for their place in God's story, can they discover it by watching us? Have we discovered our global and individual identity in the story—our solidarity, our hope, our resources to live the story from day to day? Is it possible for us to show people with our lives why we choose the Bible over other holy books, rather than trying to tell them by resorting to clichés or religious language (that no one understands and few believe)? People the world over yearn to know their place in the story. How unfortunate if we are sitting on it, dissecting it, debating it, but have not learned how to live it.

The questions I hear people asking about the Bible today are, "What makes the Bible better than the Upanishads or *Conversations with God*?" "Does anyone still believe in the Bible?" "If I don't want to waste my time on the whole thing, what are the important parts I should read?" "What good does it do me to read the Bible?"

I believe the story of Scripture holds the answer to these questions. Perhaps we can lead people to the story if we answer their questions with questions of our own, such as, "What have you heard about the Bible? What would bolster your confidence in it?" and "What is your most pressing spiritual concern?" Then we can show them with the way we live our lives how the story answers these questions.

The Bible, rather than any other sacred text, brought spiritual liberation to the Karen people and continues to nurture a joyful faith even in desperate circumstances. The Bible continues to feed and inspire them, and their insatiable hunger for its truth makes them eager, diligent, and devoted students. The Book that their white brother brought to them keeps their hope alive, and I believe some day they will have their own nation-state, because a biblically informed imagination coupled with trust in God can literally move mountains.

The Bible in the Modern World

From the time of Constantine until around the seventeenth and eighteenth centuries, the Bible was *the* sacred book for the Western world. Even after the Enlightenment, the Bible continued to influence culture, language, thought, and politics throughout Europe and the New World. Among the founding fathers of the United States, there were many aristocrats, strongly influenced by Enlightenment thinking, who rejected the deity of Jesus and denied the inspiration of Scripture, yet they continued to use biblical language and imagery because of its pervasiveness in culture—there was simply no other language available to them. As for the common person in early America, the Bible still carried the weight of absolute (or near absolute) authority. In fact, it would be difficult to imagine any sort of public communication in the thirteen colonies, written or spoken, that was not influenced by the King James Bible. At that time most Americans were willing to accept arguments for spiritual, religious, and moral issues based on biblical quotations.

Though I may be oversimplifying American religious history, it appears that intellectual doubt regarding the divine inspiration of the Bible in this country produced two major Christian reactions—liberalism and conservatism.[2] Liberalism (also known as modernism) regarded the Bible as a human composition, which reflected ancient ways of thinking about God, humans, and the universe but required scholarly "criticism" to separate history from religious fiction. Biblical "myths" were not discarded but carefully interpreted to discern whether God's "word" was present in them in any meaningful way. Liberalism was laboring under the influence of David Hume, who defined a miracle as a "violation of the laws of nature," and Newtonian physics, which "disproved" violations of natural law. Once the miracles of Scripture were called into question, all of its other historical claims became suspect.

Opposing the liberal view, conservatism produced the doctrine of biblical inerrancy, which held that every story and miracle recounted in its pages were empirical, historical events and that the Bible was scientifically accurate in all of its statements. They concluded that Christians of the true faith should trust the Bible over every objection of science, philosophy, and history. The most vocal and visible advocates of conservatism were the fundamentalists, so named for their commitment to specific, "fundamental" Christian doctrines. Though today's fundamentalists in the media appear to be poorly educated, the theologians who wrote the pamphlet "The Fundamentals: A Testimony to the Truth" were intelligent and articulate. The so-called Princeton School, which included A. Hodge, B. B. Warfield, and at one time J. Gresham Machen, was especially influential in the theological formation of fundamentalism.

We find expressions of old-school thinking and attitudes in both liberalism and fundamentalism. There are liberals (for example, the Jesus Seminar participants) who still believe they are doing the world a service by shredding the Gospels to pieces and keeping alive the quest for the historical Jesus. The new-school liberals, however, describe themselves as "post-liberal" and recognize the exhaustion of a biblical study that tries to pare down the Bible to a few historical facts. Instead, they realize that the spiritual value of Scripture lies in its present configuration, each book appearing the way its author or editors intended, and the only way to get to the meaning of the text is to accept its integrity.

For a number of reasons, including an increase in publications and radio stations as well as grassroots popularity, conservative churches and organizations in North American culture eventually eclipsed liberal theologians, who seemed to be doing little more than pronouncing the death of God. In the 1940s (roughly), fundamentalism gave birth to a movement of greater cultural breadth and influence, which eventually assumed the title evangelicalism. Gradually a number of evangelical scholars demonstrated their intellectual ability to defend the Christian faith and Scripture, leaving behind them institutions and programs for the purpose of continuing the work as new challenges arose.

Before looking at the relationship of old-school evangelicalism to the Bible, I want to mention something John Wimber, founder of Vineyard Ministries International, once said to me in a personal conversation. For roughly sixteen years, John had worked as a consultant to dozens of churches in every conceivable environment. I think he was concerned for me and my future if I continued down the path I was walking then. "I've been in all sorts of churches," he said. "I've spoken with hundreds of pastors, and I've seen something that doesn't make sense to me: Fundamentalists have truth, but liberals have the love." What a sad observation! We would think that those people who believe they possess the truth of Jesus would also demonstrate the love of Jesus.

Fundamentalists had based their entire existence on believing right things (even criticizing the "social gospel" of engaging with culture to meet the needs of its indigents), whereas a number of liberals were committed to improving the lives of others out of Christian compassion. Wimber was not the only evangelical to make this observation. Edward Carnell, Fuller Seminary's first president, lamented the absence of fundamentalism's social conscience and argued that Christians should not abandon their responsibility to society. In even stronger language, Francis Schaeffer warned believers that once they claim to have the truth, people watch them to see if they treat other humans as humans. According to Schaeffer, if believers were not meeting real human need, yet professed to be a community of love, they were merely "producing ugliness." Right doctrine, he claimed, was not enough to earn a hearing in popular culture. He had seen too many churches fight for "purity," yet they were "hotbeds of ugliness."[3]

Francis Schaeffer, a graduate of Westminster Seminary, was trained and steeped in the fundamentals, including biblical inerrancy. He immersed himself in the history of Western philosophy (especially modern philosophers) and became conversant in the intellectual and social world of popular culture to address the critical issues university students faced in the 1960s. After the publication of *Escape from Reason*, Schaeffer's reputation as an advocate of intelligent and uncompromising biblical faith skyrocketed.

As it was for thousands of other students in the sixties and seventies, reading Schaeffer's work for the first time was for me a thrilling and enlightening experience. Having grown up in a subculture that took pride in its anti-intellectualism, I was radically energized by a man who was brave enough and smart enough to articulate my fundamentalist beliefs in a way that was intellectually defensible. Of course Schaeffer was not the first Christian thinker to provide a strong rational foundation for orthodox evangelicals, but he was the most popular, and his writings hit the baby-boom Christian youth culture like a thunderclap. Even to this day, his writings affect evangelical thinking about cultural engagement, intellectual integrity, biblical inerrancy, Christian community, and political activism more than any other evangelical spokesperson.

Schaeffer's popular approach to a philosophically and biblically informed Christian faith breathed new life into evangelical orthodoxy, which in his writings is theologically indistinguishable from fundamentalism. The complication, however, is that an appendage had grown out of fundamentalism's theological trunk: the fundamentalist "culture," which is to some degree detached from fundamentalist theology. Schaeffer's Presbyterian background protected him from the cultural isolation that was typical of other fundamentalist sects. But burdened with revival-era ethics (made up mostly of prohibitive rules), taking up the gauntlet of young-earth creationism and the interpretive grid of dispensationalism, and having at its heart the fighting spirit of a reactionary movement, the separatist culture of fundamentalism became characterized by a kind of self-righteousness and self-absorption that Schaeffer found "ugly."

Armed with an inerrant and divinely inspired book, fundamentalists were empowered with an infallible source of absolute truth. In itself a book of this nature would be a great blessing, but the tragedy of fundamentalism is the way its adherents (mis)use the Bible. For example, there are Christians who go to the Bible as if it were an encyclopedia of religious and secular knowledge. They have a topic in mind, turn a few pages, find a verse (or string of verses) that in some way relates to the topic, and congratulate themselves for finding "the truth." As far as they are concerned, "God has spoken."

Abusing God's Word

Why is it not a good idea to treat the Bible like a dictionary or encyclopedia? Whew! Where do we begin? First, the Bible was not written as a one-volume reference work containing separate articles. It is a whole library consisting of stories, laws, poems, prophetic writings, letters, and so on. The whole Bible tells one overarching story of the Creator God, the plight of humankind, and its divine redemption secured by his Son and revealed in his people.

Second, every verse in the Bible is embedded in a context that affects its meaning, and the context of a verse includes other verses around it, the chapter, the section of the book, the whole book, the Testament, and finally the entire Bible. Context also includes such matters as history, culture, time period, and literary forms. The intended meaning is drained out of a verse if it is isolated from its context. If you gather a collection of verses that all contain the same word, you cannot be sure there is a real connection between those verses or that the word has the same meaning in each instance without a thorough study of the original language and context.

Finally, there are issues the Bible does not address because its primary concern is the revelation of God, his work, and his will. If we look for information in the Bible that is not there, we will likely miss what *is* there. For example, if we expect to find a training manual for all we need to know about raising sheep in Psalm 23 and John 10, we will miss the spiritual force of the metaphors developed in those passages (and we'll probably be crummy shepherds as well).

For similar reasons, the Bible was not meant to serve as an apologetic resource for confounding heretics or contradicting cults and other religions. Christians who go to Scripture to find a verse or passage to prove someone else wrong are like children lost in a desert using their last bit of water to fill up squirt guns to tease each other rather than to slake their thirst. Our spirits need to absorb the biblical truth God has revealed to us so that we may know him and please him, find the resources to care for others, and thrive.

Another way the Bible is mishandled—and if mishandled, it does not surrender its true wealth to the reader—is when it is picked up and read as if it were written for a twenty-first-century audience. Bible believers who feel they can throw verses at people and problems and expect good results to follow, because God's Word does not return void (Isa. 55:11), are treating the Bible as "a sort of magic book," in the words of N. T. Wright, as if its meaning can be disconnected from what the authors intended.[4]

In the first sixteen or seventeen years of my life I logged many hours listening to Pentecostal preachers. I discovered that a favorite strategy of those I heard was to read some obscure verse from an Old Testament prophet that few people had ever read or studied, treat it as if it were the most important revelation from heaven (giving it the hype it deserved), then extract from it mystical meanings that had absolutely nothing to do with anything that would have entered the minds of the author or his original audience. And though the preacher may have taken us through a universe of metaphysical enlightenment, we were always brought back to one of two actions: either go to the altar or give money.

As North Americans became more educated, the mishandling of the Bible became more obvious. First, students in college were learning critical-thinking skills that enabled them to see through the weakness of a single text presented as an argument or proof. Second, the nature of education itself, including Darwinian evolution, the billions of years nature required to produce the universe as it appears, and growing criticism of the Bible and organized religion within the academy made fundamentalism seem outdated, backward, and silly. The Scopes trial seemed to put the last nail in the fundamentalist coffin as far as the media and larger society were concerned.

The question that was constantly put to Bible-quoting Christians was, "How do you know the Bible is true?" or "How can you prove the authority of the Bible?" or "How do you explain the inconsistencies between the history of the Bible and archaeology?" and "What do you have to say about the places where the Bible contradicts itself?" To the credit of mid-twentieth-century evangelicals, they rose to the occasion, did the research, and produced a rational and scientific defense for the reliability of the Bible, while modifying some of their interpretations (which *were* dated). Of course they had to weed out a lot of foolishness and misinformation that had been invented and published by characters like Harry Rimmer, who claimed that a certain Englishman had an experience almost identical to Jonah in which the Englishman survived being swallowed by a whale shark and two or three days later was found by his fellow fishermen when they gutted the shark, unconscious but otherwise unharmed. Edward Davis, professor of science and history at Messiah College, published an article in the 1991 *Journal of the American Scientific Affiliation* titled, "A Whale of a Tale: Fundamentalist Fish Stories," in which he proved Rimmer's story to be either a hoax or a fabrication. There are still other urban myths to remove from the apologetic repertoire, like NASA "proving" Joshua's extralong day and Charles Darwin's deathbed conversion.

Because of their anti-intellectual stance, their disengagement from popular culture, and their mishandling of Scripture, by the mid-twentieth century most fundamentalists were ill prepared for the challenges of more skeptical and better educated opponents than those faced by evangelists like Dwight L. Moody and Billy Sunday in the nineteenth and early twentieth centuries. Moody could respond to the objections of unbelievers by quoting Scripture, because the Bible still carried enough weight in North American culture to end religious arguments. William Bryan could win a court case against teaching evolution in public schools in 1925 with very little understanding of either science or evolution, simply because popular opinion was on his side—at least in Kentucky. After the Second World War, fundamentalists discovered that mass culture had become more educated and had left them behind.

Darwinian biologist Stephen Jay Gould characterized all fundamentalists by relating a conversation he had with a man who told him, "The devil put fossils in rocks to deceive you evolutionists!" Certainly this was a caricature but to what degree is it true? If not for Francis Schaeffer—and I cannot think of another Christian thinker with the influence of his magnitude—fundamentalism could have disappeared before the end of the twentieth century or at the very least dwindled to small pockets of fanatics.

Nevertheless, the old school continues the heavy-handed, browbeating, Bible-thumping traditions of its past, referring to evolutionists as "fools," denigrating liberals, using the Bible as a club to win arguments (even with people who do not even believe the Bible), and attacking anyone whose interpretation of biblical predictions about the last days differs from theirs. Young believers are still receiving reprimands rather than answers when they ask troubling questions, and preachers still use the Bible to bolster their authority and force their opinions on people who do not know any better.

New Challenges to Biblical Authority

As the twentieth century ground on, biblical authority steadily declined in popular culture (having already fallen significantly in Europe and having been banned in Eastern Europe and China). Then in the sixties, an anomaly occurred in American history that set the Bible back even further. In the nearly two hundred years of our nation's existence, there had been a fairly consistent generational pattern of parents taking their children to church until they reached adolescence, at which time the children stopped attending. Later on, as those children reached adulthood with its challenges of career, marriage, and having children of their own, they returned to church for its spiritual stability and assistance. The baby-boom generation, however, did not return to church on reaching adulthood. Therefore the generation that followed became the first of a new wave of generations that had no church experience or exposure.

As if this were not enough of a challenge for people whose faith was defined by the Great Commission, the baby-boomer generation was exploring mind-altering states through a variety of hallucinogens, Asian and Eastern religions, and esoteric philosophies, replete with symbols, rituals, and meditative practices. Western society was in the throes of a great upheaval. Institutions that had been the crowning achievement of the modern era were vilified, logic and reason were undermined, and the Christian religion was perceived to be the source of many social problems and the solution to none. In the late 1970s a small number of boomers experimented with church, showing a preference for High Church liturgies that reflected their yuppie values, but this trend was short-lived. There has not been a parallel movement back to church in any age bracket since then.

So if the question put to believers in modern times was, How do you know the Bible is true? the questions today are, How do you know which sacred writings to follow? What makes the Bible better than other religious books? and Why not learn from all the great traditions? When Francis Schaeffer addressed the challenge of proclaiming the Christian message to a culture that had abandoned absolute truth, he recommended that evangelicals draw to the surface the non-Christian's presuppositions and gently lead them to the logical conclusion of the implicit beliefs that lay behind their presuppositions. With perhaps a few exceptions, that strategy will not work today. Few people are going to be won over to Jesus Christ through the force of an indisputable argument.

Old-school believers have a difficult time grasping the fact that young people have at least two options when presented with the airtight arguments that seemed to work for earlier generations. First, they can counter those arguments with their own strong logical case, supported by the incredible volume of information available to them on the Internet and in their university curricula; or, second, they can dismiss logic with a shrug of the shoulders. When young people refuse to submissively accept an argument that, in their view, does not hold water, old schoolers get frustrated and sometimes use intimidation rather than the force of reason or their own living example to get their students to toe the line.

Old schoolers have a strong attachment to logic and reason, partly because their faith was forged in societies profoundly influenced by the Enlightenment and partly because the founders of fundamentalism were influenced by Scottish Common Sense philosophy. Thomas Reid, who is often referred to as the father of this philosophy, was one of the few Christian intellectuals capable of challenging David Hume's skepticism that had devastated the case for miracles and the design argument for God's existence. Reid proved that Hume could not live by his own philosophy once he left his study and walked out into the street, a fact that Hume acknowledged.

Reid's commonsense approach to the Bible and Christian apologetics was the backbone of Schaeffer's evangelical method, as it has been for others into the present time (for example, John Warwick Montgomery, J. P. Moreland, and Philip Johnson have used it). Some Christian apologists would like to turn back the clock to a period when their case for Christianity, which leans heavily on commonsense logic, worked. Today many young people believe logic is a Western way of oppressing and devaluing other cultures and thus reject it.

I am not saying there is no place for Western philosophy, Aristotelian logic, or a rationally constructed theology in Christian thinking. In fact, it is perhaps more important than ever that Christian teachers have this sort of solid foundation. There is a time and place for presenting reasons. But in terms of the day-to-day exchanges we have with people, our relationships with others, and intentional evangelistic endeavors, concentrating all our effort on logical arguments will simply not have the same effect on people or popular culture that it did in previous generations.

New-school believers, by and large, are comfortable with chaos and with a worldview that does not need to be logically ordered. They were, after all, born into this world as it is today—it does not scare them. A worldview that is informed by experience as well as logic is not so different from the worldviews of a number of other cultures. The old idea that *we* are more "civilized" than the rest of the world because we value logic and reason is now considered ethnocentric and imperialistic. There is room in the worldview of the youth in popular culture for ambiguity. There is also room for sacred texts, but many cannot understand why one holy book should be valued above the others.

Rigid Control and Inquiring Minds

Old-school believers used to protect the impressionable young minds of their children and students from any material that was not written by someone within their camp. In fact, sometime around 1976, I suggested to a Pentecostal youth minister in Sweden that he and his high school students begin a study group using the works of Francis Schaeffer, which seemed particularly relevant to the educational challenges they faced at the time. He shook his head saying, "We're not allowed to do that; he is not Pentecostal."

I will venture a guess as to why old-school believers pro-hibit their students from reading anything outside their small circle. They are afraid that exposure to other ideas would weaken their commitment to their fundamental beliefs and values. But I wonder—if someone can easily be led astray by acquiring more knowledge, then how "true" were her beliefs and values in the first place? Increased knowledge of the facts, even if facts alone cannot lead to the knowledge of God, should strengthen true belief not undermine it. But old-school believers resort to religious "purity" language to describe the "defiling" nature of theology not rooted in their tradition.

If that is so, then there is good reason for "fundamentalist institutions [to] exercise careful control over the secondary reading material of the laity."[5]

But is the old-school rejection of information sources outside its own circle in keeping with biblical faith, historic Christianity, or the beliefs of the Reformers? Fundamentalists tend to reject the phrase "all truth is God's truth," because they see it as the devil's way of getting his foot in the door of a believer's heart and mind. In general they believe that certain educated or gifted individuals are able to read theological, philosophical, psychological, technical, and religious writings without being corrupted by them, but the average believer had better keep his distance for fear of being deceived and "led astray from [his] sincere and pure devotion to Christ" (2 Cor. 11:3). When Paul wrote those words, Christians could not help but be exposed to other belief systems and pagan sources of information. His admonition was not that they refuse to listen to other people but that they exercise discernment when doing so and learn how to sift truth from error.

There is no need to belabor the point that biblical characters, such as Joseph, Moses, Daniel, and Paul, certainly had education that was nonbiblical. Some fundamentalists will object, saying Paul and the others did not have a "complete Bible," but since we do, we no longer need any other source of information. Yet Christian theologians of all ages have seen the value of education in subjects not covered in Scripture. St. Augustine compared Greek philosophy and secular wisdom to the gold that Israel took from Egypt, which "they did not create themselves, but dug out of the mines of God's providence which are scattered everywhere abroad," and that no matter where this gold is found, it is God's.[6] Justin Martyr, while noting the difference between the teaching of Jesus and the teaching of Plato, remarked, "Whatever things were rightly said among all men are the property of us Christians."[7]

John Calvin regarded God's Spirit as the "sole fountain of truth" and therefore refused to reject or despise it "wherever it shall appear, unless we wish to dishonor the Spirit of God." He listed various disciplines in which God's truth emerged in the works of non-Christians, including civil law, nature, rhetoric, medicine, physics, dialectics, and mathematics, and encouraged believers to "use this assistance."[8] New-school Christians have this same fearless attitude when reading from a variety of different sources and viewpoints. They do not read these works in search of salvation but for other purposes, such as making themselves aware of popular books that are much discussed, looking to see if an important truth is stressed that may have been neglected by their church, finding a different language for communicating their faith to others, learning, and stretching their minds by facing challenging or difficult ideas or trying to better understand human and social behavior, the sciences, and so on.

There are many new-school Christians who are as curious as anyone in their peer group regarding books with spiritual themes that are celebrated in popular culture. They are as likely to read books by the Dali Lama or Thich Nhat Hahn as books by Rick Warren. Sometimes they simply want to know what all the fuss is about. We should not assume they believe everything they read or that they treat every religious book like the Bible. Should an old-school believer feel it her duty to warn them away from a potentially dangerous book, the old schooler had better know what she is talking about, forego using a heavy-handed approach, and have something more substantial to say than the clichés or stock arguments new schoolers have already heard and deconstructed.

The Bible, Alive and Powerful

New-school believers who have grown up in the church will show greater interest in having questions answered regarding such issues as free will and predestination than those who do not have a church background. Regardless of their peripheral reasons for studying the Bible, the majority of new schoolers will come to it hoping to hear God speak to them, wanting its truth to enter them and produce transformation. If the church gives them tools and training for properly interpreting Scripture, then on their own they will be able to discover its depth, beauty, and power. New-school Christians are looking for a Bible-reading experience that is spiritual, enlightening, practical, and filled with wonder.

As Matt suggests, the real test of our knowledge of Scripture is not how many questions we can answer correctly on a Bible quiz. I have met many loveless Christians who equate spiritual maturity with Bible knowledge. The critical issue is the *effect* the Bible produces in the lives of those who read it. Consistently through his prophets, God complained that the problem with his people was that they did not know *him* and did not *do* his will. New schoolers are concerned with both of these issues. In the hands of an angry preacher the Bible has provoked more deserved mockery and parody in the last four decades than has almost any other expression of Christian faith. If there is more to the Bible than what is found in the holy texts of other religions, the proof of it will be in the loving lifestyle of people who travel through this world demonstrating the kindness and integrity of Jesus.

What is it that we humans hope to find when a Hindu turns to the Vedas or Upanishads, a Muslim turns to the Koran, Krishnas turn to the Bhagavad-Gita, neo-Gnostics turn to The Egyptian Book of the Dead or The Gospel of St. Thomas, New Age devotees turn to *A Course in Miracles*, and so on? No doubt we are looking for truth, enlightenment, the right way to live, and above all, for God. We need a reasonable story that not only makes sense of the universe and human history but also helps us locate our place within the story.

Matt began this chapter with a lavish description of the biblical story that not only spans the ages of ancient history but continues to write itself in the lives of believers today, even in those whose circumstances seem intolerable. What is it about the plotline of *this* story that gives us the hope of God and personal transformation? As briefly as possible, I want to tease you with some elements of the biblical plot. The rest is up to you, because if you do not learn the story for yourself, it will have little effect in your life and you will have nothing worthwhile to say when asked, "Why do you prefer your Bible over other sacred texts?"

First, the biblical story takes place in the real world, the world of our experience. The story world of the Bible is unsanitized, ambiguous, unjust, material, and its characters are mostly unconscious of their Creator (until he terrifies them with an unexpected visit). If a number of characters in the plot had encounters with God or other spiritual beings, that certainly was not their normal experience or the experience of the majority of biblical people. The biblical world, like ours, is one into which order, justice, and mercy must be *imposed*, because those things are not there inherently. So it is a world in need of fixing, of rescuing and redeeming.

Second, the characters too are in need of rescuing and redeeming. Like us, they are not predisposed to the kind of selflessness that will resolve the tensions in the plot—tensions between good and evil, desire and sacrifice, hope and despair. Like the world in which they lived, biblical characters needed intervention, a solution to their problems that was greater than their mental, spiritual, and physical resources—a solution greater than their problems.

Third, as the plot slowly unfolds through history, it reveals a theme of salvation in which the Creator is involved. Unlike any other sacred text, the biblical story includes a Redeemer who, even though he is transcendent, steps into the human story, embraces it as his own, and loves the characters within it to the point of self-sacrifice. The death of the Redeemer makes possible a spiritual life and enlightenment for all other human characters, leading to the resolution of their tensions and problems. Those who recognize the presence of the transcendent Creator in the immanent Redeemer and trust him to rescue them are transformed to become like him. Then their lives have the effect of his life, bringing healing and resolution, shining his truth, and showing others the way to salvation.

I may have given away the whole plot in those last three paragraphs, but you will have to know the story for yourself and come to terms with its truth if you are going to live the kind of life that answers the question this chapter raises. And only a real life can provide people within popular culture an adequate answer for this question. Do not think you can get away with *telling* the story—you must live it. When the story of your life is defined by the story of the Bible, people will see the power of the Word.

If Francis Schaeffer's logic-dependent evangelism strategy is not likely to be as effective among new-school Christians, his biblical model of a loving community has the potential to convince many people of the truth and goodness of the Christian faith as revealed in Scripture. Of all the available religious literature, what makes the Bible unique? Well, what does it do in the lives of those who read and live it? Does it make them more generous and compassionate, more hospitable and merciful?

Though I cannot comment on the nature of Schaeffer's spiritual community at L'Abri—my one visit lasted less than forty-eight hours—my friends and I felt welcomed there. Our hosts encouraged us to participate in the Saturday night discussion (which Schaeffer led sitting atop the mantel over the fireplace, as I recall), and the next morning after church, Dr. Schaeffer made a point to walk over to us, shake our hands, and ask if it was possible to extend our trip and stay another week. That simple gesture meant more to me than anything I have ever read in any of his books, for it reflected the heart of One who said, "I was a stranger and you took me in."

3

Do I Have to Go to Church?

What Is Church?

I drive a white Toyota truck. If you were to visit the most popular church in my town on a Sunday morning, you would not find my truck parked in the lot. In fact, you would not find my truck parked on the street. If you arrived thirty minutes late, you still would not see my truck anywhere in the vicinity of the church. Where is my truck, you ask? At whichever local surf break is offering the best waves that Sunday morning.

You might be thinking, *But, Matt, I thought that you were a Christian and you work for a Christian university.*

I have certain expectations about church. I do not expect church to entertain me, but I do expect it to motivate me in my spiritual journey, to give me an opportunity to worship God, to serve the world, to develop strong relationships with other Christians, to be able to ask questions that really bother me, to greet others with the same love with which Jesus greeted the crowds that came to him. It was never about what "the church," as an institution, organized service, building that protected you from the weather, could do for you. It was always about the people and the opportunity to interact in deep fellowship. Does what we call "going to church" provide that today?

It's not that surfing is more "fun" than going to church, it's just that "going to church" does not bring me any closer to other Christians or to God, beyond those 120 minutes on Sunday morning. In my experience, churches have burdened me with guilt when I attend and burdened me with guilt if I miss a service. I do not have a spiritual need for what many churches have to offer.

For instance, a lot of what is called *worship* does not seem worshipful. It does not encourage me to give the best of what I have to God. In fact, the choruses we sing express what I need *from* God. The service hardly gives me an opportunity to "present my body as a living sacrifice."

When I am floating on the ocean, however, I experience a genuine sense of communion with God and am able to worship him. It's also an opportunity to minister Jesus Christ to other people. Many times the people around me in the water and in coffee shops need to be ministered to, and isn't that what we as the church should be all about?

I have had the following conversation quite a few times in the last year or so, not with my peers—who immediately have a better understanding of my choices and behavior—but with more mature people with greater life experience than me.

"What do you mean you surf on Sunday morning rather than go to church? Oh, I get it; you go to one of those Saturday night services. Right? What? You don't? Why not?"

"Well, on Saturday night I had church."

"Okay, so you did go to church Saturday night."

"Nope."

"Huh?"

"I *had* church Saturday night, but I did not *go to* church."

"Wait, so what exactly did you do?"

"I went to the local coffee shop with some friends to chill."

"But I thought you said you went to church last night."

"I said I had church last night. I didn't say anything about going to church."

Unfortunately the phrase "go to church," which describes a routine that many Christians follow, usually involves *attending* a weekly meeting that is program-driven, permits limited opportunity for personal participation, and is controlled by the few people who stand in front of the rest.

I am interested in church as family, as community, as a mutual sharing of spiritual gifts. I am interested in face-to-face encounters with other Christians and with God. I am interested in learning what the Bible has to say to the practical issues of my daily life so that I am better able to know God's will for me. I am not interested in learning a denomination's pet doctrines merely because they think it necessary to stress why they are right and everyone else is wrong. I believe the essence of *church* should be to love God with all our heart, soul, and mind, and love our neighbors as ourselves. To me church is a loving community of believers where God's presence is revealed, we are free to express our love to him, and we are encouraged to care for one another so that the strong support the weak, the wealthy take care of the poor, the leaders pray for the sick, the wise counsel the simple, and the lonely are welcomed into the family. I believe church should be an event shared with other people and should offer more grace than guilt, hope than despair, and freedom than slavery.

You may be thinking, *Don't we have a responsibility to the entire body of Christ, not just to those we enjoy being with?*

Does it make sense that most Christians are concerned and protective of their little corner of the earth and have no global understanding of God's kingdom? If a person chooses to go to a particular church, and drives past many other churches on her way, is it possible for her to know what goes on in those other churches? Does she have a sense of solidarity with those other believers? Or does she judge them as she drives by? Is it possible to belong to one denomination—or doctrinal viewpoint—without thinking that the others are a little less right?

Look for me in a church in my community on Sunday, and you probably will not find me. On the other hand, there are many other times—every day of the week—when you may find me worshiping with Malaysians, Indonesians, Burmese, Brazilians, Koreans, and others in a variety of denominations around the world. At these times I have the wonderful opportunity to share with others what God has given me and receive from them the ministry of God's Spirit.

There are, of course, people who believe strongly that I should attend church on Sunday morning, even though I explain how little I benefit spiritually from sitting in a row of people, looking at the back of other people's heads, yawning through hymns that are pitched too high for me to sing, and listening to a sermon that has little to do with my deep longing for God or the pain I feel inside regarding people I love who are suffering.

Though there are churches that sing choruses rather than hymns, show movie clips for sermon illustrations, and try to keep things lively—or "spiritual," depending on their tradition—the majority of the population in North America, of all ages, find the services of their local churches either incomprehensible or unattractive. Otherwise, why is it that religious polls repeatedly reveal the disparity between the number of Americans who identify themselves as Christians (currently about 77 percent of the population) and those who attend a Christian church on Sunday (less than 50 percent)? If churches were really meeting our spiritual needs, their attendance would not be on the decline as it has been for the last fifteen years.

Still people tell me I should be in church on Sunday, and if I ask why, they remind me that the Bible says, "Let us not give up meeting together, as some are in the habit of doing" (Heb. 10:25). I wish more Christians would take a closer look at this verse, because it definitely does not tell us that we have to "go to church." We are not to forsake assembling, but nothing in Hebrews 10 says anything about Sunday morning meetings for music, prayers, and lectures. Rather we are to "draw near to God," "spur one another on toward love and good deeds," and "encourage one another" (vv. 19–25). To get our current form of Sunday church out of that passage is certainly a stretch. This leads me to ask: When did church become more about *bodies* in a building than Christ being *embodied* in his people?

I have a memory of going to church when I was around twelve years old. One Sunday morning everyone filed in as usual. A worship band played in the background, people engaged in friendly chatter, and ushers passed out bulletins and gave special greetings to visitors. The pastor entered, had everyone sit down, and we all began to go through the motions of "church."

When it came time for the sermon, the small children were dismissed to children's church. I was too old for that much-needed relief, so I had to tough it out for the next hour in the adult service. The pastor read his Scripture text, prayed, then launched into his speech. Everything was perfectly, dreadfully normal. I leaned back, squirmed a little, and sought a comfortable position to begin my head-bobbing sessions, from almost asleep to awake to almost asleep again.

About halfway through the sermon, something absolutely bizarre happened. I will never forget the reaction of the church members when this one person did something that was totally unprecedented, uncalled for, and apparently forbidden. Judging by the disturbance in the congregation that morning, you would have thought someone had flipped off the pastor or torn off his clothes and run around the church cheering for his favorite football team. Nope. What happened—and it happened in *my* row—is that for the first time in the history of that church, a man raised his hand to ask a question. I knew that person! He was my father.

It's funny; when I try to remember the pastor's sermon or my dad's question, I draw a blank. What I do remember is the look on the pastor's face and the chagrin on the faces of everyone else. Now why would it create such a fuss to ask a question during a sermon? Are we not allowed to ask for clarification or ask where the preacher gets his information? Is the person speaking never supposed to be questioned? Have we confused the preacher's voice with the voice of God? Is church like a theater, where no one is allowed to speak during the performance? I would love to attend a church where I could raise my hand, have a dialogue with the teacher, or ask pertinent questions. Why are we not free to do that?

What about church membership? I have always been confused about that issue. Why is it such a big deal to be a member of the church? Why do I have to sign a document or attend evening classes to qualify for membership? What is church membership anyway? Do members get a special Bible or an identification card? Do they have special privileges none of the rest of us knows about? Do I get the one-day-only service of prayer and teaching unless I sign up for membership class?

Why make church a Sunday event? Why place the pastor on a pedestal, then try to knock him off, then get furious when he falls off? Why do we think pastors have to be sinless? How did people come to think that the Christian life consists in a one-hour meeting once a week? How did we come to believe that the only way to enter God's presence is with a Sunday-morning formula that usually does not work anyway? Why do some Christians look for their spiritual identity in going to church or church membership rather than in Christ?

These questions lead to a host of other questions people are asking about church. Do I have to accept the religion to have the experience? Do we need to hear a sermon every week? How boring does our music have to get before we are allowed to change it? Does church have to be on Sunday morning? Can church be fun? Or is that not right?

To me church on Sunday morning is impersonal, boring, and usually a charade of make-believe. It starts the moment I dress up or drive in the parking lot or give the greeter at the door a fake smile. The chairs are arranged to discourage conversation among members, and we adopt an educational environment without providing a real educational process. I can name many more times when I felt God was present in a conversation with my friends than when occupying my assigned seat in a church. I don't see the point of going to church when, for example, a vulnerable conversation with a close friend can be so much more nourishing.

So many people have told me they feel as I do about going to church, I cannot count them all. Some of them go anyway, but why? What is the draw (or fear)? Others stopped going to church, and then because they never learned how to have a relationship with God outside of the institution, they gave up on him too. Then there are those who have found greater community, richer worship, and more beauty in other Christian traditions that go about church in a way that is very different from the average evangelical model.

The nature of my work at University of the Nations and the training I provide for ministers overseas has required me to spend several years studying the Bible. It is there that we should get our understanding of church. But it seems like the church today and the church of Paul and the disciples have completely different purposes. It is because of this underlying purpose that the church today has resorted to a college lecture format with an offering at the end.

The church of the New Testament was organic. It was loose and mobile, enabling it to grow. But its growth was not because there was a hot new teacher in town. The growth came from people who needed what the church had to offer. They needed a place to *belong*. It was a place of peace and serenity, a place to find love and mercy regardless of what you believed or did. It was hospitable and was held in familiar places, like people's homes. You joined a family rather than a membership class for a denomination. You did not have to leave at a certain time or feel like you were imposing because you wanted more dialogue. You were invited into the family.

Think about the time in the church's early history when Christians were being martyred. A raving psycho, Nero, burned down a city and blamed the new Christian movement in Rome. No one understood the Christians. They seemed atheistic because they had no temple in which they worshiped. Many thought they were cannibals because they talked of eating Christ's body and drinking his blood. During periods of persecution, believers were dragged off to coliseums and killed because of their identification with Jesus Christ. Paradoxically, though, as the persecution grew, the faith spread. Why? I think it was because of the community that these early believers developed. They found family and belonging. This fellowship was so deep that they were not able to deny that something existed beyond themselves, and therefore they were willing to die for it. These Christians had no Bible, no fancy workshops, no Christian bookstores, but they were part of a loving community. I believe this is what they died for—an undeniably deep relationship with their fellow believers and ultimately with God.

Would we die for the community of believers we worship with at our local church? Does our local church facilitate belongingness for people who have never belonged? Maybe I am missing something, but I cannot shake the feeling that church as it exists today is on its way to becoming a museum exhibit, whereas the spiritual community that will rise in the next ten years to replace today's church will consist of people living 24/7 in friendship with God and each other. Isn't church more about the people than the building? If that is a fact, do I have to go to church? Do I have a choice?

C   From Center to Margin

Both Matt and I have had difficulty with this chapter. We both know that the Bible does not make going to church a requirement for being a Christian. In fact in the New Testament the church was not something people *went to* but something people *were*. Church, according to Scripture, is something that happens when Christians live, work, pray, and obey God together, the emphasis being on *together*. Yet going to church is such a well-established tradition in our religious subculture that it is difficult to see how we can do without it. We anticipate an angry backlash for even suggesting that it is not necessary to go to church.

The unpleasant ordeal (I've heard some call it "Protestant purgatory") of going to church has become even more tedious in the last fifty years than it was two hundred years ago when ushers had to carry long poles to wake up those who had "fallen asleep in Christ." Going to church was more tolerable in the days when people lived in stable communities. Going to church meant sharing your life with people you rubbed shoulders with every day. There was a lot more to attending church than merely enduring a boring sermon and bad music. Church was integral to the fabric of a community's social life.

In early America—at least in the New England states—churches were built on greens that were almost always at the geographic center of town. The property of the building and common area were generally owned by the church but treated as public property. The church doubled as the town hall where community issues were discussed, important announcements were made, and public records were stored. Everyone was in some way connected to the church—the community hub. Therefore, going to church was like the evening news, continuing education (ministers belonged to the professional class and were well educated), political engagement, family gathering, spiritual nurture, and socialization of local residents all rolled into the nucleus of city life. The town's leading families lived nearest to the green, so the church was truly the heart of the community.

Churches no longer exist at the center of towns or cities in any sense—geographical, cultural, or spiritual. Urban sprawl has erased any center, creating instead decentered sites for specific activities, such as shopping malls, county recording offices, educational campuses, and so on. The mobility of employment and even corporations prevent people from experiencing community with their neighbors. Why get to know the family across the street if you are not going to be living near each other in a year or two? Therefore people look to other environments for community, like country clubs, sports events (including children's sports), churches, and bars. The advent of Internet connections to every conceivable commodity, news and information source, and religious teaching has an even greater decentering effect on public life.

People today are not as committed to church as were former generations, because the time is long gone when church was the only show in town. Community is not automatic in churches, where the members see each other only one day a week, and it is all but impossible in megachurches (unless community is redefined so as to be quickly, easily, and strategically achieved through classes or seminars). No doubt, whatever sense of community any church will enjoy today, it will not be at the center of a town or public culture.

Churches tend to be resistant to change because many Christian leaders assume (or believe they can prove) that the form of their organization and the format of their services are God-ordained and supported by Scripture. Ministers and worship directors who assume they still have captive audiences deliver presentations and perform rituals that are irrelevant. They have managed to bore people out of their churches, because there are too many options that promise to be more interesting, more entertaining, and even more helpful in the day-to-day needs of real life.

An Inadequate Model for the Future Church

Ever since the 1950s when national and now multinational corporations began to uproot families and move them around the country (not to mention military dependants who attended five or six different schools before reaching the seventh grade), the church in general has taken a less central role in neighborhoods. People who go to church in mobile communities are constantly sitting next to strangers. The friends they made last month have been transferred to another city, and the people who have moved into their spot will be leaving in six months or a couple of years.

Losing its position as the center of the community, the church has been reduced to the programs and services it offers its members. This is the church of the modern era. It measures its effectiveness, according to Pete Ward, by "the number of people who attend on a Sunday."[1] If membership is not a measure of effectiveness, then budget; if not budget, then longevity. There was an assumption running through the late modern era that if an institution had been around for a long time, it must be good at whatever it does for its customers. Old corporations proudly displayed their elder status with the prominent statement "Founded in 1899" or "Established since 1976." The implication is that older is better. As the authors of *Funky Business* illustrate, "The prevailing view has been that permanence is good. This explains why companies build such vast headquarters buildings. The bigger the better; the deeper the foundations and the higher the tower, the better the business."[2]

Change the term *companies* to *churches*, and we can better understand the need that many North American pastors have for endless building programs—a spiritual disorder my cousin refers to as "edifice complex." In the late modern period, when corporate leaders believed management methods held the keys to accomplishing anything one could dream, megachurches looked as if they would be the wave of the future, and the pastor as CEO was the new model. Churches with sprawling campuses became the envy of every church leader from inner-city churches to rural country parishes. The sheer size of the megachurch facility seemed to scream, "God is doing something in this place!"

I have been a pastor for thirty-two years. My dad's church is one of those megachurches, which has also spawned other megachurches, from California to Florida, not to mention hundreds of smaller churches (like mine) around the world. I do not have negative feelings about "the fastest growing churches in America," but I am not enamored with them either. The most authentic Christians I know serve the smallest churches in America—rescue missions, recovery homes, or refugee camps in foreign countries. These men and women, without the rewards of a big-digit income, recognition in the media, or socializing with celebrities, dedicate their lives to caring for the world's poor and suffering. In doing so, they reveal the truth of Christian experience: what we do outside church, rather than "going to church," is the chief expression of our faith.

Visit my church on a Sunday morning and you will find people sitting in rows, singing, praying, and waiting for me to talk to them about biblical solutions to our practical problems. This is the modern configuration of "church." There is a true spiritual community at the heart of our church, but I'll be the first to admit that many people come as consumers, "shopping" for services that they hope will meet or at least supplement their spiritual needs. So "church" occurs within the institution, but it is not the institution, which is something more organic, relational, intangible.

Old schoolers apply Hebrews 10:25 to going to church: "Let us not give up meeting together, as some are in the habit of doing, but let us encourage one another—and all the more as you see the Day approaching." But as Matt pointed out above, some of our most powerful experiences of giving and receiving encouragement from one another occur in living rooms, parks, and restaurants while we are hanging out with Christian friends, rather than while we are sitting in church, listening to someone tell us his or her opinions about God, the world, the Bible, politics, and so on. Seldom does going to church include the richness and honesty of deep conversations about God, faith, and personal struggles that we enjoy with close friends in informal settings.

Every week I receive catalogs from companies that promise to increase the attendance or income of my church. Some catalogs have glossy pictures of mammoth church sanctuaries with large video screens and garish stages, featuring an inset of a famous preacher and a glowing recommendation for the company who designed and built his church. But something I find horrifying in each image is the chairs aligned in straight and ordered rows—to maximize the number of members in the audience—all facing the stage with a direct line of sight on the one person who will be speaking. The photograph reinforces the assumption that the role of the average Christian *in church* is to be a spectator who sits passively watching and listening as the one spiritually gifted person speaks. Perhaps we would do well to meditate on Jeanne Halgren Kilde's *When Church Became Theatre: The Transformation of Evangelical Architecture and Worship in Nineteenth-Century America* to see where we may have gone wrong.[3]

We are living in a time when ministers no longer have a captive audience. People vote with their feet. This is the reason so many megachurches have to keep the glamour and hype going, having to constantly introduce new programs. They experience so much leakage as people who hunger for authentic community and a freer spiritual experience go searching elsewhere, newcomers have to be attracted to fill the empty seats of those who are leaving. After all, a megasanctuary shows a decline in attendance very quickly. Aggressive churches strategize ways of attracting people to their buildings and, once they show up, ways to keep them coming back. These churches often promise "community" but provide their members with nothing more than structured small groups. They promise seekers the opportunity to find God but supply them instead with programs (discipleship, membership, Bible training, and so on). The fact is, many churches, whether consciously or not, structure their small groups and programs to *control* people.

The control these churches exercise is meant not only to keep people coming back to the church building but also to prevent them from developing relationships outside the church that might lead them away from the church. Also they are designed to meet all the believers' spiritual needs (or at least keep them too busy to do anything else) so that members will not attempt to develop spiritually on their own, which is a risk that they will learn and grow in ways their particular denomination does not want them to learn and grow. The old school wants to monitor and control the spiritual progress of their members.

Of course, some old-school churches are not this sophisticated, have not implemented the membership programs developed and marketed by the megachurches, and therefore use more primitive systems of control. The most typical control factors are exclusion and guilt. "We are the only church who understands the truth, follows all the commandments, and has the full work of God going on in our ministry." "Leave us, and you've left the kingdom of God." And "If you really loved God, you would be more involved in our church."

There is an old-school myth that I have never heard anyone call into question, but it deserves some critical attention. The myth is that getting more and more involved in the institution of the church is the same thing as growing closer to God. Some churches provide pathways for people to become more active in the life of the church, which oftentimes means nothing more than volunteering more of their time, talent, and income. By stages they become embedded in the life of the institution, partly because huge churches require tremendous resources to keep their lights turned on and their programs rolling. It's sad that church members are bamboozled into equating this institutional entrenchment with spiritual progress.

The New Old Church

I believe there is spiritual value in meeting together regularly with other believers at a particular time and place. But when churches are guilty of spiritual or emotional abuse, boring sermons, uninspired worship, and attempts to control the spiritual experience of their members, then "going to church" is definitely optional, and I cannot blame Matt or anyone else for opting out.

Christians need to rethink and reconfigure the whole idea of "church" if we hope for it to have a viable presence in the future. Popular culture and young Christians are neither impressed nor put off by church, mega or otherwise; they are indifferent to church. For the last thirty or forty years we have been tinkering with modifications, but we are rapidly getting past the point where bandages are going to mend our wounds. We're losing too much blood.

The problem with "going to church" is that it is not authentic—that is to say, attending church is not an authentic expression of spiritual community. The church form—sitting in rows, looking at the backs of heads, hearing announcements that affect fewer than 5 percent of the listeners, and so on—needs to be overhauled. Churches are in the same situation as many corporations that have discovered, just because they have been around for many years or at one time produced a hot-selling item, there is no guarantee that they will have any customers tomorrow. Companies that want to survive into the future cannot make slight adjustments, but have "to be reshaped along entirely new lines."[4] Lyle Schaller noted three decades ago that people are no longer faithful to the religious denomination of their parents or ancestors. Denominational brand loyalty is extinct. Church leaders have learned to appeal to the felt needs of people in their area, but little objective research exists proving that the real spiritual needs of people in their churches are being met.

Here is a well-kept secret: thousands of active Christians who work in almost every imaginable parachurch organization, including seminaries, campus evangelistic organizations, Christian publishing companies, youth organizations, and so on, do not go to church. The list includes authors, recording artists, professors, even evangelists and missionaries. While the policy of most Christian organizations is to encourage their employees and volunteers to be active in local churches, many of them opt out. They entered a Christian organization to pursue a spiritual calling, and now much of what they do "feels" like church—maybe even more so than attending a local church. Also they know that bad music and boring sermons do little to improve their spiritual vitality. In other words, they do not see the value of going to church.

Will we in our lifetime witness the demise of church? No, but we will continue to see a steady decline in the number of evangelical Christians in America until enough of us finally figure out that we had better do more than rattle our sabers. More important, and this has already begun, we will see a post-evangelical reconfiguration of church that will take many different forms that believers might not have acknowledged as church twenty or thirty years ago.

Communities of people are forming around the country with a variety of agendas. Some shelter and feed the homeless, others care for AIDS patients, others are writing screenplays, and so on. And their commitment to each other has become the basis of a spiritual community in which their gifts are put to work, their conversations contribute to their growth in Christ, and God's presence is manifest. They enjoy a communal and spiritual experience that is not dependent on rigid hierarchies, expensive technology, or temperamental musicians. They have come to the realization that music is not the only "sacrament" of Christian worship, but that prayer and praise can take a variety of forms. For example, a friend of mine goes monthly to a prison for juveniles who have been sentenced for violent crimes. She is permitted to lead a chapel service for the teenage gangsters who are already hardened to most forms of evangelism. One evening she announced that she was going to play a song by DMX (who was well-known by the inmates for the profane lyrics of his rap music). She let them know that what they were about to play was a prayer, then she played "Ready to Meet Him." The spiritual dialogue DMX wove into that song became the communal prayer in chapel that evening.

Once a believer feels the freedom to look over the denominational fence to see how other Christians are interacting with God, they become exposed to alternative expressions of prayer and worship that may inspire their own creative innovations. Some new-school Christians have learned the practice of passive prayer in which they listen to God while surrendering their bodies to him as living sacrifices in complete silence. Others are writing prayers and posting them in the places where they meet. In fact, in some meetings, prayers are thrown into a fire, nailed to a cross, passed to a neighbor, or secured to a refrigerator door with magnets (this last example symbolizes our prayers on "God's refrigerator"). I have heard prayers composed for public worship that incorporate genres like beat or slam poetry. Some new-school believers prefer more candles and rituals, some prefer fewer; some want worship that is streamlined and simple; others want lots of technology; and still others want to experience ancient Christian liturgies and rituals—at least once in a while.

While not all the new forms of worship will work for everyone—such as blowing bubbles as prayers, Celtic prayer circles circumscribed with rocks, or messages in bottles—merely having the attitude that imagination and creativity can play a role in the church's prayer life is helping people find a more meaningful and gripping way of communicating with God. Those who have been jaded or disenchanted by either extemporaneous or written liturgical prayers discover a breath of fresh air at a window opened toward heaven that is new to them. Will the new forms become old some day and in need of renovation or replacement? Of course they will, because every generation needs to find its own voice before God.

Two constants of the church's worship are time and space. Location in space does not come to us, but we must go and seek it out. Time passes by us, but we pass through space. Occasionally time and space converge—a particular moment in a particular place. Consider worship in the story of Jesus: "They went to Capernaum, and when the Sabbath came, Jesus went into the synagogue and began to teach" (Mark 1:21). The Sabbath "came," but Jesus "went" to the synagogue. The location in space changed from the tabernacle in the Old Testament to a synagogue in the New, but the example remains constant: God meets with his people at particular times in particular places, which we identify as sacred time and sacred space. To forfeit that pattern is to lose the rhythm of life and our sense of place.

Nevertheless, many churches will shrivel and die, as they should, if their leaders do not wake up to the new challenges and realities of the world as it is today. We cannot deliver boring lectures in stuffy buildings, nor can we meet in rooms that look like hotel lobbies and claim to be honoring sacred space. If our church meetings (including architecture and artful expressions of worship and word) do not evoke a sense of reverence, we cannot pretend they help us touch the sacred. The very nature of sacredness is that it produces reverence in those who approach it. People are hungering, starving, for the sacred and the reverence it evokes.

Church in the Threshold

Ministers especially will have to understand the nature of "liminal zones," those in-between spaces where God meets with people and reveals himself. For instance, we speak of "threshold" experiences. Why thresholds? Because when we stand in a threshold we are neither inside nor outside, yet we are participating in both the in and the out. A liminal space is a kind of nothingness, a nowhere and no time, a crack in reality through which heaven appears to mortal beings. Falling asleep and waking up are liminal times, when we are neither awake nor asleep but a little of both. God often speaks in these strange moments when we are not in our normal state of consciousness.

Think of dawn; it is neither night nor day but both. The same is true of dusk, which is neither day nor night but some of both. God instructed Israel to offer sacrifices every morning and evening in those liminal spaces. I have personally experienced the richness of morning (matins) and evening (vespers) prayer while visiting a hermitage of Camaldolese monks. We learn from Israel's daily sacrifices the importance of liminal zones, which like the sacred, exist in both space and time. Worship is a liminal experience. I have long been fascinated by the fact that the cloud of God's presence descended over the *doorway* (or threshold) of the tent of meeting whenever Moses went there to speak with God, and that at the same time all the people stood in the *doorway* of their tents (Exod. 33:7–11). There is something spiritual about the idea of a doorway, a threshold, and perhaps that is one reason Israel was to inscribe the commandments of God on the doorframes of their houses and on their gates (Deut. 6:9).

Despite their difficulty in connecting with life in the world of today, Orthodox churches have an advantage over evangelical churches in that their architecture, rituals, art (icons), and liturgy create liminal space. Another advantage is that their ancient liturgy guarantees that every week in every church the service will take its course even if the priest should die, which spares them the personality cult that is the bane of evangelical churches with charismatic leaders. Russian Orthodox worship—scented with incense, illuminated by candles, framed by symbolic architecture, adorned with biblical symbols, shrouded in mystery, informed by Scripture readings, and accompanied by a cappella singing that in the domed roof sounds like a choir of angels overhead—can be a liminal event that is strong enough to knock a Protestant boy off his feet. I do not think I fully appreciated the magnitude of this rich experience until I stood in an Orthodox church for the first time in Kostroma, Russia. As I listened and prayed, the realization came over me that they had designed everything to give the worshiper a taste of heaven. But this was not heaven as theme park, mall, or food court; this was heaven at the edge of eternity with the Creator robed in unspeakable majesty. Everyone honored the reverence of that place.

In the Orthodox churches I have attended since that first experience, worshipers mill around during the service, going from icon to icon, lighting candles, signing themselves, bowing, singing, and so on. They do not sit, but stand, kneel, or walk according to their spiritual response, impulse, or longing. The focus of the worshipers is not on a lecturer but on liturgy—the ritual form of confession, prayer, Scripture reading, praise, and personal participation. For all the intimacy we enjoy with God in contemporary Christian worship, we are missing a huge element of worship in regard to reverence, and I do not think we can get from here to there. Theology that stresses God is personal leads to intimate worship. Theology that stresses God is mystery leads to reverence. New-school believers will experiment, fail sometimes, succeed sometimes, go back and research, borrow traditions, experiment some more, happen on to something, and be led by the Spirit until they manage to merge a theology of person and mystery and release their souls into a worship that is reverent and intimate, sacred and relevant, spirit and truth.

Church on the Margin

The majority of towns and cities in North America are not likely to return the church to the geographical center of the community. There are many Christian leaders who have yet to come to terms with this fact and act as if the nation should be consulting them on all moral and spiritual issues. But the church has been pushed to the margin of society. What are we to make of this new geographical location? We are to make the most of it, knowing that everyone else on the margin is exactly the kind of person who has been invited to enter God's kingdom. We are going to see more churches on the margins, expressing their faith in worship styles that reflect their culture and, hopefully, the theological substance of Scripture and tradition.

If the corporate model of church creates discomfort for people on the outside, what other model should we expect to

see on the horizon? We should not expect to see any *one* configuration but a variety of small communities in every city. They
will probably tend to be connected along relational lines rather
than membership rolls. In other words, people will feel they
belong to a family rather than a company. When their church
contacts them, it will be a person who loves them and not a
computer that tracked them. In fact, groups of friends who go
camping together, work in food lines together, take pilgrim-
ages to holy sites (or Christian concerts) together will come
to realize that they are church and Christ is with them.

Do you know of a church that desperately wants to reach
young people? Not only do we worry about the coming generations, but their presence and participation in a church bring
to it a living energy that brightens every activity. So the typical
thing to do is plan special events and programs or attend seminars and subscribe to publications to draw in the youth. The
problem is that older people have designed most of these programs! Few people trust the youth enough to ask them to do
it. If a focus group is gathered, it often consists of the wrong
people, or else those present are not really encouraged to think
radically enough. Christian leaders do not generally pay any
attention to or endorse what young adults have to say. People
from eighteen to thirty years old do not pay the church's bills,
so their concerns are not as critical as the forty adults with
median incomes who can provide more revenue than four hundred young adults. One big reason the church does not listen
to the next generation is simple economics; money talks.

I am tempted to say that our youth are the future, but the
truth is, our youth are the present. The churches that need
to be planted today (or taken over) require youthful leadership with a solid connection to God, a strong link to popular
culture, and an honest desire to satisfy their spiritual longing
with something different than what they have been fed. Keep
your eyes open and continue to surf the Web. The prototypes
are beginning to emerge even now.

4

Do I Have to Sell God?

How People Believe

Have you ever sat in a restaurant and strained to hear the conversation at another table? Once when I was in a café, a few guys my age a couple tables over burst out laughing. One of the bigger guys was laughing so hard, his whole body shook and made the silverware dance in front of him. I went into "daredevil" mode, extending my listening skills in their direction to eavesdrop.

"Dude," one of them said, laughing, "remember the Power Team?"

"Totally!" the big guy was nodding his head, "I fully *rededicated* at that church."

"Oh, man, remember that guy named Carmen?" another chimed in.

They all broke out into laughter again.

They continued to crack jokes over their lunch, adding up all the times they "rededicated" their lives to Jesus. I began to laugh inside too as I recalled the time I was dragged off to a Power Team event. Several times that night we were urged to rededicate our lives to the Lord. While sitting there watching the muscular exploits, hyped by the ring-master-type preacher and applauded by the audience, the words "how lame" continued to flash on the screen of my mind. The evening was geared to Christians, who would understand the religious jargon, rather than to anyone outside the subculture.

The conversation I overheard in the café reminded me of all the other schmaltzy events I had suffered through in various churches. Though we were urged to invite our high school friends so they could hear the gospel, I would have been humiliated if any of my friends had ever caught me at one of those meetings. When I was a teenager, there were several times when I was at a party drinking or smoking weed, and people would start a conversation about God. Their thoughts and language were nothing like the religious vocabulary of my parents and their friends from church. My parents' religious talk embarrassed me so much, I found excuses to keep my friends away from my house. I always preferred spending the night at someone else's house. I was not about to expose my friends to my parents who would mortify me by blasting cheesy, Jewish-knockoff music with Christian lyrics, speak only in Christian slogans and clichés, and feel duty-bound to save my friends' souls. And you know what? Somehow I gained much more, spiritually speaking, from my pot-smoking friends than from my fundamentalism-smoking parents.

There was a period of my life when I hated Christianity because our church leaders prohibited us from having non-Christian friends. If we knew any nonbelievers, we were obligated to pressure them into converting to our faith. Youth pastors told us to start a Bible club at school and separate ourselves from the "worldly" kids. While other students are loafing through their lunch period or smoking on the baseball field, the message went, Christians should be praying and studying the Bible. The Christians who did as they were told tended to seem arrogant, as though they were better than everyone else—an attitude they most likely picked up at church. They seemed to think belonging to the Bible club was the only way to be good. For these reasons everyone made fun of them on campus.

Unfortunately, our youth leader thought we still lived in the eighties and so his program was hopelessly irrelevant. The worst time of the year was Halloween. My friends would ask me what I was doing, and I would change the subject or tell them to shut up so my parents would not hear them. When my parents did happen to overhear them, they quickly responded, "Matthew is staying home because Halloween is Satan's day. We don't worship Satan, we worship Elohim, Yahweh the God of Israel," and on and on they would go in a language that left my friends totally baffled. *Were Christians supposed to do this sort of thing? Would I have to do this to my children and their friends?* My parents' ravings were confusing even to me. All I knew for certain was that while my friends were out having fun on Halloween, I would be forced to attend the church Harvest Festival, where Christians dressed like farmers rather than demons, and the highlight of the evening would be a hayride—the holy alternative to our Satan-worshiping neighborhood's ritual of trick-or-treating.

Despite how uncomfortable my parents and youth group made me feel, I thought Jesus was cool. He seemed like a rebel; he lived outside the norm. He was criticized by the "good" people for hanging out on the margins and for socializing with sinners. But I was being raised in a religious subculture where we were forced to separate ourselves from the very places and people where Jesus would have been involved. The only time we associated with our community was one weekend a year when we went out to convert them. This was our church's big chance to point out everyone's sins and tell them, "Repent! For the kingdom of God is near." I was not the only person who felt conflicted about my admiration for Jesus and my embarrassment with the church. Every young person in the church felt this way, and they probably still do, because they left as soon as they could and have never returned.

Reflecting on that time of my life, I realize how different my view of Christianity was from that of my baby-boomer parents. They felt compelled to evangelize people, whereas I wanted to simply be with people. While hanging out with my friends, I did not need an agenda to convert them. I wanted to know them. When the topic of God came up in our conversations, I contributed my thoughts, but it was a lot of work, because the only vocabulary I had for religious topics was the hyperspiritual jargon of my church. I did not really know how to explain my beliefs. I knew certain behaviors were wrong, because that is what I was told, but I did not know *why* they were wrong. Nevertheless, my friends were graciously interested in what I had to say and asked a lot of questions. We had the kind of conversations you can have only in a close relationship, and that is something that cannot be formed at a one-time evangelistic event.

This brings me to questions I am always asking myself. Is mass evangelism the most effective means of introducing people to Jesus and the Christian faith? To me this seems like a mechanized Scotty-beam-me-up salvation, where everything happens in a matter of moments. But were the disciples saved when Jesus said, "Follow me"? Or was it a journey that they took with Jesus that ended in salvation? If the disciples were saved after their journey with Jesus, what implications does that have for my winning people to him? Do I have to be strategic with every conversation I have, always inserting a salvation message? I am unable to find where Jesus used the "four spiritual laws" or a salvation cube to win followers. What role does my life play in evangelism? Is it morally or biblically justifiable for preachers to pressure Christians to try to convert others? Does evangelism need to be anything more than building a relationship? Is evangelism reducible to effective tactics, or is it more about God's grace and a changed life? Do we have to talk about Jesus for the world to *see* him?

With all my heart I believe in Jesus Christ and his power to transform people. Elissa and I have devoted our lives to making sure people in all parts of the world and in every class of society have an opportunity to hear the story of Jesus Christ. By "hear the story," I do not mean that we merely expose them to a sermon, religious pamphlet, or a public broadcast. Instead, we interact with people so they have the opportunity to ask questions until they thoroughly understand the message. But at the end of the day, we are not the agents who work God's revelation into their hearts. We cannot control their response or force them to make the decisions we have made.

How Christians Convey the Message

What if Christians received training to become skilled *listeners*, to be people who create an atmosphere of dialogue wherever they go, with any type of person? What if we knew how to ask the questions that matter to others and encouraged them to ask us questions? I do not mean that we should have a list of stock questions, but we must have enough love for and interest in other people that we allow them to lead the conversation, and in this way *show us* what it is they need to hear about God. What if God wanted us to engage people in conversation the way Jesus did in the Gospel of John?

I would never toss out mass evangelism, because many believers I know credit one of these events with the beginning of their Christian experience. I have seen some amazing productions move audiences of all ages and backgrounds. Also I believe that mass evangelism can sometimes be a catalytic event to get people out of the comfy chair on Sunday morning and bring salvation to the streets. After all, that is where it belongs, not locked up in a bell tower or steeple. But I will never have enough money to put on a big show or the staff to organize a massive rally, and I am fairly certain God does not want average Joes like me to bring amplifiers and microphones into the office, stand on our desks, and at ninety-eight decibels announce that the kingdom of heaven is near. The reality is that average Christians live, work, learn, and play among more nonbelievers on any given day than will be affected by ten thousand years of mass events. We need to build relationships with the people who live within our orbit; we need to show them love, and we need to learn how to converse with them.

Recently I spent the weekend in Waikiki with Elissa. We had the chance to stay right on the beach for free. While cruising the strip I saw some hilarious things. First there are the entertainers, men and women who are completely painted in silver and gold, posing as statues. The person who really caught my eye was a musician who was playing his guitar while his friend was handing out flyers. As I got closer, I realized it was a familiar tune—one of those cheesy evangelical praise and worship songs.

I kept walking and saw something that seemed to me like such an act of injustice. It so disturbed me, I wanted to scream. I wanted to tear my clothes and run through the street naked to stop this injustice. A group of fourteen-to-seventeen-year-old kids were singing yet another praise and worship song, holding a box for offerings and a stack of directions for saving your soul. *Who is making them do this?* I wondered. You could see the embarrassment on their faces. You could feel the utter horror that was inside them as people walked by and laughed and snickered. I am sure it was a youth pastor who put them up to it. "Kids, people need to hear the gospel," I imagine him saying. "Jesus was slapped, beaten, and killed; we can at least sacrifice our Friday night and sing a song on the street corner." It's interesting that I did not see the pastor anywhere around, but I noticed something else. As these kids were singing, their eyes were drawn up the road to another group. Five black kids were ripping rhythms with their drums. They were holding down the beat while people joined in battling each other. Black kids, Asian kids, and Hispanic kids were all using their quick minds to create the smoothest flows for one another.

Why can't the church get hold of what is happening in our culture? When will we start to understand that if we like something in our church, like a song or dance, most likely the average person cruising down the street won't be able to relate to it? When are we going to get it? When will we understand that kids in our choir would rather be playing music on the street? Could it be that God has put in them the ability to create flows that are better than those of the average rapper out there? When will we start letting a younger generation lead us out of our pews and into the streets?

Evangelicals Evangelize

The evangelical label comes from *evangel* (Greek, *euangélion*) and is translated in our New Testament as "gospel." Evangelicals are Christians who have dedicated their lives to communicating the gospel to the entire world. Though the Bible says nothing about a Great Commission (it does have something to say about the "greatest commandment"), evangelicals interpret the last three verses of Matthew's Gospel as a requirement and priority for all believers. In the broader sense, to evangelize means "to make disciples"—presumably to turn Gentile pagans into full-fledged Christians, but its narrower and common-use meaning is "to tell others the good news that they do not have to go to hell, because Jesus died for their sins."

Around the middle of the twentieth century, a number of young men, who were eager to win the world to Jesus Christ and were frustrated with the procrastination and ineffectiveness of churches, moved outside the church and founded a number of important parachurch organizations. These new institutions tended to specialize in reaching certain demographic sectors, such as college students, people in the armed services, and substance abusers. Though these leaders had the best intentions, there were a number of unfortunate developments.

1. Many Christians came to think of evangelism as "delivering a message." The idea of *listening* to others neither occurred to them nor seemed important. For that reason, evangelism could be performed en masse, over the radio, or through pamphlets handed randomly to strangers. Christians who engaged in this type of evangelism seldom worried about how their words were perceived, because they felt they had done their job if they got the message "out there."

2. The message that evangelicals communicated to non-Christians was often a distilled version of the faith and therefore an oversimplification that not only missed important elements but actually misrepresented the truth. They reduced the profound message of the New Testament to bite-size pieces of information, supported their assertions with biblical quotations (from Rom. 3:23; 6:23; and John 3:16, for example), and then delivered an urgent appeal for a response.

3. Individual believers were given the impression that their job was to "close the deal"—to pressure others to make a decision regarding Jesus after being exposed to the Good News, even if this was their first encounter with the Christian message. The hard-sell aspect of witnessing or evangelizing is what average Christians found the most uncomfortable and disturbing part of the process. They felt like they had to be hucksters or telemarketers for Jesus.

4. Christians were often made to feel guilty if they did not take every single opportunity to force the topic of salvation into every conversation and encounter with family, friends, coworkers, fellow students, and strangers. After all, if the hallmark of being a Christian was evangelism, then every believer should be forcing the issue all the time. People were on their way to hell unless we intervened by letting them know that Jesus died for their sins. So Christians felt obliged to do things that on some occasions seemed socially inappropriate, rude, unnatural, and beyond their abilities. Understandably, their presentation was generally perceived as forced, awkward, and obnoxious.

If the faithful Christian attempting to convert a stranger on the street is confronted with a scientific or philosophical objection, there are all sorts of no-nonsense, apologetics-made-easy answers that are available to him. Generally this includes a pseudo-scientific refutation of evolution (which will not work if the other person has had a college-level course in organic chemistry or geology) or an incredibly deficient theodicy (an argument for why an all-good, all-powerful, all-loving, all-wise God would allow pain and evil). Christians who pride themselves on their personal evangelism skills are often guilty of providing cheap answers to serious questions. Some such questions take philosophers a whole lifetime to sort out, let alone answer.

New Testament scholar N. T. Wright has argued that if we want to understand the teachings of Jesus and Paul, we need to read them in the context of first-century Judaism. The starting point for interpreting the New Testament, according to Wright, is in the socio-historical, theological, and literary context in which it first appeared. So even though evangelists have commandeered the word *gospel* in reference to their short-form message of salvation, the full range of meaning that John the Baptist, Jesus, or Paul had in mind may have been somewhat different. Wright says:

> "The gospel" is supposed to be a description of how people get saved; of the theological mechanism whereby, in some people's language, Christ takes our sin and we his righteousness; in other people's language, Jesus becomes my personal saviour; in other languages again, I admit my sin, believe that he died for me, and commit my life to him. In many church circles, if you hear something like that, people will say that "the gospel" has been preached. Conversely, if you hear a sermon in which the claims of Jesus Christ are related to the political or ecological questions of the day, some people will say that, well, perhaps the subject was interesting, but "the gospel" wasn't preached.[1]

Though Wright is comfortable with the way evangelists use the word *gospel*, he does not believe Paul used the word in the same way. He had something more in mind. To do justice to the gospel, we should be aware of its wider meaning and not assume that the way we have used it in our subculture reflects its full depth or tells the whole story.

If, on the one hand, evangelicals have misrepresented the gospel through oversimplification or formulaic steps to salvation, they have also made the concept all but inaccessible to the average person. Why do many Christians insist on using terms found in the King James Version of the Bible to describe the various facets of salvation, such as *repentance, redemption, atonement, justification, righteousness, reconciliation, propitiation*, and *sanctification*? The New Testament was written in a common (*koine*) language, but we continue to use an outdated and inflated vocabulary to talk about God's work in our lives, which almost guarantees that no one will understand us. In fact, given a pop quiz on a Sunday morning, my guess is that many evangelicals would not score well if asked to explain the theology behind words we hear and use all the time.

While theologians struggle to fine-tune the theological definitions of these key terms, who is bothering to translate them into the common language of average Christians (let alone people outside the church who have no Bible background)? Is the typical vocabulary used in evangelism really necessary? What of believers who live in impoverished and war-torn parts of the world and have not heard these evangelistic terms? Is their faith less real, less rich, less genuine than that of believers in the West? Many Christians in the United States admit that believers they have met who suffer for their faith are more authentically Christian than the armchair variety here at home, who constantly debate the finer points of doctrinal nomenclature.

Though theological knowledge may be important, what is the essence of the Christian life? Have we concentrated too much on being well informed when we should have been developing well-formed character? Lifestyle changes can be made long before Christians have answers to all their theological questions, and their lives can influence others even if they haven't mastered all of the evangelical terminology or shortcut apologetic answers.

The New Evangelism

Evangelism in the new context necessarily emphasizes dialogue rather than monologue, relationship rather than impersonal contact, a life that is lived and a story that is told. Dialogue is, of course, two-way communication. Living in a pluralistic society requires Christians to listen as much as they speak and sometimes to listen more than they speak. Our right to speak in public is earned, in part, by our willingness to listen to others. Jesus's apparently free-flowing conversations with Nicodemus and the Samaritan woman are models of how the new school concerns itself first with people and then with the message we present in ways they can understand so they will discover its application to their needs.

We also have a new understanding of the Good News. It calls for radical change and allegiance. In the New Testament we find communal, social, and political concerns, as well as personal concerns (as in, personal Savior). The fact that Jesus addressed human physical need as well as spiritual need, that he cared for people on the margins of society and turned a critical eye toward hypocrisy, expands our understanding of what the gospel *is* and *does* in community.

New-school Christians have a high regard for the greatest and second-greatest commandments—to love the Lord our God with all our heart, strength, and mind; and to love our neighbor as ourselves (see Matt. 22:36–39). The application of these commandments is evangelism as Jesus demonstrated it and comes before any sort of methodology, publication, or script. The type of evangelism that is concerned only about winning souls, while neglecting the needs of individual men, women, and children, is a contradiction of Scripture, which tells us that God made humans in his image and that salvation means *wholeness* as well as rescue.

According to new-school believers, it is not their job to convert people. The word *convert* has gone through a conversion since the time of the King James Bible. The Latin origin of *convert* simply meant "to turn," and in the New Testament, it is the believer who *turns himself* away from sin and toward God. The contemporary definition of convert is to "change something," and in religion it means to change people to your religious point of view, but that is not how it was used in the Bible. I think we will always have a sense of doom if we go through life thinking we have to convert people. We have the choice to turn our own lives around, but God has not given us the power to turn around anyone else. What we can do is live a *changed* life and explain to others how God worked that change and that he is willing to do the same for them. But we cannot change them.

New-school Christians do not put much emphasis on programs, such as discipleship classes, where believers receive more information than they can retain, are challenged to strive toward impossible goals, or are given the whole Christian life in neat sequential stages that have little to do with real-life development and spiritual warfare. Instead of worrying about how much information believers can acquire and disseminate, new-school Christians concentrate on the type of person Christianity produces. Are we merciful, generous, kind, full of love and integrity? In a word, are we *good people*? Those who live outside the church do not care what we believe, but they watch us to discover what Jesus does with a person's life when it is given to him.

What does new-school evangelism look like in popular culture? It looks like *you*. Every Christian is an advertisement for the faith. The most effective evangelism is a life transformed by Jesus Christ, a life that reflects his goodness and love, a life that is dedicated to alleviating pain, redeeming society, and taking care of the planet and its ecosystems. If we are not transformed into the kind of people who reflect Jesus Christ, then what is the point of talking other people into becoming Christians? Either it works or it does not work. If it works, the evidence will be in your life; then people may ask you to explain "the reason for the hope that you have" (1 Peter 3:15).

5

Can Christianity
Be Reduced to
Steps or Stages?

The Problem with Structure

My work in Youth With A Mission includes teaching in discipleship and leadership training schools around the world. A recent engagement brought me to one of our schools in the heart of Mexico, which was nice for me, because I had not been in Latin America for several years. All the arrangements for our trip went smoothly and Elissa and I were soon airborne.

When we arrived in Guadalajara, Mexico, two people from the school's staff met us. Our ride from the airport was the typically wonderful tour through the countryside, passing horses, cows, and small farms, while raising a dust cloud. I had forgotten how much I enjoyed earlier trips to this rich part of the earth. We rounded a corner, drove along a dirt drive, and entered through the gates into the campus. Usually there were no more than seven to fifteen staff members living in this facility, but when we got there, the campus was in a frenzy of activity. More than three hundred people had registered for this particular semester.

As we climbed out of the van, people were everywhere. A friend we had not seen in a long time stepped out of the chaos of the bustling crowd, and her first question to Elissa and me summed up the situation on campus: "Have you guys come to take me home?" She then described the ordeals of the previous four weeks: sharing one room with thirty-six other women and three bathrooms with three hundred people. Crazy, right?

The philosophy behind these leadership schools is to provide the students not only with a classroom education but also an exposure to other cultures. So the leadership school is a *floating campus* that moves to different locations around the world. In this way the school can accommodate local leaders (who do not have the means to travel out of their area) while at the same time training the more mobile students. The implicit assumption behind this philosophy is that God will provide enough buildings and facilities to train, feed, and house everyone who attends. When the school completes its session, it leaves behind a large number of trained leaders as well as new buildings that are available for further ministry.

Time flies when you have a busy teaching schedule, and suddenly we realized our week of lectures was over. The last day we were on campus, the staff asked me if I would take a few minutes to "share what was on my heart" before leaving. I wanted to oblige them, but there was one major problem—I had *many things* on my heart. During the week of ordered chaos, sleeping in a room the size of a closet, looking out a clear plastic window with a hole cut in it for air, God had been speaking to me—louder than I had heard him for several years. The four nights we were there, I had hardly slept because my brain was trying to process everything it was learning.

Before we left our home, bound for Mexico, I had grabbed a cheesy-looking journal that had been on our shelf for months. I blew the dust off it and tossed it into my backpack. I am so grateful now that I brought it along, because I was not able to write fast enough all the new thoughts that came to me. While I listened to the other lecturers, I scribbled notes, feeling I was going to explode with all these insights and wanting to scream them out to the attentive students. So that last morning in Mexico was my big chance. But how could I possibly condense all this information and pack it into a five-point lecture? What acronym could capture my experience of God that week? My thoughts and feelings were all over the map. I decided to leave my Bible and journal in my room with our suitcases all packed and ready to go. I would simply stand in front of the students and let the words flow. To the best of my ability, I would tell the story of what God had been doing with me and showing me.

After I was given a brief introduction, I went on stage and stood before three hundred people representing fifty-two nations. With no notes, I breathed an urgent prayer that God would not let my mind go blank, paused briefly allowing the room to be cloaked in silence, and then I set free the words rumbling in my heart. Fifteen minutes later I was finished. Without making a formal conclusion, I walked off the stage. I cannot explain the following forty-five minutes, except to say God worked in ways I had never seen before. The students and faculty felt vitally connected to God, we had moved beyond the academic culture, and we sensed something going on inside of us, healing deep wounds and the damage of many years.

From this experience and others I have learned that oftentimes our well-prepared sermons leave little room for the prophetic; our busy retreats give us little time to listen for God's gentle whisper; our organized church service can hinder the flow of conversation and normal community building. Are we more certain of logic than we are of God? Do we tend to substitute logic for experience?

Many of us want to marvel at God's infinite and awesome nature. We can tell when a preacher is speaking from his notes, his stored-up clichés, or his heart. We want to meet with God in worship (or else we should stop claiming that we do). We are tired of the song and dance and yearn for the real deal. Do highly structured and formalized relationships mask our doubts, insecurities, and the truth of just how messed up we actually feel inside? Does the ten-step program give us an illusion of being in control, when what we really need to learn is to surrender our lives to God's control? Is it possible that if our lives were less ordered, the world would see a refreshing realness in our lives that speaks of grace rather than grids, service rather than success, and God himself rather than pseudo-people putting on pseudo-events?

You may be thinking I am completely against planning and all about intuition. This is not the case. I spend hours preparing lessons and messages. I have organized many university courses and training models. But the point I am making is that I try not to let the structure lead. There is something organic that occurs when you are open to the creativity in other people, open to their last-minute input, or open to those moments when your mind, heart, and soul kick into a high gear of new understanding. It is in those times that I lay aside my plans for the sake of greater revelation.

C It's Not Rocket Science

Ask twenty Christians how they came to believe in Jesus and you will hear twenty different stories. Ask a hundred Christians and you will hear a hundred different stories. Every time someone describes his or her spiritual journey to God, I am amazed. No one could have programmed such a strange and roundabout route to the Creator. Everyone who turns to God in truth has come to him by a path that includes many diverse events and encounters that, in retrospect, are obviously the work of God's Spirit. So why do we think we can *engineer* evangelism, spiritual growth, or encounters with God? We have to understand a few things about the last two hundred years of Western culture to answer this question.

By the dawn of the twentieth century, science had intruded into every aspect of personal and family life. The positive result of this intrusion was protection and relief from such debilitating illnesses as polio, whooping cough, and cholera. As the technology of communication systems advanced and spread, more and more households were informed of new medical solutions to age-old problems. The assumption of the modern age—that all progress is good, especially if it occurs rapidly—ensured that more and more labor-saving and life-enhancing commodities would appear in thick catalogs and newspapers on our doorsteps and later intrude into our living rooms through radio and television. Science, in service to the world, promised a continuous stream of solutions to human problems, needs, and desires.

Perhaps that early enthusiasm for all the new gadgets, medical triumphs, communication, and transportation technologies blinded people to the fact that they were not only buying what science invented, but they were buying into science itself—that is to say, a worldview. The scientific method—observation and description of an "event," formation of a hypothesis, prediction, experimentation, and so on—yielded a process for unraveling the mysteries of the universe. The physical sciences focused attention especially on cause-and-effect relationships in the universe. Therefore, if one knew the process that caused an event and had the resources to duplicate the cause, then one could replicate the effect over and over again. The basic idea was rather simple: the secret to producing the effect is knowing and engineering the cause.

As a worldview, the scientific method produces an unconscious assumption that, given enough information and material resources, there is a solution for every problem, every mystery can be solved, every goal achieved, every mission accomplished. Do you want to be a success? Listen to the person who has discovered the steps (cause) that have been proven to produce success (effect). It is all so *scientific*!

If you wonder how far the scientific method has shaped our worldview, consider how many "methods" are sold to help us order our personal lives. There is no end to the books that claim to teach the science of this or that. For example, there is *The Science of Cooking*, *The Science of Selling*, *The Science of Happiness*, *The Science of Mind* (which is not a science and has nothing to do with cognitive science or neuroscience), and even *The Science of Harry Potter*.

Did the church resist the scientific worldview and immunize itself against the assumption that science was the answer to every question, problem, and challenge? If you know the church, you know the answer. We have been assured that even as "there are physical laws that govern our physical universe, so there are spiritual laws that govern our relationship with God."[1] We have been offered steps ranging from all kinds of spiritual disciplines to personal and practical matters—peace with God (are these *all* the steps, and has everyone who has peace with God taken these same exact steps?), a successful marriage, discipleship, evangelism, and on and on. In fact, there are many preachers who give us the impression that each department of our lives can be sorted out, inventoried, and managed in such a way as to achieve whatever goal we desire. They go so far as to claim that the Bible itself provides the scientific principles for effective Christian living.

Borrowing from the worldview of modernity, Christian authors, preachers, and leaders have offered their faithful followers rational guides to spiritual development. By following logical steps, we can all reach desired goals, such as maturity, humility, patience, or even spiritual gifts. Through such teaching, the Christian life has suffered the same reductionism as everything else that can be dragged into a laboratory, dissected with a scalpel, and placed under a microscope. We can know how a machine or living organism works by breaking it down to its smallest components, examining their functions, then forming a hypothesis that explains how all the pieces work and go together to form the whole. Everyone appreciates the value of these experiments—except the frog.

The scientific method became the dominant mind-set in North American culture because it worked. We have always been a pragmatic people, eager to adopt the easiest, quickest, and surest route to our goal. But the question is this: can the scientific method be applied effectively to *everything*? We can understand how useful it is when we need to figure out why our bedroom clock stopped working or if we need to learn a new computer program (there are some things we can learn and master by steps), but when it comes to other, less material, issues, we find that our current sciences have not yet collected enough data for us to draw conclusions or we are dealing with spheres where the scientific method breaks down.

The scientific method works in situations in which there are constants. For example, if water always boils at 212 degrees Fahrenheit (at sea level) and always freezes at 32 degrees, then we can make stable predictions about ice cubes and boiled eggs. But any parent who has more than one child can tell you there are few constants from child to child. One sibling will eat like a shark and another like a bird. One will teethe at five months and another at ten months. One will not respond to discipline regardless of the method used, while the other collapses into tears when spoken to in a harsh voice. Perhaps there is a general constant, that all children need discipline, but to be effective, the form that discipline takes varies from child to child. If we understand the New Testament correctly, God's grace determines and shapes the course of an individual Christian's life rather than the constants of the Mosaic law.

Laboratory Faith

Christian faith created "in a lab" is a manageable faith rather than a scary and uncertain faith. So the temptation to reduce the process of becoming a believer to simple steps is difficult to resist. But among the various Christian traditions and evangelistic organizations, there is a wide divergence of teaching on these topics. For example, what are we to do with the fact that one expert's method for discipleship differs significantly from another's, or the process that requires "three stages" for one teacher requires "ten stages" for another? We can see that the number of steps or stages depends entirely on the person selling those steps.

Regardless of the number of steps a preacher tells believers they must take to pray effectively, achieve intimacy, beat depression, become successful, or whatever, the scientifically inspired attempt to *clarify everything* leaves little room for mystery. Where there is no mystery, there is no reverence. Perhaps the loss of mystery was one of the motivations for the way some old-school evangelicals romanticized their relationship with Jesus—even as the philosophical romanticism of the eighteenth century was a reaction to neoclassical art. When the life of the spirit is rationalized or objectified, we long for subjective experiences. But over-romanticizing a personal relationship with Jesus plays into the hands of philosophers who deny that God's existence can be proven and must be accepted only through blind (imaginary) faith.

The modern assumption that Christian virtues or disciplines can be acquired through a series of steps has been haunted by a nagging problem: *the steps do not work*. Even for those people who have faithfully and diligently followed every step, the promised results fail to materialize. Too few people acknowledge this fact. Of course, if the technician who invented the steps is going to troubleshoot the problem, he will find a flaw in a person's performance rather than in his system. People are therefore berated for not trying hard enough or not being sincere enough to make the program work. It is their fault. But when a great many people are told that if they use a particular method to get rich and only one in a hundred actually makes any money, we should question the method. I should also add that in most cases the preacher who presents the steps to this or that desired goal has not done any real scientific or field research to verify the process. To be honest, preachers and authors pull a lot of this stuff out of the air.

Really, this sort of thing is so easy; it is cheap. For example, right off the top of my head, I am going to come up with the four necessary elements of prayer—I am making this up as I write:

P*ersuasion*. You must be persuaded that God can handle everything you bring him (2 Tim. 1:12 KJV).

Reliance. You must completely rely on God, without doubting or leaning on your own understanding (Prov. 3:5; James 1:6).

Ardency. You must be fervent in your requests (James 5:16 KJV).

Yieldedness. You must surrender your will to God (Mark 14:36).

Okay, so I had to make up a word. (Do you know which one? Not *ardency*, that is a real word.) The scriptural references came to mind immediately (as they would to any minister). I could do this sort of thing all day, but in terms of *real value*, no one under my care would receive any substantial help. I am not saying there is no truth in the PRAY elements I made up, but they do not tell the *whole* story about prayer, and enough is missing to confuse and trouble a sincere Christian who is trying to make prayer work in her life.

Many well-meaning and dedicated believers have made their best effort to do all they have been told would help them achieve assurance, hope, stronger faith, answers to prayer, or any number of personal successes, but they have failed. Life, faith, relationships, and anything relating to mental or emotional states are not so easy to simplify. Still, there are preachers who insist their program works, and for a handful of people it may work. But that is not proof that we have uncovered the one, true biblical methodology. My suspicion is that more often than not, the speakers who oversimplify the message of the Bible are like the religious leaders criticized by Jeremiah: "They dress the wound of my people as though it were not serious. 'Peace, peace,' they say, when there is no peace" (Jer. 6:14).

If the spiritual programs based on rational or scientific procedures are flawed, why do they work for some people? I am not qualified to give a final answer to this question, but I can suggest three possibilities. First, it may be that enough truth is embedded in the process that it will work for some people, especially those with little training or understanding of Christian faith; young Christians are especially susceptible to believing everything they hear from a preacher. Second, some people are so optimistic, everything seems to work for them—their career choice, their parenting, their diets—no matter what plan they use. Nevertheless, the success they tout is no more universal than their optimism.

Third, for many people a structured approach to spirituality seems to work but only superficially. In other words, people who have a shallow commitment to God jump through all the hoops as if earning a merit badge, but in the end they are no more serious about their faith or closer to God than when they began. The results of applying oneself to the engineered stages of spiritual progress may be nothing more than finishing a guidebook or manual and doing the exercises at the end of each chapter. The process may have little effect on one's daily life.

The Work of Grace

The methodology underlying the idea that people can become right with God by following certain laws, taking steps on their own volition, or performing religious "works" runs counter to the teaching of the New Testament. Christian faith insists that humans are absolutely incapable of saving or justifying themselves (Mark 10:23–27; John 1:12–13; Rom. 3:20; 9:31–32; Gal. 2:16; 3:1–3, 21–22; Eph. 2:8–10). If there are definite steps every Christian must take to accomplish spiritual goals, then we have reverted to a performance-based religion that negates faith, grace, and the hand of God. I am not saying that God's grace does not call for our cooperation, only that his grace takes us places we cannot go on our own (no matter how many steps or stages we master). If we are convinced that we can achieve some kind of spiritual success by following the rules outlined for us, our confidence rides on our own effort and works.

I do not question whether we are to "work out [our] salvation with fear and trembling," but no one could plot all the steps the Holy Spirit takes any individual through to bring out the full implications of salvation, nor does the Spirit follow any particular order or have everyone matriculate through the same process (see Jude 22–23). The way of the Holy Spirit in a person's spiritual life is less like walking up a stairway and more like riding an elevator that makes apparently random stops until the person reaches his floor.

There is no effective movement toward God, unless we have first had an experience of God working in us "to will and to act according to his good purpose," or we are living something other than the Christian life (Phil. 2:12–13). Preachers who imply that Christianity is simple and can be mastered by following their principles, secrets, or keys minimize the importance of grace. There is nothing worthwhile in the Christian life that can be had or accomplished apart from grace. There is no way to predict or program how God's grace will enter our lives or from which direction. To give grace lip service, then try to achieve spiritual maturity through an outlined program, is to wander from grace into a works-oriented religious lifestyle. Grace is not an "add on" that we include in our list of steps.

How often have we missed the force of Jesus's teaching: "With man this is impossible, but not with God; all things are possible with God" (Mark 10:27). The inner transformation of a human life that makes a person a "new creation" is purely an act of God. Science as we know it in the West is rooted in *naturalism*; it does not acknowledge anything outside the objects and forces of the material universe. Perhaps modern Christian thinking was subtly infiltrated by the idea that God did not mess with his creation, does not actually perform inner transformations, and therefore it is up to us to devise methods for improving our spiritual lives on our own.

Does the Bible contain specific instructions on how Christians are to believe, behave, pray, treat others, and so on? Yes, of course the Bible has much to say about these things. Does the Bible promise benefits to those who will follow its instructions and commandments? Most certainly. But contrary to the promise of many preachers, we may not see any tangible benefits in our lifetime. Nor is it the intent of the Bible that we turn its teaching into formulas.

Do you ever wonder if Christian authors and preachers have missed the point when they tell us there are biblical, even "heavenly," strategies for material success? Does the message of the New Testament in any way suggest that believers should be living examples of success in every facet of life? Jesus's and Paul's teachings were intended for an impoverished people—many of whom were slaves—who were more concerned with survival goals than material success goals.

If business, corporate, financial, marital, and parenting "success" were as simple as preachers imply in their "Ten Biblical Principles," then there would be many more Christians funding humanitarian and relief organizations around the world and fewer Christians living in poverty.

But the balance of poor to wealthy Christians has always been pretty much the same, and Paul did not seem as concerned about Christians acquiring wealth (or being successful centurions or successful craftsmen) as he was that believers learn to be content with their situation in life. Much later, during an era of unprecedented affluence and self-interest, success principles were developed, and preachers began to declare that every Christian could (or should) be high achievers in every walk of life.

One of the many traits that typifies old-school authors is the tendency to hype their particular formula. Pick up one of their books or listen to their spiel, and what you find in the introduction is an exaggerated promise of the benefits you will receive by following their program. Have you ever wondered why we have been so vulnerable to this blatant self-promotion? Have you ever glanced back after reading one of these books or attending one of the seminars and realized you were sold empty promises? No doubt there are many leaders, indoctrinated into the scientific worldview, who sincerely believe that they hold the keys to the kingdom. But there are many hucksters who know they can draw crowds of desperate people who need to believe the promise of financial freedom or spiritual victory, even though there is often a huge gap between the speaker's own life and the promises he sells. "Unlike so many," Paul said, "we do not peddle the word of God for profit. On the contrary, in Christ we speak before God with sincerity, like men sent from God" (2 Cor. 2:17). Paul! He is always a breath of fresh air.

A Simple Comparison

Mike Yaconelli died too soon. For more than thirty years I have known of his ministry, yet I was unprepared for the gentle wisdom and reassurance I found in his book *Messy Spirituality*, released the year before he died.[2] His book hit a nerve with new-school believers (a quick search on the Internet for blog sites where his book is discussed will reveal not only its popularity but the strong response of young people who fully identify with its theme). We love Mike's book because he describes Christian faith in a way that is true to our experience.

In *Messy Spirituality* Yaconelli tells stories about himself, others, and his church that sound familiar. People who love God, yet sin; people who take two steps forward in Christ, then slide three steps backward; people who swear, yet demonstrate incredible generosity. Messy spirituality is unstructured, unpredictable, unstable, like the real life most people know. The Christian experience Yaconelli talks about is transparent regarding its struggles, honest about its failures, carried forward by God's infinite grace, and totally impossible to manage.

I also love Rick Warren's book *The Purpose-Driven Life* and have a deep respect for Rick as a Christian leader and trainer.[3] However, I agree with Justin Baeder who on his blog said, "I really think its message is pretty good; it's just that the packaging is not well suited to the emerging generations. . . . This book was written to get Boomer churchgoers to do more than warm pews; it's not an evangelistic tract for 20-somethings."[4] Here is the difference between old school and new school in regard to spiritual growth. Old school continually simplifies the process, breaking it down into stages, whereas new school sees the process as a complex whole, beyond sorting. Yes, some things you can control, but the demand for continual grace (on God's part) and faith (on ours) is extremely high.

Science has been with us long enough for us to realize that it cannot create happiness or utopia. It cannot even solve all of the problems it created. For new-school believers, the Bible is more story than science. Treating the Bible as information from which we draw ideas and principles to engineer a spiritual life seems foreign to the emerging generation of Christians. For them the Bible generates life, opens their minds to the experience of God, or at the very least enables them to hear God's voice. The fact that the predominant literary form of Scripture is narrative (followed by poetry) is not lost on them.

I need to clarify one point. People who teach Bible studies for new-school believers cannot get by with less research, reading, and study into the background of the biblical text—history, theology, literature, worldview, culture, language, geopolitics, and social science. Rather, they must do more! What is needed is not less scholarship but more scholarship. We need teachers who understand that Scripture, like life itself, is complex and multifaceted, and its meaning is not always self-evident. Instead of oversimplifying the riddles of the Bible, teachers should work alongside students who are struggling to understand its message, to sort out its difficulties, to grasp its truth, and to make the most honest application of its meaning to their lives. We do not need teachers who pretend to have all the answers and then spell them out for us with charts, diagrams, and alliterations that purport to make the Bible easy to digest and simple to put into practice but do not work.

Old school's steps and stages, keys and secrets, methods and programs look too packaged for tomorrow's Christian. Like the military's MREs (meals ready to eat), the contents may provide necessary nutrition but lack the flavor of real food. In the same way, a by-the-numbers approach to spirituality is unappealing to kids who invented extreme sports. The unknown, the unanswered question, the potential risk, and the adrenaline rush that follows the adventure tell them they're alive. They discern in the pages of the Bible an extreme engagement with *life*. A Savior who lives so boldly as to risk crucifixion on a Roman cross and who dies so courageously as to impress his executioner is not likely to be the kind of person who commits himself to the seven habits of other people—effective or otherwise.

For a generation raised on television, the promises of Christian authors and preachers are indistinguishable from self-help gurus, motivational speakers, and infomercial hucksters. No one takes advertisers seriously any more, not even advertisers. Who told us, "Image is nothing"? It was a television commercial, trying to create a thirst-quenching "image." They understand popular culture's skepticism toward ads and attempt to use it. In an environment where most every message is a sales pitch, the grandiose promises of preachers appear thin. Older Christians may take the bait on the book jacket, but new-school Christians doubt that answers for their troubled and chaotic lives are available for twenty dollars.

Individualized Curriculum

Every person's life is complex, difficult, and fraught with challenge. New-school believers acknowledge that there are universals, such as sin, truth, right/wrong, good/evil, and so on. But what they doubt is the universalizing of lived experience, which is subject to many varying factors from individual to individual. Theologian George Ellis makes this point when he says:

> There is always a tension between universal principles and the particular situations in which they are applied. The specific circumstances applying in any particular case give it specific identity, and still allow universal principles to apply; the related underlying questions are whether the model is appropriate to the particular situation at hand (a meta-question that cannot be answered fully by use of the model itself), and whether all significant particular circumstances have been taken into account by the model used.[5]

How does the illiterate person fulfill the criteria for discipleship that requires daily Bible reading? Important differences between races, genders, socioeconomic groups, mental abilities (and disabilities), aptitude, and interest in learning and an almost infinite host of individualizing factors throw the standardized "simple steps" into a tailspin.

New-school believers don't want to manage life as much as observe it, discover what emerges, and respond accordingly. Their lives seem as random to them as Abraham's must have seemed to him (or Ruth, David, Paul, or just about any other biblical character). For example, it would be difficult to believe that Paul planned on being imprisoned, shipwrecked, stoned, and chased from one city to another (2 Cor. 11:23–27). Paul could not predict where his message would be accepted or how long he would be in a particular city. At one time he wanted to go with his traveling companions to Bithynia, but "the Spirit of Jesus did not permit them" (Acts 16:7). On other occasions he was directed in a vision to go to Macedonia (vv. 9–10), instructed in a trance to go to the Gentiles (22:17–21), and told by an angel that he would appear before Caesar (27:23–24)—methods for discerning God's will that you are not likely to find in the typical "key to success" Christian books. On his last trip to Jerusalem, Paul admitted he did not know what would happen to him there (20:22), and it is doubtful that he expected the events that followed or his eventual imprisonment in Caesarea. After telling the Roman Christians that he planned on coming to them, he did not come the way he said he would, not realizing that he would arrive as a prisoner (Rom. 15:22–26). The image of Paul being led by the hand into Damascus is a rather fitting symbol for the way he lived the remainder of his life (Acts 9:8).

In the same way, new schoolers are confident that God is in control, so even unexpected and painful events somehow fit into the whole design. In fact, the unplanned events are sometimes the most crucial life-defining moments in one's journey, and for new-school Christians the journey metaphor is more dominant and believable than the "I have arrived" pose of some teachers. New-school disciples are looking for teachers who are on the road, traveling with them, and admitting their own weaknesses and flaws as everyone helps everyone else.

Few new-school Christians are looking for manuals that boil marriage, parenting, discipleship, or evangelism down to a science. They are looking instead for mystery, beauty, passion, love, and, in a word, God. Not a totally comprehensible god, dissected into minuscule doctrines and from whom all mystery has been drained, but the unpredictable and consuming fire of a God whose presence engulfed Abraham in dread and made Moses tremble. Ambiguity is not a deterrent for these believers, because their lives are already filled with unsolved riddles they have learned to take for granted. They do not feel the same pressure that drove previous generations to reason their way to the last word on debated doctrines or interpretation of Scripture. They are content not to know everything, because their faith is in the God who knows all.

The objective of new-school preachers and teachers is a changed life, and that means that a new set of commandments is not going to be any more effective than the originals (see Rom. 3:20). Spiritual transformation does not work from the outside in, because "church people are like other people; we are not changed by new rules." If preaching new rules will not change people, as Old Testament theologian Walter Brueggemann claims, then what? "The event of preaching is an event in transformed imagination."[6] Brueggemann's point is that if a person can begin to imagine a different life, a different world, then breaking free from the current condition becomes a possibility. If people never imagine a life other than the one they live, they will not take the first steps toward freedom.

> The deep places in our lives—places of resistance and embrace—are not ultimately reached by instruction. Those places of resistance and embrace are reached only by stories, by images, metaphors, and phrases that line out the world differently, apart from our fear and hurt. The reflection that comes from the poet requires playfulness, imagination, and interpretation.[7]

Given this context, the parables of Jesus make perfect sense.

If preachers and teachers seriously want to change lives, rather than lay down rules or standardized growth stages, they should consider transforming imaginations and altering worldviews by way of storytelling. As N. T. Wright has observed: "Stories are, actually, peculiarly good at modifying or subverting other stories and their worldviews." In *The New Testament and the People of God*, he explores the way Jesus used stories (parables) to alter or replace the dominant worldviews of his time.[8]

Walter Brueggemann says preaching is not therapy, yet in several ways preaching is analogous to therapy. For example, the preacher does not attempt the enormous project of undoing and reconstructing the church's consciousness in one sitting. Rather, the preacher goes after "the little, specific details that hold hidden power over us." Then again, like the therapist, the preacher "does not have to see everything or know everything in advance."[9] If the little flaws in the inner belief system of the community are brought to the surface, it is enough to patiently wait for these revelations to do their work. The work of preaching makes use of Scripture to destabilize the old mental script that has defined our lives (or in Paul's terminology, the "mind of sinful man" or being conformed to this world, Rom. 8:6; 12:2) and write a new script "in accordance with the truth that is in Jesus" (Eph. 4:21–24). But this approach to the ministry of transformation is a long and painstaking process.

> What is yearned for among us is not new doctrine or new morality, but new world, new self, new future. The new world is not given whole, any more than the new self is given abruptly in psychotherapy. It is given only a little at a time, one text at a time, one miracle at a time, one poem, one healing, one pronouncement, one promise, one commandment. Over time, these pieces are stitched together into a sensible collage, stitched together, all of us in concert, but each of us idiosyncratically, stitched together in a new whole—all things new![10]

What, then, is the difference between the old-school promise of achievement, blessing, and character development through simplified formulas extracted from the Bible and the new-school message? One big difference is the way the two schools approach the Bible. New school goes to the Bible to learn what it actually says, not to find the key chain of life's secrets to wealth, happiness, and piety. As believers grow in their knowledge of Scripture, they become suspicious of people who quote verses apart from the setting that reveals their true meaning. They realize the danger of twisting Scripture to support a philosophy, theory, or practice that contradicts the overall message of the Bible. So rather than using the Bible as a self-help book that promises remarkable achievements, new-school believers are learning to read, study, and listen to Scripture to know God in Jesus Christ (John 5:39–40).

6

Does God Speak outside the Bible?

A Profound Realization

I am not a tough guy, but neither am I one to cry. I do express my emotions, but in other ways. I have noticed, however, that in the last couple of years, tears come more readily. On a few occasions, surprisingly, I have had to exert all my willpower to keep from looking like a blubbering baby. One of these took place on a recent flight with Elissa.

We boarded a plane, looking forward to returning to the large rock in the middle of the Pacific that we call home: Hawaii. Once we were situated and buckled in, I grabbed the airline magazine to check out the movie listings. I'm always a little nervous that they'll run a movie I have already seen. Nothing is worse than discovering the in-flight movie is one you saw two days before your trip.

Okay, there it was: "Westbound Flights from the Mainland to Hawaii." Yes! A movie I had never seen. Unfortunately, the summary of *Fighting Temptations* did not excite me. I thought about the handbook on spiritual growth in my backpack. I could force myself to read my book, or I could watch a lame movie. Hmmmm, choices. I chose the movie.

The experience I had during the next two hours is not easy to explain. I will not give away the details of the movie, but it included sex, broken relationships, lying, cheating, debt, church, and bad language. The characters consisted of pimps, unwed mothers, jailed gangsters, and southern legalistic church folk. But there was a message in the movie that communicated hope, reconciliation, grace, mercy, love, and redemption.

For the entire movie I was either choking back tears, laughing out loud, or empathizing with the characters. I felt sorrow, pain, joy, and relief. It was an amazing experience. The feelings it stirred in me were familiar, like the playground you can remember from elementary school. When the movie ended, I wanted to stand up and applaud, but I restrained myself, because I would have whacked my head pretty hard on the stupid reading lights people use when I am trying to sleep.

While the credits rolled, I dropped into a state of deep reflection. Thoughts of God's awesome nature hovered in my mind like the angels in Isaiah's vision of God. I had such a strong impression of God's love and mercy that for the first time I saw with crystal clear vision the truth that it doesn't matter whether I measure up to others' expectations of me. God loves me as I am. He sees me differently than others see me, differently even than I see myself. And he does not see me worse than I see myself but better. Nothing matters, not my race, my lifetime achievements, my successes or failures. God loves me simply because I am me and he is God. It was a profound realization.

I looked over at Elissa who, I'm happy to say, was crying too. We talked about the movie, the meaning we drew from it, and our emotional response. I realized after eventually reading the "spiritual" book in my backpack that I learned a lot more about life, God, and myself from the "secular" movie than from the "spiritual" book. Why is that? Why and how could I learn so much more from a movie produced by MTV than from a best-selling Christian author?

I heard a Christian speaker say once, "Unredeemed people can make beautiful things." Is this true? My personal music collection consists mostly of secular artists. Though Christian musicians may write good lyrics, the music itself is often inferior to what people outside the church are doing. Usually I listen to the music without paying much attention to the words, but there are times when my heart opens up to the lyrics and then the artist is speaking to me. More often than not, I would rather listen to songs that honestly wrestle with life's hardships than about the magical way love and grace make every hurt go away. The world is filled with pain (as are the Psalms), and I have known my share of it. Sometimes I want to know that others out there feel the same way, that though we suffer, somehow we'll make it through the darkness.

MTV versus the popular Christian author—which one should I choose? Which one would God choose? I can tell you what a local pastor might say: "Matt, you can't be filling your mind with things of this world. Fill it with *spiritual* things." Surprisingly, my mind was drawn to everything eternal that somehow emerged in *Fighting Temptations*. Why was I so deeply moved? Why did this movie reach me at a deeper level than could months of attending church? Why is it that God spoke to me through a "pagan" movie much more than through the last ten "spiritual classics" I have read? Why is it that next Sunday morning millions of Christians will listen to sermons based on biblical texts that will not affect them nearly as much as the movies they watched the night before?

These are the sorts of questions I hear people asking. They also want to know if it is possible to learn anything from other religions, whether God ever uses nonbelievers to speak to believers, how they can improve their ability to hear God speak, and how they can know when God has spoken to them.

God spoke to me that day, as I was hurtling forward thousands of feet in the air, crammed in a tiny space next to a tiny window. God spoke to me while I watched a movie forged in the furnace of Hollywood, a cesspool of sex, drugs, and rock 'n' roll, or so I've been told. Many Christians say the movie industry is going to hell in a handbag, but God used that film to speak to me. Why is it that others in my Christian ghetto get hung up on the unwed mother or the sex scene and miss the message?

Another confession: I hear God, not just in movies, but when I am surfing, camping in the open countryside, having a dialogue with someone immersed in New Age belief. I hear God while reading a book from the *New York Times* best-seller list.

We search for truth, but our individualism keeps us from finding it. Individualism is so rampant, both in the church and outside it, that we all have become our own gods. We think we don't need God and we don't need each other, and we end up going through life with almost no interaction with anyone. The band Black Eyed Peas picks up on this brilliantly in their song "Where Is the Love?" Even if we search for what is true, our search and our definitions end up being shallow because we have isolated ourselves, but that doesn't keep us from unloading on everyone else the "truth" we find. Actually, the liberals and pagans and people in the margins of society could deepen our understanding of truth considerably if we would just listen to them. They may not have found the truth of the gospel, but they can pick up on the absence of truth right away. It's sad that they often detect this absence in the church.

Chuck and I do not question the fact that God speaks to individuals and churches through the Bible. Nor do we question the importance of the Bible and its centrality in Christian theology, belief, and practice. We firmly believe that every message a person receives should be evaluated in the light of biblical truth. We further believe that generations of Christians who have gone before us have done well to stress the importance and primacy of the Scriptures. But sometimes we hear the voice of Scripture speaking in other places too.

You Talkin' to Me?

C

If we say, "God has spoken," we may mean nothing more than God has revealed information to humans through the agency of his Spirit and has inspired writers and the biblical text they produced. Most conservative Christians agree that God speaks (communicates his truth) through the Bible and, less clearly, in nature. Some Christians, however, limit God's speech to the biblical text and the meaning found in it through exegesis—careful analysis of the original language, grammar, historical situations, and so on. Other Christians believe God's voice can be heard in that way but also through reading Scripture devotionally, with an open heart and mind (without the aid of Bible study helps), but the true fundamentalist is wary of devotional interpretation of Scripture or *anything* that may produce a feeling.

Christians in the charismatic and Pentecostal camps share fundamentalist beliefs, but they are convinced God's Spirit speaks through prophets or people with the gift of prophecy or some other speech gift (listed in 1 Corinthians 12). Some evangelicals believe God may also speak through literature. Almost all old-school believers agree that God often speaks through preachers, Bible teachers, and some commentaries, usually "ours" but not "theirs."

If an old-school couple had marital problems that were serious enough to send them to counseling, they would look for a Christian counselor who would guide them from the Bible, citing chapter and verse. Psychology might have limited value for people who are "crazy," but since God invented marriage in the book of Genesis, who knows more about it than he? As far as the old school is concerned, everything that humans need to know for life, health, relationships, religion, politics, science, history, you name it, is all right there in the Book.

Because the old school tends to build and fortify a thick wall between "us" and "them," the tendency to demonize the world that exists outside the church is pretty strong. Therefore we have light to share with the world, but they have nothing for us. Some old-school Christians raise their eyebrows when I quote philosophers. They remind me that Paul warned the Colosse believers away from "deceptive philosophy" (Col. 2:8). Whatever you hear from the world will be tinged with deception, they warn, but whatever you hear quoted from the Bible is God's truth. The simple categories of truth and lie, right and wrong, good and evil establish the lines along which you can expect to hear God speak.

I have heard young Christians gently and sometimes not so gently corrected when they tell their church that God has spoken to them through media other than the Bible. They are counseled to be more discerning, that there are many spirits in the world and not all of them are from God. They are told about angels of light who mislead believers, false teachers, and false doctrines. Cold water is poured over their experience, often without anyone listening to their whole story. The message is clear: God speaks through the Bible and the church; anything else will be contaminated with enough error to make it dangerous.

Those Who Have Ears to Hear

God certainly speaks through the Bible, yet the Bible itself tells of a God who communicates to people through a variety of characters, circumstances, events, and states of consciousness (for example, dreams, visions, and trances; see Acts 10:10–13; 22:17–18). Sometimes fundamentalists argue that God spoke through these other means before believers had a complete Bible, but now this is no longer necessary. However, the Bible never says that God would at some point limit himself to speaking exclusively through the written text and abandon any other form of communication with humans.

God speaks everywhere, through everyone and everything, and all one needs is ears to hear, eyes to see, and a heart to perceive. Jesus found messages from God in a shepherd's lost sheep, a merchant shopping for pearls, a field planted with both good seed and weeds, a rich man's greed, a sparrow, and so on. He also uncovered spiritual revelations in common objects, such as water, light, bread, salt, and leaven. In fact, the reason the disciples did not understand what Jesus meant by "the leaven of the Pharisees" is because they did not hear what God had to say through the loaves of bread and the fish that they had passed out among the crowd (Mark 8:14–21).

God speaks through the voice of nature and every living thing (Job 12:7–10; Ps. 19:1–6; Rom. 1:19–20). God speaks in dreams, pain, and by way of angels (Job 33:14–15, 19, 23). Would you say God cannot speak through a rock, a plant, a donkey, an ant, a lizard, a false prophet, or a maniacal king? If there is anything in the universe—object or event—that we believe God would definitely not use to speak to us, then we leave God out of that part of our existence. To refuse to listen to God through whatever media he chooses to communicate diminishes our experience and awareness of him—we lose God. One of the roles of the church is to act as God's redemptive agent in the world, and that includes everything, for even the "gates of hell" cannot prevail against God's spiritual community (Matt. 16:18).

The issue for new-school believers is not how God speaks to us or what means he uses to give us assurance and direction, but how his message is to be heard, interpreted, and applied. They draw their theology from the Bible alone, but encouragement and understanding—sometimes by way of analogy—can come from a variety of sources. After all, well-meaning people can draw lies from the Bible (what is heresy, after all?) if they are not careful in the way they read and listen. New-school believers are not as concerned with whether the message came from "us" or "them" (distinctions that are less important for new schoolers than for old schoolers) as they are with the impact of the message, the way God intends it to be heard and obeyed, and the results that follow.

David Dark represents new-school thinking when he encourages his readers to look for the revelation of the sacred in what he terms "everyday apocalypse" in the literature of

Flannery O'Connor, the music of Radiohead, such movies as *The Matrix* and *The Truman Show*, and episodes of *The Simpsons*.[1] Dark tells us that a close reading of popular culture reveals how it deconstructs itself and proves that "its claims about itself aren't true."[2] Yet at the same time, God manages to insert his own messages into popular culture that have something to tell us about our world, our neighbor, ourselves, and our relationship with God.

Many times visual artists, poets, playwrights, composers, directors, actors, authors, and musicians say more than they realize. Like Caiaphas in the Gospel of John, they prophesy without knowing the deep and profound truth they have articulated (John 11:49–52). A director may be looking for perfect shades of light and camera angles to intensify a dramatic moment or produce a visual effect, but in the creative process a secret comes to the surface of the film and revelation occurs.

Unlike old-school believers, the new school does not assume that Christians have a corner on the truth market or on God. Instead, they assume he is larger and more bountiful than our intellectual boxes or theological constructs. Like Paul, who said that God did not leave himself "without testimony" (Acts 14:17) but deposited trace amounts of truth in every culture, the new school believes that God is working in popular culture, speaking, revealing, leaving fingerprints everywhere and drawing people to himself.

I'm tempted to tell you about an experience I had in a theater. Maybe I will.

Both Christians and people who do not call themselves Christians can tell you about a time when God spoke to them through a song they heard on the radio. Even though the song had nothing to do with Jesus Christ, a line in it, the soulful sound of the singer's voice, or just the musical hook woke something within them, told them God knew their name, comforted or challenged them. God's voice has also been heard in art galleries, beauty salons, airports, malls, and bookstores. In fact, his voice "goes out into all the earth," because creation itself is a divine speech act (see Ps. 19:1–4).

Matt's description of the effect *Fighting Temptations* had on him is important. Old school said, "Your feelings are irrelevant. All that matters is the objective truth of God. People are misled by their feelings." Not only does that response fall on deaf ears, it misrepresents Scripture and is in fact an accommodation to Enlightenment rationalism. In modern times rationalism was pitted against romanticism, which eventually resulted in a cleavage between science and art—the poet and the engineer. In accommodating itself to modern culture, the church also became rationalistic. That is how the negative attitude toward feelings became so strong in twentieth-century Christianity. Go back and read Christian authors before the Reformation (and even the writings of the Reformers), and you will find a warmer attitude toward human emotions.

God Has Your Address

Which is more important, the way we think people ought to come to Jesus or the way they actually come to him? If we insist people must come to Christ through reason and truth, are we going to stand at the entrance to the kingdom of God and prevent those who are coming through feeling and faith from entering? The truth is, we are not the rational creatures we think we are, and that is why our attempts to engineer evangelism and discipleship ultimately do not work. Real life is too chaotic, unpredictable, and at times emotionally overwhelming to go back to our three-ring binder for the correct response. We have to learn dependence on God—trust. We do not live on principles alone any more than we live on bread alone, "but on every word that comes from the mouth of God" (Matt. 4:4). Perhaps the majority of the time we will hear words from the Bible, but many other times, if we are listening, God's words will come to us from a magazine article, an advertisement, or the lips of a stranger.

What is God saying in the world? All sorts of things. He is reminding people that the world is a broken, oftentimes twisted place, and their own self-centeredness is the problem not the solution. He is communicating his nearness and love. He is sending encouragement to people who cannot seem to hold their lives together. He is letting others know that the world would be in no better shape if they were God. He is showing off his splendor and might, revealing his "eternal power and divine nature" (Rom. 1:20), and giving a host of people better thoughts of Jesus than they would ever get from Christian television.

Okay, here's my theater story. Ever since high school I have lived with a low-grade depression. I am sure it is partially neuro-chemical, and I am aware of other contributing factors from my early life. Anyway, I have to keep myself going every single day, because the temptation to just stay in bed, escape the world, and avoid all responsibility is tremendous. My inner voice constantly tells me I am a failure, hopelessly flawed, and worthless.

Periodically I experience an urgency to walk away from my life in the ministry. The thought of all the people in my church who find encouragement, spiritual insight, or personal benefits in my "talks"—public and private—overwhelms me. I have done all right to this point, but I am always expecting the ground to give way under my feet and to be publicly exposed as someone who has no business in Christian leadership, which is quite true for a number of reasons. For about five years, every Sunday afternoon as I walked across the parking lot to my car after our third service, I would tell myself, *I have to resign. I'm going to resign this week. I can't do this any more.* I did not realize how sick that thinking was until just now as I wrote it out.

Maybe a year ago I hit another spell of depression and longed to flee Orange County and the ministry forever. Keep in mind that everything was going well for me; my teaching was becoming more refined, greater numbers of people wanted to listen to my talks, my second book was due for publication, and all the time I was receiving encouragement from a variety of people that my efforts were effective. Still, the feeling of wanting to run away was so strong that I decided to spend a day fasting and seeking God. Normally I am not one to fast, and I do not necessarily think that it works all that well. So the few times that I have fasted, it has been sort of a hit-or-miss type of thing.

It was my day off, with another round of normal activities. I prayed and read my Bible in the morning, exercised a little, caught up on some email, did a couple of chores, and ran a couple of errands. By the evening I had not received any revelations, but that did not surprise me. I had fasted and my life was in God's hands. That was good enough.

My wife, Barbara, asked if I wanted to go see a movie and let me know it was my turn to pick one. I chose the thriller *Along Came a Spider*. It would be hard to find another movie in 2001 that garnered more bad reviews than this movie. No matter. Morgan Freeman is one of my favorite actors, and I am fairly easily entertained. So we sat there and watched an apparent friendship develop between Freeman's character, Alex Cross, and Jezzie Flannigan, played by Monica Potter. Sitting in Jezzie's apartment, Alex was trying to console her, because a child was kidnapped on her watch at an upscale boarding school. Jezzie was ready to give up her job with the secret service, and Alex was about to respond.

At that moment, time stood still for me. Something inside me said, *Listen closely to this next line*, and I could swear that there was a light shining down on me. Morgan Freeman's deep, resonant, articulate voice said, "You do what you are, Jezzie." Here is the dialogue that follows:

Jezzie: You mean you are what you do.
Alex: No, I mean you do what you are. You're born with
           a gift. If not that, then you get good at something
           along the way. And what you're good at, you don't
           take for granted and don't betray it.
Jezzie: What if you do . . . betray your gift?
Alex: Then you betray yourself. That's a sad thing.

I doubt that there is any way God could have made a stronger impression on my heart that evening—well, perhaps a burning bush. I understood with certainty that I was where I was supposed to be, doing what I was supposed to do. When I arrived at church for the staff meeting the next morning, I was ready to face a new week of challenges with energy, creativity, and the confidence that I would not betray my gift.

Even more recently God spoke to me again, this time in the Denzel Washington movie *Man on Fire*. (Why does God use the cheap flicks to get to me?) Everything in this movie is cliché, which works for me. A burned-out ex-CIA operative, drinking himself to death, is hired for the dishonorable job of bodyguard to a small girl. He makes a commitment not to get personally attached to her so that his emotions will not impinge on his professionalism. Nevertheless, she is totally precious and wins his heart (of course). They bond intimately, and then she gets kidnapped, which gives him motive (and justification?) to go off torturing and murdering anyone who may have benefited financially from the girl's death. You get the idea: one cliché after another.

Rewind for a moment. During our church preparations for Easter this year, I felt God impress on my heart that I was not to celebrate Easter like another day on the Christian calendar, then move on hastily to the next holiday. He told me, instead, to stay with the themes of resurrection and life. The weekend after Easter, I found myself in a hermitage on the central California coast. Bells called us to worship at 5:30 a.m., 7:00, 11:00, and then again at 5:30 in the evening. I learned in the brief time I was there how to live in the rhythm of the bells. During worship, I noticed that the songs, Scripture readings, and prayers were all about Easter, resurrection, and life. This was wonderful for me, because it reinforced the message God had been giving me. Then while reading my Bible and observing silence one morning, God told me that he wanted to resurrect something in me. *So that is what all these messages are about*, I thought, *something God is bringing to life in me*. I was excited at that prospect.

A few hours later I remembered the flip side of resurrection—death. Something in me had to die so that God could bring to life something else. I had to give up a dream I had held on to for twenty years, a prayer, a desire, a longing, for God to reveal himself to me in a specific way. I had to die to what I wanted God to do in my life to come alive to what he was already doing. (Imagine that! God is already doing something inside of you that you may not have realized, all the while you are asking him to do something else, which is less spectacular.)

I was home a couple weeks, and one Sunday after church I was exhausted and wanted to give my brain a rest in a movie theater. Barbara was busy with something else, so I went up the street by myself to see *Man on Fire*. I have already told you about the graphic gore, so do not rent it if that sort of thing bothers you. I also mentioned that the plot was built on a series of clichés. But what was not cliché was the way Washington quoted Scripture in one scene, read from a Bible in another, and when the mother of the kidnapped child borrowed his Bible, he encouraged her to read it with the promise that it would give her comfort. Cool!

You have to know who Christopher Walken is to appreciate this next scene. Walken plays an ex-CIA friend of Washington. He is in the office of a high-ranking official in the Mexican government. Walken explains that if the official allows Washington to carry out his vendetta on the kidnappers, he will single-handedly do more damage to crime in Mexico than the entire police force could do in twelve years (or something to that effect). The official then wanted to know why Washington cared so much for the little girl, and at that moment I once again heard God say, "Pay attention!" Walken lifted his index finger in front of his face and in his inimitable voice he said, "Because she taught him he could live again." There was God's message, and it was the Easter theme again. He was reminding me and reinforcing his promise. He was teaching me it was all right to live again, to let him bring to life in me the thing that pleased him most. He wanted me to be a "man on fire."

There is no book I love and treasure more than the Bible. Every morning as I read, I am struck with a thought, discover an insight, come across a truth that either addresses a personal need or provides me with wisdom and understanding. In this way, I can say God speaks to me every day, and I have more than thirty notebooks collected for more than a dozen years in which I have stored my daily meditations on Scripture. But it would be a shame if God spoke to me only in the morning, then said nothing else to me while driving, counseling, reading, talking with my friends, or watching a movie. New-school believers want to *see* when they look, *hear* when they listen, and *understand* with their hearts what God is saying to them everywhere and at all times (see Mark 8:14–21).

7

Is Forgiveness Real?

God's Response to Our Sin

Lynn was raised in Yonkers, New York. Both her mom and dad were successful, wealthy entrepreneurs. Her father, who had owned several jewelry stores in Manhattan, proved to be a better businessman than he was a family man. After years of his long hours at work and fewer hours at home, his wife kicked him out of the house. Lynn was eleven years old. About the same time, Lynn's mother began slipping deeper into alcoholism, and Lynn followed suit. At fourteen, pumped up on drugs and alcohol, Lynn wandered around at a huge open-air event called Woodstock. At seventeen she left home, traveled, and dabbled in meditation and Eastern religions. She entertained herself with drugs and sought comfort with men. During this season of restless wandering, Lynn became pregnant on four separate occasions, ending each pregnancy in abortion.

Like many other young people in the early seventies, Lynn did not know what to do with her life. She worked every day, partied every night, and probably would have continued to do so until she either died of an overdose or became so strung out that any hope of a normal life would have passed her by. But one evening a domino fell that started a chain reaction of dominos falling that eventually led to a radical life change.

At twenty-three Lynn lived on her own, supporting herself by working in a bar on Central Avenue in Yonkers, New York. Usually the bar was quiet and Lynn just went about her business. But when a construction company began a major project across the street, everything changed. The crew that was hired for the job worked for a company owned by an Italian man who had two sons; one was married and the other was single. Lynn knew this because the crew ate lunch every day in the bar. The owner's son was attracted to Lynn, and each time he came by, he asked for a date, and each time he asked, she politely declined. One afternoon when he invited her for the hundredth time to have a traditional Italian dinner with him at his family's restaurant, she gave in and agreed to follow him to his house so he could change his clothes. She was still not sure about him, so she insisted on driving her own car to give her a sense of control.

The young man asked Lynn if she would like a drink while she waited for him, and he poured a scotch for her. When she finished her drink, she began to feel strange, unlike any other drinking or drug experience. She must have fallen asleep or passed out, because the next thing she remembers was waking up on his couch and hearing his shower running. As her head cleared, she realized what had happened. She had become a victim of the too common abuse known as date rape.

Three months later she was throwing up every day at work. She purchased a home pregnancy test at a nearby pharmacy and groaned when it indicated "positive." She began planning her next trip to the abortion clinic. Since she had done this before, she knew all the ropes. Her first stop was at a Planned Parenthood office where a blood test confirmed the pregnancy. She then called the clinic to schedule an appointment, but while she was on the phone, she noticed a chart on the wall of the office that illustrated the stages of fetal development and found the picture that matched the month of her pregnancy. She had never before thought about what was actually taken from her body in an abortion, and the resemblance of this tissue in her womb to a child shocked her.

Several phone calls later Lynn discovered that an abortion at this stage of pregnancy would be complicated and expensive. But those thoughts had less influence on her thinking than the chart she saw hanging on the wall. The picture of that tiny bit of life is what made her decide against abortion. As soon as she made the decision, she prayed that God would take care of her and her child. Within a few days an old friend invited Lynn for a visit to her home in the suburbs, and while there Lynn found a new job. A month later she joined a Bible study and prayer group, and within a short time she gave her life to God.

You may be wondering what Lynn's story has to do with the title of this chapter. I will explain. If Lynn had gone through with her fifth abortion, you would not be reading these words, because I would not be here to write them. Lynn is my mother, and I am the child she spared. So now that you know the background, I will come to the point. Within an hour of my birth, a nurse laid me on my mother's stomach to look me over, examine me, and make sure everything was normal. My mother, however, wanted to give me an even closer look to see if I was deformed in any way. She was afraid that because of the circumstances surrounding my conception, God might punish her with the lifelong responsibility of raising a deformed child.

God's Grace

What in the world would cause a woman to think that God would do something to her child to get back at her?

Where do people get the impression that something terrible will happen—like a car accident, losing a limb, or cancer—if they break one of the Ten Commandments? And why do some people ask God, "What have I done? Why are you mad at me?" when they have been diagnosed with cancer or lose a close relative? Unfortunately, many people have been led to believe that every sin (at least every *big* sin) is followed by some kind of disaster, and so they live in constant fear of God's punishment. Is this an accurate picture of God? Does it do justice to his nature, his love, his mercy?

We need to understand that sin produces its own spiritual, psychological, and physical consequences. Sin is a form of self-destruction that sometimes rebounds quickly and other times corrodes a life over many years. Sin is also an alienating behavior that tends toward narcissism and an inability to form strong bonds with others. Many of us will carry the scars of our sins for the rest of our lives, even though we are forgiven and spiritually healed and restored to God.

Without a doubt God disciplines us in some of the same ways and for the same reasons that parents discipline their children. He trains and instructs us in the proper way to live, because he loves us (Heb. 12:4–11). God disciplines us with the intent of restoring us to himself and to good works, for which he has created us in Christ Jesus (Eph. 2:10). If God is not always just, it is because most of the time he is merciful, but he is never cruel or vengeful. Nevertheless, the image some Christians have of God is that of an angry stepfather with a quick temper. I know people who are constantly begging God for grace, even weeping and whining, like they have to show him how pitiful they are before he will answer their prayer. I wonder if they think some days he is in a better mood than others.

Bad things happen to us—terrible things—but we live in a world that is not right, a world that is fallen and in need of God's transforming grace. Until the day that the earth is "filled with the knowledge of the glory of the LORD, as the waters cover the sea" (Hab. 2:14), people will suffer. But God is not the direct cause of all the horrible suffering in the world, nor does he "willingly bring affliction or grief to the children of men" (Lam. 3:33). We tend to condemn ourselves and each other much more than God does, and that is why we need reminders not to judge others but to show mercy.

Do we withhold forgiveness from others because we believe God is withholding his forgiveness from them as well? I am thinking right now of people in our churches who have been caught having an affair, who are going through a divorce, whose children are on drugs, who came to church one night tipsy or even drunk, or who even flipped out and embarrassed everyone because they ran out of medication. I am not thinking of someone who personally injured you through molestation, rape, theft, or domestic violence. Forgiveness in those situations is complex, and I wouldn't dream of making light of it.

I don't mean to suggest that we act foolishly when we demonstrate God's love (like the Corinthians who were apparently proud of their tolerance in 1 Cor. 5:1–8). There is a way to love and forgive people, to show them mercy, and at the same time act toward them in wisdom. We would be pretty stupid to make a repentant pedophile a crosswalk guard. Yet at the same time, the spiritual community can find a way to forgive, work with, and monitor the repentant molester. If not us, then who?

Recently a friend of mine made an excellent point. He was sharing from the story of Adam and Eve and how sin entered the world through their poor decision. Now they may not have known the implications of their decisions, but God sure did. I cannot even imagine the heartbreak God felt when after the fall he returned to walk with his creation in the garden. Adam and Eve must have expected God's wrath, so they ran and hid. But what did God say when he entered the garden? He called for them and asked where they were. Of course, he knew where they were (he is God, isn't he?), but he called anyway. What an amazing picture of grace. In spite of all Adam and Eve did, God called for them. Would we be so quick to call after those who have afflicted us?

Is it possible for Christians to be more forgiving than judgmental? Does a divorced single mother have as much access to the services, community, and ministry opportunities in a church as a mother never divorced? In what ways can our church extend forgiveness to a woman who has had an abortion or a man who has been on drugs? Is forgiveness available to everyone or is it only for some people and certain types of sins but not for other people and other types of sins?

C Graceless Communities

Forgiveness is a complex issue. On the one hand, there is God's forgiveness for us and our recognition of his forgiveness for others, which is sometimes difficult for us to accept even as it was difficult for the Pharisees to watch Jesus associate with "sinners" (Luke 15). Then there is the forgiveness we extend to each other. In some cases that means clearing the account of an act that did not affect me personally, while in other instances it involves a personal affront or insult. There are times that we forgive but tread cautiously, and other times when we forgive with total abandon. There are people whom we forgive but rarely ever see again, and there are others we must forgive because we want our relationship to be restored or continue to grow in intimacy. Every spouse, parent, child, and good friend must learn to be forgiving; otherwise, human relationships are not possible, because at times we all fail to fulfill the expectations of others.

So what are Matt and I concerned about in this chapter? We are thinking of the average Christian—like us—who cannot live a healthy life if his mind and heart are darkened by an excess of guilt and shame. We are thinking of people who love God and want to serve him but make one serious mistake (like having a child outside of marriage) and are forever blackballed from Christian service. We are thinking of people who arrive at our churches in clothing that is immodest, with alcohol on their breath, or decorated with tattoos and piercings. We are wondering if old-school believers are fixated on sin rather than grace and on guilt rather than mercy.

Old-school Christianity developed an obsession with sexual sin. For some reason, sins having to do with the body and its functions have attracted more attention (and more shame) than other forms of sin in the North American religious subculture. Sins that are less physiological—like greed, pride, injustice, self-indulgence, stinginess, and just plain meanness—are frequently ignored. We can hear echoes of Jesus's denunciation of the Pharisees who were hyper-conscientious when it came to tithing but "neglected the more important matters of the law—justice, mercy and faithfulness" (Matt. 23:23).

Because of the old school's preoccupation with sexual sins, the gravest punishments and most severe criticisms have been reserved for people guilty of premarital and extramarital affairs, abortion, divorce, and pornography. The old school is certainly correct in its reading of Scripture that promiscuity and sexual immorality are forbidden in both Old Testament law and New Testament doctrine, but the selectivity of the old school in condemning a young woman for having an abortion, while honoring the donor of a large charitable endowment whose life is characterized by conspicuous consumption reveals an unbiblical double standard. The negative attitude of the religious subculture in which I was raised was disproportionately severe toward men and women who had committed adultery compared with that shown to people who indulged in gluttony, hatred, materialism, and even domestic violence.

Our sensitivity to sexual misconduct tends to eclipse other moral and ethical considerations and create a lopsided system of values. For example, Christians raised in the worldview and tradition of the old school tend to focus on the sexual liaison between David and Bathsheba, whenever their story is told, and miss God's greater concern for justice, faithfulness, and the use and misuse of power. Perhaps the most serious consequence of our lopsided system of values is the fact that many churches have thrown stones at the very person Jesus tried to protect when he said, "If any one of you is without sin, let him be the first to throw a stone at her" (John 8:7).

The old school has tended to accentuate a predictable set of sins—drunkenness, drugs, gambling, swearing, and so on—that are fairly easy to identify and condemn, do not affect most people raised in Christian homes, and make for graphic illustrations. The sins that lie closer to our heart may be mentioned on occasion, but any real investigation of our cherished vices is quickly dismissed. So we go on polluting the air, exhausting the earth's resources, hoarding our possessions, ignoring orphans and widows, supporting oppression and slavery through our purchases, shopping as if the world were not filled with starving people, gossiping, slandering, and maligning others. The old school has practiced an un-Christian selectivity when reviewing New Testament sin lists, highlighting sexual sins in particular and meting out punishment without mercy, while ignoring other violations.

Untouchables

Old-school churches can be very unforgiving. For example, when Leslie's husband (not her real name) became violent and physically abusive after he suffered a stroke, she tried her best to stay with him, care for his needs, and protect the children. Leslie's husband was a big, muscular man who could no longer control his raging and destructive anger. When her physical and mental health were jeopardized, as well as the safety of the children, Leslie filed for divorce and had a legal restraining order imposed on her husband.

Leslie's church did not understand her reasons for divorcing her husband, and she was told she could no longer attend services or consider herself a member of the church. Most of the other members would have nothing to do with her and treated her as though she had caused them the deepest disappointment of their lives. More than twenty years later, Leslie has not remarried and has never received an apology from the church for the way she was treated.

Leslie's story has been repeated many times in old-school churches. Some Christians seem incapable of tolerating any other situation than one man and one woman married for life. Any sort of deviation from that model is condemned, and many of these old-school believers don't seem to know how to apply mercy and forgiveness to fellow believers who fail to live perfectly according to the biblical standard. Thousands of children—not to mention the mothers—have never even entertained the idea of attending church because of the merciless way their mothers were treated and the ensuing suffering they observed when their mothers were excommunicated after a divorce.

From the old school and from parents with perfectionist tendencies, we have learned how not to forgive ourselves. If the church and its Christian leaders cannot extend God's forgiveness to me, how can I forgive myself? As Matt said, we keep waiting for some horrible thing to happen to us because we sinned and have no concept of God's mercy or forgiveness.

Forgiveness has been taught, analyzed, and stressed for many years. Christians have been told that in not forgiving others, they are damaging themselves. We have been told that forgiveness has psychological value as well as personal and communal value. Still, there are many Christians who apparently have no pangs of conscience about holding onto old offenses and resentment. The old school is notorious for creating two classes of Christians—the first-class Christian, who has never been divorced, never had an affair or abortion, never looked at pornography (or has never been caught); and the second-class Christian, who is guilty of one or more of these actions and is therefore unfit for church membership, let alone ministry.

Few people born in the last twenty or thirty years have come of age without some kind of moral failure or defining experience that revealed their imperfection as a human being. The social mask of moral perfection that church families wore in the first half of the twentieth century has completely eroded. Therefore new-school believers have a clear understanding and deep appreciation for Jesus's prohibition against looking at the speck of sawdust in your brother's eye while paying no attention to the plank in your own (Matt. 7:3). New-school Christians are radically aware of the planks in their eyes.

For the same reason, new-school believers cling to Jesus's teaching, "Do not judge, or you too will be judged" (v. 1). They wonder, *How dare I judge someone else, seeing how messed up I am?* This does not mean that new-school Christians are cavalier about sin or unable to talk to their friends who are slipping into sin. Rather, it means that when they do talk with friends, they talk with compassion and understanding, almost as if they share the same prison cell—as one sinner to another. They are not afraid to confront or embarrass someone else, but they are deathly afraid of becoming hypocrites, of judging someone else while they still have so many flaws that need fixing. They have a deep concern over the way their lives affect others. They want to follow Christ's example of not breaking a bruised reed or snuffing out a smoldering wick (Matt. 12:20). In other words, they want to be gentle.

New-school Christians are more likely than their parents or grandparents to give their fallen heroes a second chance and see the value of a person's gifts, even if the person is imperfect. They appreciate the greater transparency, candor, and humility of leaders who have stumbled but recovered their footing and therefore no longer attempt to strike a saintly pose. Those who have never been through the disgrace of having their sins publicized and smugly condemn those who have strike new schoolers as arrogant, self-righteous, judgmental, and less helpful than the "more human" people who have been caught in the same traps that the majority of North Americans know too well.

Mercy *and* Truth

Forgiveness is very real for new-school believers, and they understand the importance of giving it as much as receiving it. Coming from broken homes, living in a permissive culture, growing up in a world where millions of their siblings were aborted, and confronting the most drug-infested period of human history, they are well aware of sin and evil. They are survivors, but they also carry their scars. They are looking for leaders who carry scars and who are not ashamed to confess their mistakes and share their growth. They do not trust leaders who pose as experts who have mastered Christian living, leaders at the end of the trail who say, "I will teach you how to get to the level I have achieved." Rather, they follow leaders who reveal their wounds as Jesus did to the disciples and say,

"I am on the road with you. We will grow and learn together." They want to walk with people who struggle, do not give up hope, and make steady progress.

New-school Christians strive to live in full compliance with the Ten Commandments. They are aware of Paul's strict warnings against sin and do their best to apply themselves to his teaching. When it comes to the way they treat others, they make every effort to follow the example of Jesus Christ. They understand that only his mercy can heal the many wounds—self-inflicted or otherwise—caused by sin. They love the way Jesus generously forgave sins without even being asked to do so. They are enchanted by the fact he could be accused of being a friend of sinners. They rejoice in his refusal to condemn those whom others condemned. They take hope in the fact that Jesus kept the door open for outcasts and people with questionable reputations, because that means the door is open for them.

Seeing in color rather than black and white, new schoolers approach the issue of sin with greater sensitivity and compassion than people who think of it in only legal terms. New-school believers understand the way social, psychological, and interpersonal factors play a role in sin and that these issues need to be addressed for full repentance, recovery, and lasting change to take place.

Forgiveness, mercy, and understanding in this new context do not translate into freedom to disregard the Bible's moral code, permissiveness, or failure to address sin. New-school Christians, like believers in all generations, take a strong stand that believers must walk the walk, confess their sins, repent, and abandon sinful practices. They are committed to spiritual growth in grace, purity, and devotion to Jesus through a lifestyle that honors him.

Christians who identify with the new school still practice Jesus's teaching: "If your brother sins, rebuke him, and if he repents, forgive him" (Luke 17:3). But they have learned to deliver the rebuke in the gentleness and humility Paul recommended rather than the conceit, anger, or self-righteousness that often characterized the old school (Gal. 6:1). At the same time, new schoolers appreciate the fact that Jesus taught his disciples to forgive their brother seven times in a day if each time he returns and repents. If we must be this forgiving with each other, certainly we can return to God again and again for forgiveness, and each time he will pardon and restore us. Some days it takes seven times to get it right. So although their intent is not to condone sin, to accept it as a way of life, or to compromise with sin, when someone is caught in a sin, the new school tries immediately to understand why this is so, is not quick to condemn, but strives to love first, ask questions, then extend mercy and help (in whatever way it will be welcomed and received).

Mercy Not Sacrifice

On two different occasions Jesus quoted Hosea (a book most evangelicals' Bibles do not fall open to) and gave them a brief application based on the lesson in the verse. On the first occasion he told his critics, "Go and learn what this means: 'I desire mercy, not sacrifice'" (Matt. 9:13; Hos. 6:6). He was challenging them to study the words of the prophet and apply them to the current context. On the second occasion he said, "If you had known what these words mean, 'I desire mercy, not sacrifice,' you would not have condemned the innocent" (Matt. 12:7). He is telling them that they would have modi-fied their attitude and actions if they had really understood Hosea. In light of all the attention given to Christian wor-ship, do we really understand that Jesus would rather have us showing mercy to each other than standing with hands held high singing praise songs?

Not only did Jesus demonstrate mercy and command his disciples to be merciful (see Luke 6:36), he also told parables that highlighted mercy and demonstrated the way he wanted his followers to treat others, forgiving them from the heart and rejoicing when they return to God (Matt. 18:21–35; Luke 15:11–31). He warned them that if they would not forgive others, they would not be forgiven (Matt. 6:14–15). This last teaching is so strong on forgiveness that many old-school commentators have tried to tone Jesus down by suggesting he did not really mean what he said. But for just one moment suppose that Jesus did mean what he said, and Christians will not be forgiven their sins unless they forgive others. How much mercy do you want God to show you? That is how much mercy he wants you to show others.

When a woman caught in adultery was brought to Jesus, he had a perfect opportunity to apply the clear teaching of Scripture to her case (John 8:3–11). The scribes and Pharisees were correct in saying that the law of Moses commanded that people guilty of adultery were to be stoned. The biblical commandment was clear, and a literal application would mean that Jesus was in favor of the woman's execution. But he did not condemn her or apply the literal teaching of Scripture. Instead, he showed her mercy and instructed her to leave her life of sin.

Christians who always want to apply the literal commands or teaching of Scripture may be correct in their understanding of what the Bible says, but they are out of step with Jesus. Sometimes the demands of Jesus were greater than the literal application of the law (for example, he taught that hatred is as severe a crime as murder) and other times he was more lenient than the literal command. No matter how stringent the requirements of God's kingdom, Jesus constantly extended mercy to all sorts of people to help them enter the "straight gate." From David to Peter, God provided biblical characters with recovery after a fall and restoration after sin and repentance.

New-school believers are anxious to see what a church would look like if all of its members really practiced mercy to the degree Jesus taught and demonstrated. They believe that there is an element of restoration in forgiveness, that God will repay them "for the years the locusts have eaten" (Joel 2:25). Authentic forgiveness includes healing, in the one doing the forgiving, in the one being forgiven, and in the relationship between them. The show of forgiveness that is typical in the church is in word only and does not heal anything. According to Vincent Brümmer, forgiveness "costs you something." He goes on to say, "One of the basic characteristics of forgiveness is therefore that the one who forgives is the one who suffers."[1]

New-school Christians find this proposition to be accurate, acceptable, and Christlike.

My Story

Matt has suggested (okay, insisted) that I tell a bit of my own story at this point. I promise to keep it short.

My childhood was as different from Matt's as the geographical environments where each of us grew up—East coast, West coast. My father was a minister before I was born. Both he and my mom preserved their virginity for marriage and after more than fifty years they are more deeply committed to each other than ever before. I was born in 1951, a radically different era from the seventies, when Matt was born. I grew up in the calm before the storm, just before LSD, student riots, and free love. Matt was born after the storm had passed through and damaged every social institution on the cultural landscape. I was much prayed over, and my mother dedicated me to God and his work before I was born.

By the time I was twenty-three, I had already started two churches and was laying the foundation for a third. Eight weeks before I turned twenty-four I stood at the altar and pledged my love to a girl I had adored in high school but did not get to know until three years after we graduated. Whenever I was near her at school, I was always too nervous to put a coherent sentence together. But there we stood, in love and looking forward to a lifetime of shared memories.

A year later our first child, William, was born. His sister Jennifer and brother Michael followed like stair steps, each of them two years apart. After a hiatus of four years, a miscarriage, and the decision that we would not have any more children, the twins arrived, Karen and Scott. God had blessed the church we started when we were first married, and my parents helped us get into a home large enough to accommodate the seven of us. Everything was perfect, except for a low-grade depression that had stayed with me since high school and flared up on occasion. I easily found my identity in being a husband and a father—a family man. When I look at my children's baby or school pictures, my heart still swells with the deep love I felt for them at each stage of their development.

I remember learning one day that the wife of a local minister was filing for divorce. Though surprised and saddened, I was nonetheless convinced that had the minister really wanted to save his marriage, he could have applied himself to loving and serving his wife, and she would have stayed. After all, he was attractive, brilliant, gifted, and he had a secure income and future. He also seemed like a nice guy, so in my heart I held him responsible for the breakup of their marriage, even though I never talked to him about it or had any knowledge of the details. In my mind divorce was an alien behavior that could not touch true Christians, let alone a minister; it simply could not happen. Honestly the thought of divorcing my wife never entered my mind.

In January of 1993 I realized suddenly that my wife and I were facing a severe crisis in our marriage. I was one of those thick-skulled husbands who was the last to know. Three months prior to our eighteenth anniversary, my wife told me she wanted a divorce, that it was the only way to resolve our differences, and that her decision was not negotiable. I was devastated by her announcement and sank into the most painful season of my life; really, I did not know that humans could survive such intense emotional pain. I scrambled as fast as I could to try to fix our relationship. I found a professional female counselor who was willing to see us and was not "one of those reborn people," as she informed me on the phone. I wanted my wife to feel comfortable if she ever were to come to counseling with me and not think she was being ganged up on by me and a male counselor who quoted chapter and verse. If my wife had felt the counselor was using Scripture to coerce her back into my arms, she would have bolted the first session. I made many other attempts to recover our marriage: romantic cards, manipulation, attestations of my love, and groveling. I had no pride left. Without my family I had nothing.

Without going deeper into the details of our split up, I need only say that our marriage was free from affairs or infidelities.

A year after our separation I reminded my wife that she did not have biblical grounds for divorcing me—another classic blunder when I would have been better off keeping my mouth shut. If it sounds like our divorce came suddenly, out of the blue, that is exactly how I experienced it. My wife, however, informed me that I should have seen it coming, and looking back I do think she had been unhappy for a long time. It just never occurred to me that I could have been the source of that unhappiness. After all, as one of my close friends put it, she was my solace, my closest and most intimate friend. I assumed I was the same to her.

Informing the church board of our divorce was a terribly sad task. I was surprised when one of the board members expressed his deep sorrow for what was happening in my life, but immediately added, "Chuck, we still want you to continue on in your role as visionary and senior pastor of the church." Then the other board members gave me their unanimous support. Now, I have to say that going into that meeting felt like walking up the scaffold to the hangman's noose. I fully expected them either to ask for my resignation or not wait for it. To tell the truth, I was not at all sure that I wanted to continue on in the ministry and was prepared to leave it that night for good. In fact, I did not see how I could be a minister now that my wife was leaving me. But their encouragement and support gave me the impression that it might be possible to carry on in my role and duties. I remember thinking several days later, *Well, at least God didn't strip this away from me, the one thing that still gives me a sense of identity and a reason to live.*

Did my board of directors make the right, the most biblical decision? Did I do the right thing in accepting their offer of support and staying on through my personal storm? At first, I was not sure I could go through the agony (and humiliation) of divorce and continue to minister to people. Three months after the board of directors guaranteed my job, I went into the office of my executive pastor and resigned. But Craig would not let me. He knew my emotional turmoil and cried with me often, as I informed him of the latest developments. People who are dying inside as they journey through divorce feel a need to talk about every little detail—a lot! And over and over! Craig pulled together a couple friends and board members that evening. Together they told me that I was in no condition to make big decisions, that I could take as much time off as I needed, but they would not accept my resignation for at least a year. Then, if with a clear head I still felt as though I wanted to resign, they would regretfully let me walk away.

I was fortunate enough to have several ministers living nearby with whom I met on several occasions, and I hope they do not mind that I mention their names, because their gracious support is a tribute to the largeness of their hearts and Christlike compassion. Kenton Beshore had arranged for all of us to spend an afternoon with John Stott, whom he had befriended some time earlier. Before Dr. Stott arrived, I mentioned to Kenton and the other pastors present—Denny Bellesi, Rick Warren, and Bob Shank—that I was giving serious thought to resigning from the church. The five of them encouraged me to take time off but advised me not to leave the work that God had blessed under my care. Their support meant a great deal to me, as there were many other ministers in our area who were convinced I should leave both my church and the community—in disgrace.

A day came when I had to sit down and write a letter to the local minister, whose divorce had occurred only a couple of years prior to mine. I apologized for secretly blaming him. I told him that I now realized that when one spouse decides to end the marriage in divorce, there is nothing the other spouse can do, no matter how much effort, love, or prayer one puts into salvaging the relationship. I greatly regretted my lack of understanding and sympathy for his situation. Quickly he returned a kind and generous response. We now belonged to the same fraternity, and the initiation was hellish.

How is it that I continued on as a minister when my house was not in order (see 1 Tim. 3:4–5) and I had failed in my marriage? To this day I will not say that I did the right thing or that I am either an example or crusader for other ministers who go through the same situation. I will say only that God had cultivated mercy in our church. We had received hundreds of people whose lives had been wrecked by divorce. Our meetings were filled with broken people whose lives God was piecing back together. We had come alongside them in their hour of crisis, and when they saw me collapse, they came to my side. Of course not everyone was supportive. There were several families that left the church, and I do not blame them. What did I have to say about marriage that was worth hearing? I felt I had learned a few things I could tell husbands they should *not* do. For example, *husbands, don't get irritable and fret over money every time you sit down to pay the bills; it's better to go into debt with your wife at your side than alienate her with lectures about how you're trying to be a provider while it all leaks out through her checkbook or credit card.*

That whole period of my life was surreal. I have no doubt that, in spite of my daily suffering and longing to just die and be through with it, God was using me to inspire hope and do something in the lives of others. Every week I received several letters from people who described what good things were happening in their lives or families through my preaching and teaching. I read a letter one day that opened a valve in my heart and dumped a bucket of tears, because the man who wrote explained in detail the wonderful way God had put his family back together through our church and my ministry. The irony crushed me. I was broken yet mending others, grieving yet helping them find joy, lost but guiding them to God's light.

Yes, there are unforgiving Christians who desire sacrifice and will not be merciful, but new-school Christians wear their wounds well, never forget the debt they have been forgiven, and know how to extend mercy when mercy is what God wants them to give. How is it that eleven years after a brutal divorce I am still in the ministry today? It has to be God's mercy working in my life and in the lives of those who are in my care. I am forgiven. I hope that every believer will be able to experience mercy and forgiveness when he or she needs them. Mercy is definitely new school.

8

What Makes
the Christian
Experience Unique?

Examining the Faith

Did you know the Hawaiian Island chain is the most remote place in the world? We are thousands of miles from any other inhabited piece of land. We actually have some of the most diverse cultures, climates, and spiritual traditions in all of the United States. We are Polynesian, Melanesian, Micronesian, Asian, and "haole." Haole is the friendly term we have in Hawaii for those who "flew here versus grew here." Out of the fourteen climate systems in the world, twelve of them exist on our islands, and humans cannot survive the other two systems. Also we are diverse in religion. Take your pick: Buddhism, New Age, Bahai, Islam, local Hawaiian, Christianity, Naturalism, and many more. Mormonism thrives in the islands, and the Moonies recently landed on our rock as well.

About four years ago I met Dayn, a single twenty-something who had recently moved to Kona from Seattle. We both were in Kona, staffing and teaching biblical studies here at the University of the Nations on the Kona campus. Due to the intense scheduling and grueling time spent in the classroom, we were on campus a lot and so had time to bond. After hanging out and working together for a while, we became close friends. During this time the program's leadership asked the three of us (Elissa, Dayn, and me) to start an internship program for our students who graduated from our biblical studies courses. This meant taking a couple of trips in and out of Asia together. During one of our semester breaks, Dayn went to Oahu for a week to meet some of his friends who were students at Brigham Young University.

I have never known any Mormons, and I wanted to learn something about their beliefs. I told Dayn to ask a lot of questions and bring back as many publications as he could get his hands on to share with me when he returned. But there was no way I could prepare myself for everything he brought home.

As soon as Dayn was back in the office, we got together to catch up. He began the conversation with a travelogue, citing all the places he had visited—Waikiki, the North Shore, Pearl Harbor, and so on. I had been to all those places myself, so it was all "blah, blah, blah" to me. I wanted the goods. Then he showed me some pictures to give me a context for the stories he told me about his friends. When I looked at the photographs, I saw people who looked like me—young, wearing T-shirts, board shorts, and flip-flops. *Mormons look like us*, I thought.

Then he got to the goods. He held in his hand a fistful of letters. When Dayn left for Oahu, he knew only two of the students at Brigham Young—the two friends he went to visit. But by the time he returned home, he had met several other people and all of them had written him letters telling him how much they enjoyed spending time with him and letting him know they were praying for him. What? Praying for him? Can they do that? One letter was extremely "evangelistic." The writer used the same language that my Christian friends and I used when sharing our faith with others. I was shocked. "Can they do that?" I asked again. I thought that language was exclusive to my religion.

Both of us were stunned. The writer began by urging Dayn to recognize the void that was in his heart, then explained that God created him like a puzzle with a piece missing. Mormonism was the missing piece. He could not be satisfied by any spiritual experience other than the Mormon experience, because it was the real one. He went so far as to use the "chicken skin" terminology—that warm feeling one has when opening his heart to God. My assumptions about the uniqueness of orthodox Christianity began to wobble a bit. As we read on, letter after letter contained the same evangelistic themes. These young people were very thorough; they hit all the heart strings, covered all the bases, told him how desperately he needed what they had.

A few months later a Mormon temple opened on our island, followed by an assault of Mormon evangelism in our community. A year or so later another friend and I were on the north side of the island for a spear-fishing adventure. On the way we planned a quick stop to help Ernie get his car running. While there, a car pulled up and two young guys stepped out, probably in their early twenties. From the way they were dressed, I would have mistaken them for waiters if not for their badges with the word *Elder* printed next to their names. When I saw them coming, I stepped behind the truck for cover yet stayed within earshot.

They began with typical small talk, the weather, car repairs, life on the island, and so on. But then the missionaries got down to business. Little did these eager elders know they were baiting two Spirit-filled, born-again, evangelical Christians. However, the knot in my stomach told me what was about to happen would not be pretty.

As the dialogue progressed, two things became clear: First, my friends had no clue about Mormonism. They instantly at-

tacked Mormons for polygamy. I could not believe it! What a
lame way to (mis)represent Jesus. The two elders fired back,
and though they knew their faith, they had little understanding regarding the beliefs of orthodox evangelicals. Also, after
an hour or so, it became obvious that neither my friends nor
the missionaries were the least bit open to hearing what the
other side had to say. Instead, the four of them took their
stand, two on one side and two on the other, ranting at each
other, using their own religious terminology.

When the Mormons had had enough, they headed my way. I
guess they figured they would work the shy guy hiding behind
the truck. I could hear my friends congratulating themselves
on how well they whooped those elders. The next stage of the
conversation surprised us all.

Before they reached me, I decided to tell them what I believed, ask them what they believed, let them explain why
they felt I was wrong, and ask them about their beliefs that I
thought were wrong. So when we began talking, I walked them
through thousands of years of history, told them the story of
Jesus and the apostles as they appear in the Gospels, and then
described what Jesus had done in my life. I asked them to tell
me their story and explain why they believed it to be true. Next,
we took turns interrogating each other's beliefs, arguments,
and basis for knowing the truth about God. Fortunately, there
was more fun than fight in our conversation.

Our conversation eventually turned toward our experience
of God, and it was at that point they began to fidget and act
nervous. They told me their "testimony" of how the Holy
Spirit gave them a "burning sensation" in their hearts that the
god of Mormonism was true. But when I described various
God-encounters I had experienced and the closeness of his
presence that I am frequently aware of during my workweek,
they had less to say. In fact, the older elder cut off the conversation abruptly with the announcement that they had run
out of time and needed to be going elsewhere.

Thinking back to this time, I wonder what made my religious experience different from theirs. In some ways they
seemed the same. But in our conversation it was obvious that
they felt mine was more valuable. Looking back, I don't think

it was my experience that shocked them but rather what led to my experience. I showed them that my faith was not fragile, but I was still seeking and asking my own questions. I had a faith that was based on a lot of seeking and searching, which gave it a depth that was foreign to them.

Here we were, five young men, roughly the same age (I was twenty-two at the time). They were doing their missionary work, and I had spent the last two years doing missionary work. We all were on the front lines of our respective faiths. So what happened next was remarkable for many reasons. The younger elder turned around, walked back over to me, and stretched out his hand. As we shook hands, he thanked me and said that our conversation had taught him more about the truth than all his years of religious education. He returned to their car, and they drove away.

For a minute or two I watched as their car made its way back to the main highway. My friends and I were silent and dumbstruck, as if we had just looked into the future and were not yet able to absorb what we had seen. No one spoke a word as we went back to work on the car. *Our* religious training had also been revised by this chance meeting. Competing religious beliefs and experiences were thrown into the ring and were interrogated, assaulted, and torn apart. We discovered that our Christian experience of God in Christ according to the Bible is unique, desirable, and threatening to alternative religious claims.

Not long ago our university surveyed our community to learn what people thought of truth, whether it was absolute, relative, or if it even existed. We included questions such as, "Would everyone agree that the earth is round?" and "Is 1+1=2 a universal truth?" We expected most people to argue that truth is relative but that there are some absolutes. What we discovered is that people over forty tended to lean in that direction, but people in their teens and twenties believed everything was questionable, including the equation 1+1=2. They resisted any piece of information presented to them as absolute truth. The harder we pressed them, the more they resisted, because they were not fighting for a concept but for what they perceive to be freedom and justice.

This begs the question: How can we communicate our faith to a culture that does not believe there is absolute truth? If people have given up on the whole idea of rationale, what good is it to offer reason after reason for the validity of Christian faith? Should we spotlight our experience instead? Is this a time to hide our God encounters or bring them out in the open? If God is all the Bible says he is and if Christianity is all we say it is, why is our experience of God so weak that we often fear having it examined?

C Spiritual Experience

The whole issue of spiritual experience has become a hot-bed of evangelical controversy. On the one hand, Pentecostal/charismatic believers make outrageous claims of having visions, angelic visitors, or divine messages put in their mouths. On the other side of evangelicalism, fundamentalist Bible teachers accuse Pentecostals of being demon-possessed and are skeptical of any sort of feeling or experience. Nevertheless, for people who have God encounters, the experience is incredibly self-authenticating, and no matter what the logicians say, humans long for God "as the deer pants for streams of water" (Ps. 42:1).

It is important for us to see how many old-school Christians, who otherwise resist the dominant values of mainstream culture, simply take for granted the status, privilege, and authority of human reason. Repeatedly, old-school preachers and teachers drummed into the heads of their followers: "Do not trust your feelings!" Subjective, personal experience had to be tested and verified by objective measurements, something in the real world, outside the individual. Emotional states are unstable and unreliable, the old school teaches; people hallucinate; the devil induces false visions. Even spiritual feelings may have other causes than God. Private experiences are not to be trusted. In fact, the general impression I received from some fundamentalist ministers regarding salvation, prayer, worship, and discipleship was, "If you experienced it, it was not of God."

This obsession with reason may have roots in the thought of the Reformers. In Luther's famous "Here I am" speech, he took his life in his hands before the Diet of Worms, boldly stood his ground, and said:

> Unless I am convicted by the testimony of Scripture and plain reason—I do not accept the authority of popes and councils, for they have contradicted each other—my conscience is captive by the Word of God. I cannot and will not recant anything, for to do anything against conscience is neither right nor safe. God help me. Amen.[1]

Protestants often cheer the brave monk-turned-Reformer because he held out for a Christian faith derived exclusively from the Bible. *Sola scriptura!* We can hardly imagine what would have happened to Christendom if Luther had backed down before those who accused him of heresy and threatened his life. Given this critical moment in history, we cannot overemphasize his courageous declaration. For this reason, his choice of words fascinates me.

The irony in our enthusiasm is that Martin Luther did not take his stand on the basis of *sola scriptura*, as we often assume; he made it clear he was willing to concede either to Scripture or "plain reason." The significance of this addition is so great, I am amazed that few people have commented on it. It is quite possible that we in Western society have become so indoctrinated in human reason, we fail to notice when it takes a seat next to Scripture. But if we do not even bat an eye when reason is fastened irrevocably to the Bible, we're in trouble. Luther had no way of knowing that the Protestantism that broke away from Catholicism through Scripture and reason would soon break away from *Scripture* through *reason*. Even as Reformers exalted Scripture over tradition, Enlightenment intellectuals exalted reason over Scripture and faith.

Though I am neither a historian nor an expert on Martin Luther, I will venture a guess that his elevation of human reason had something to do with general currents of thought at that time, especially within the academic community. Luther, it seems, was ambivalent about the role of reason. On the one hand, reason sets humans apart from other animals. On the other hand, as he famously said in his last sermon in Wittenberg, reason is the devil's whore. The problem arose when people chose reason over faith or when a person was unable to reason well—due to lack of intelligence.

The reality is that we run into a number of problems if we reduce the source of Christian truth to Scripture, reason, or both. For example, to assume that all humans are endowed with the same level of reasoning ability may be democratic, but it is not true. Also, if the testimony of reason is as valid as that of the Scriptures, then what is to prevent reason from operating independently of the Scriptures and establishing its own criteria for truth (as, indeed, it did)? Another problem is the assumption that God intended all of his truths to be accessed by reason. Is this a valid assumption? Perhaps God intended to reveal some things "to little children" that the "wise and learned" could not discern (Luke 10:21; see also Matt. 16:17 and 1 Cor. 1:17–31).

John Calvin was also ambivalent regarding reason, believing it to be one of the "natural gifts" God had given humans and, though seriously impaired by the fall, it was not "completely wiped out." Like Luther, Calvin believed reason separated humans from "brute beasts." Calvin realized the importance of believing that "the testimony of the Spirit is more excellent than all reason," and Scripture is superior to all human reason; otherwise, "its authority will always remain in doubt." Nevertheless, he provided a number of proofs to satisfy "natural reason" of the credibility of Scripture.[2] Reason had become too important a topic for the Reformers to ignore or dismiss.

Should reason be set beside Scripture? Should it be used only in the interpretation of Scripture? Should it be discarded? Or should it operate outside of Scripture altogether (in the way that Francis Bacon separated reason, which he said was for the study of nature, from faith, which he said had to do with God)? Is it legitimate to say experience has no place next to the Bible, but human reason does? The path we take regarding this challenge is rather precarious and will not be resolved here. We are certainly not interested in an irrational faith, but what does it mean to know God with all of our being? Does that include our emotional self as well as our rational self?

Reason, Religion, and Rigidity

Part of the problem old-school Christians have with spiritual experience goes back to the Reformers' insistence on *sola scriptura*, rationally interpreted and applied, and their antipathy toward Catholicism. Although the Reformers rejected tradition, apparently they did not reject *all* church traditions. Both Martin Luther and John Calvin had deep respect for early Christian theologians whose work they knew well and quoted freely. Their rejection of tradition was, in fact, rather selective. If they discounted every decision of every pope and council, Protestants would have had to rediscover the doctrine of the Trinity and figure out all over again how the two natures of Jesus Christ coexist in one person, to say nothing about which writings constitute Scripture, which Luther *did* dispute.

Rather than eliminate reason from the Scripture-plus-reason equation, we should probably rethink the role of councils and tradition, because studying the Bible in community is one of the safest ways of protecting ourselves from errors and misinterpretations, while keeping human reason in check. There is no question that the development of Luther's and Calvin's theology benefited greatly from the scholarly communities to which they belonged. After all, they did not single-handedly bring about the Reformation. Christian tradition, in general, is a good plumb line, though it does have a record of severe abuses, theological oddities, and some questionable practices that need to be taken into consideration. This is also true of the Protestant tradition since the time of the Reformers. Tradition, by its nature and momentum, stubbornly resists change when new information comes to light or reform is needed.

Fundamentalist theologians went further than Luther in their esteem for human reason and their denigration of spiritual experience. For example, Charles Hodge argued theology was a "science" that required a "system," because the human mind cannot help but reconcile and systematize such a large volume of "undigested facts."[3] This belief is, of course, thoroughly modern and somehow overlooks thousands of years when the human mind was able to assimilate and reconcile Bible facts within the framework of its story, which revealed not only the meaning of those facts but also how they were worked out in everyday life. Hodge's goal was to create a science of biblical study that challenged and refuted the liberal theology he had studied in Berlin. If German liberalism began with a religious feeling common to all human beings, Hodge faithfully reversed the order. "The feelings come from spiritual apprehension of the truth, and not the knowledge of truth from the feelings."[4]

In an article written for *The New Schaff-Herzog Encyclopedia of Religious Knowledge*, Hodge's successor, B. B. Warfield, said that God's gift of faith is not "an irrational faith" but has a recognizable foundation in "right reason." He continued, "We believe in Christ because it is rational to believe in him."[5] Warfield's reference to "right reason" has generated a recent controversy, because historians say it places him squarely in the modern rational mind-set, while his defenders argue he was merely helping believers become more certain in their faith.

We should not be disturbed if Warfield and other modern-era believers represented Christianity in the intellectual context of their times; we all must do so. That Warfield had a high regard for reason is apparent from another piece he wrote: "Confident that [Christianity] is the only reasonable religion, it comes forward as pre-eminently the reasoning religion. The task it has set itself is no less than to reason the world into acceptance of the 'truth.'" How can a believer determine the "limits of controversy for the saving truth of God"? Warfield answered, "Solely in objective considerations."[6]

The lingering influence of fundamentalist rationalism can be seen in its desperate need to be doctrinally correct. Today doctrinal statements abound, and it appears as though a believer cannot open a bookstore, run a café, create a website, or help orphans, without publishing her "doctrinal statement" for the satisfaction of tightly wound sentinels who do not wish to share money with someone who is not a "true" Christian.

Old-school believers give the impression that the quality of your relationship with God depends on how much you have stored in your brain. You simply cannot memorize enough Bible verses, attend enough Bible studies, read enough books, or sit through enough seminars. The more orthodox your views, the safer your soul. And Bible teachers continue to accommodate this ravenous appetite for biblical information.

A few years ago I had the privilege of auditing one of Chuck Kraft's classes at Fuller Seminary, where he is a professor of anthropology in the School of World Missions. I remember noticing him slightly smirking when one evening he asked in an off-handed way, "How much information do you need in order to be saved?" I was still a card-carrying fundie at the time, so his question threw me. *Is it even possible to get enough information?* I wondered. *What am I doing in this classroom if information is not the key to the kingdom?* But then I thought about the people in the Gospels who crossed paths with Jesus only briefly, who never read anything in the New Testament yet were transformed by a fragment of his teaching or the power of his touch—the blind man who did not know whether Jesus was a sinner (John 9:25), the demoniac who had less than twelve hours with Jesus yet wanted to follow him (Mark 5:1–20), and the thief on the cross who knew little more about Jesus than what was written over his head, "This is the king of the Jews" (Luke 23:38–43).

We live in a society that pays a premium for correct information. Students spend tens of thousands of dollars for an education. Corporations are willing to pay outrageous fees for consultants, specialists, or subcontractors to have the benefit of their knowledge of marketing, management, computers, or whatever. The worship of knowledge spills into the church when Christians assume that knowing is as good as being or doing. In other words, if a believer reads a book on prayer and assumes he is ready to move on to other things because he now knows about prayer, he has mistaken information for experience. Prayer is something we do, not a lesson we learn. If we are not praying, biblical definitions and doctrines of prayer are irrelevant.

Holding Truth in Humility

New-school Christians are learning to take a humble attitude toward truth. They do not embrace the postmodern relativism that old-school believers frequently criticize, but they understand that their own grasp on God's truth is imperfect.[7] One of the delusions of the rational mind is its conviction that it is capable of figuring everything out, solving all riddles, clarifying all mysteries. New schoolers refuse to go down that path. On the one hand, they are not interested in clarifying all mysteries, because mystery itself is necessary for their experience of the sacred and for evoking reverence. On the other hand, they remember that "the man who thinks he knows something does not yet know as he ought to know" (1 Cor. 8:2).

The new-school attitude toward absolute truth is that it exists, but no living human has direct access to it. As Paul said, our best apprehension of absolute truth is "but a poor reflection as in a mirror" (1 Cor. 13:12). Therefore, new-school believers leave enough slack in their beliefs to be corrected, to allow God to teach them even more, and to make room for discovering the truth with clearer and clearer vision. They believe that people who spend their lives trying to prove the truth they know rather than striving to live truth do not grow.

Perhaps the best metaphor to describe the new-school attitude regarding truth is spiritual journey. We know some things for certain, and we hold this knowledge in common with all believers who subscribe to such statements as the Nicene Creed. But since we are not God, we cannot know the truth perfectly; therefore, we are constantly journeying closer to the truth, and new schoolers assume that the closer we get to truth, the more it transforms us. That is why few people believe that the religious person who constantly loses his temper while debating his faith is very close to the truth. There is too much of him and too little of God.

Last year I compiled a short list of changes that evangelical churches could make to have a more effective impact on the twenty-first century. One item on my list has to do with salvation. We need to think of it not merely as a forensic transaction but as an authentic transformation. Certainly in the New Testament, and especially in the book of Romans, the process of salvation is described in judicial terms, though perhaps not as much as some Bible teachers think. But now it is tragically apparent that many people who believed they were declared righteous before God's judgment bench never experienced any real change in their behavior. Oh, they broke a few bad habits and they started attending Bible studies, but beyond these cultural or superficial changes they never received the new heart that made them new creatures. The *experience* of an ever-changing life and taking on more of the character of Jesus Christ is the sort of salvation new schoolers are looking for when they ask about the uniqueness of Christianity. To reduce righteousness to a legal decision made in heaven that we can neither see nor hear is to miss the crucial spiritual, social, environmental, relational, and personal experience of redemption.

Whatever the legal transaction that takes place before God in heaven, there must be a corresponding change in our lives on earth. If we know that our heavenly Judge has declared us righteous, we also need to know that the One who declared us righteous also *makes* us righteous, which is to say we now live righteous lives. The whole idea of righteousness as a way of life has become more and more interesting to me over the last year or so. Simply put, to be righteous means to be right or to behave in a relationship in whatever way is appropriate to that relationship. For example, right with God is reverence, trust, and obedience; right with others is mercy; right in society is justice; right with nature is cooperative care; right with oneself is humility. Of course, I could say much more or be more precise, but I have found that having righteousness sketched out like this helps keep me focused.

Also, God's righteousness heals the radical breach of intimacy that followed Adam and Eve's disobedience in the Garden of Eden. Prior to the fall, they enjoyed God's company "in the cool of the day" (Gen. 3:8), the garden fed them, and they worked it and took care of it. They "were both naked, and they felt no shame" (2:25); they enjoyed intimacy with God, nature, and each other. Once they ate the fruit, they were alienated from God, who banished them; from nature, which grew thorns and weeds rather than fruit; and from each other, for now they felt compelled to make coverings for themselves. Righteousness is the recovery of intimacy—the restoration of people to right relationships. Given this general understanding, there is nothing in our lives that God does not want to redeem.

How sad it would be if all we have to offer people is an invisible and immaterial legal transaction in heaven while they are asking questions like: What do you mean, you "know" God? What is your spiritual experience like? Can you prove that your experience of God is real? Do you ever feel like you might be wrong? Do you experience God as a person? Do you think that was Jesus I saw when I had a near-death experience?

God Encounters

For many years I have heard believers minimize their experience of salvation, saying things like: "There wasn't any thunder or lightning"; "I didn't see any visions"; "There were no angels"; and so on. Perhaps these believers were trying to soften the blow new converts might feel if they were to become Christians and experience absolutely nothing. I cannot imagine the apostle Paul saying, "Well, when I first met Jesus, there wasn't any earthquake. Oh, but wait a minute; there was that heavenly light that knocked me to the ground and blinded me. Oh, yeah, and the voice." When biblical characters encountered God, they were forever humbled and transformed. People today—both within the church and in popular culture—hunger for spiritual experience. Rather than set them up for a cerebral "belief-only" conversion, what do you think might happen if we allowed the Holy Spirit to do whatever he wanted in their lives? Maybe more people would have life-transforming encounters with God if we stopped pouring cold water all over them the very moment they are about to step from death into life.

Calvinism has had a significant influence in shaping American fundamentalism and evangelicalism, so it is a good idea to revisit Calvin once in a while to examine the roots of our religious beliefs and to rummage around for what we may have missed. As I mentioned earlier, like Luther, Calvin placed Scripture over reason, so that the Bible did not require rational proof to establish its truth or authority. But if not by reason, how can a person know the Bible is from God? Calvin's answer: experience. He referred to "a conviction that requires no reasons," though the best reasons will confirm it to be true. He said that the human mind could rest in this conviction "more securely and constantly than in any reasons" and that it was "a feeling that can be born only of heavenly revelation." Not only was this feeling nonrational, words "fall far beneath" Calvin's attempt to explain it, though it is nothing less "than what each believer experiences within himself."[8]

New-school believers expect highly educated and intelligent people to talk about personal God encounters. They long for an encounter with God that is both experiential and rational. Furthermore, they live in a world where people are constantly asking, "Where is your God?" and they need the conviction of a real work of God's Spirit in their lives to meet the challenge of living for and representing a God who is not present to our eyes or ears yet who works powerfully to transform us into the likeness of Jesus (see Job 23:3, 8–9; Ps. 42:3; Isa. 64:4; 2 Cor. 3:18). God cannot be conjured and we cannot experience him at will. God chooses when, where, and under what circumstances he will reveal himself to us so that we become aware of his immediate presence. Under normal circumstances and in what seems like the routine of our everyday lives, yet always unexpectedly, the Holy Spirit arrives, bringing with him a sudden awareness of God's nearness.

Is the Christian experience better than the experience of any other religion? Who can say? Is there anyone who has experienced the depths of every religion and would know how one experience compares to another? All human experience is *embodied*—we do not know of any *purely spiritual, disembod-*

ied experience in this life. Every human thought and feeling is processed through the neurology of the brain. If we have a God-given capacity for spiritual experience, can it be triggered by mechanisms—rituals, meditation, fasting, drugs, and so on—as well as encounters with God?[9] If we experience God in a trance, would that be different from other trances (Acts 10:9–16)? Would a God-induced trance be processed through a different region of our brain than a trance produced by some other mechanism? It is quite possible that we cannot—at least at this time—know if there is a qualitative difference between the Christian and non-Christian spiritual experience. But what we can compare is the *contents of our experience*, how we interpret what we experience, and the sort of behavioral changes it produces in us. More important, we can know whether or not we have any kind of experience of God, and if we do not, then that is certainly something to mourn (Ps. 74:9).

New schoolers will not produce logical reasons for why people should not have a spiritual experience. Rather, they are likely to return to Scripture and linger over those passages where angels dined with families, divine fire engulfed a desert bush, vision was granted to servants who could not see an army of angels, and God's radiant splendor filled the temple. They will ask questions of those Bible characters who walked with Jesus, and they will read the text closely to see how the question of Christian experience is answered. They will read Paul's writings again and again to see what sort of expectations he had for the average Christian's God encounters. They will be reasonable in their search for understanding but not to the exclusion of other ways of knowing. They will exercise a radical faith in and dependency on the Spirit of God. New schoolers are concerned that their own experience of God is so deep, real, and convincing that when asked what makes their religion unique, they will smile and say, "Come and see."

Gatekeepers

A few years ago a thought occurred to me while reading the Bible. I realized that I did not want my intellect to be the gatekeeper of my soul. I was willing to have God do a work in my life that I could not understand or explain. Prior to this simple revelation, I had assumed my spiritual growth depended on the next important book I read that either revealed a profound biblical truth or explained how to have a richer prayer life. In fact, to know God better, I was driven to read as much theology as I could. Unfortunately, I only learned more *about* God. I was convinced that someone had the wisdom, the secret knowledge, or the correct assemblage of Bible verses to point the way to an ultimate consciousness of God. But when I realized that I was limiting my experience of God to what first had to flow through my brain, I knew it would never work. God is so much more than I could ever comprehend that if he first had to accommodate himself to my intellect, he would be so infinitely diminished, he would not be recognizable as God. No, my intellect could not be the gatekeeper of my experience, and I was pretty pleased with myself for coming to this realization. (I now imagine Jesus rolling his eyes and shaking his head at my naïveté.) There was more for me to learn.

Three months ago I was visiting a friend at a hermitage in central California. One night we sat on a bench, talking about our current struggles and how God was working in us through them. A stranger approached us in the darkness and smoothly entered our conversation; it seemed perfectly natural. Quickly we realized that his spiritual depth was much greater than ours, so we asked questions rather than spouting our own nonsense, except I did mention in passing my great revelation about not wanting my intellect to be the gatekeeper of my experience. The stranger said, "Yes, and you do not want your imagination to be the gatekeeper of your experience either."

His words hit me pretty hard, because I had assumed that my imagination was God's "alternative route" to my soul. I asked him to explain what he meant, and he answered, "We can imagine some pretty wonderful things—warm feelings, the breath of God on our cheek, colored lights—but we do not want to limit God to what is imaginary. His real work is much more profound, exciting, and transforming." That night I had to think long and hard about my life with God, because I had believed my imagination was capable of going wherever God wanted to take me. Gradually the light came on for me, and I saw that my imagination of Jesus tended to be controlled by romantic images and sentimental hymns and gospel stories from my childhood and the devotional writings of Christians whom I had always respected. Exercising my imagination is still good for some things—like Bible study and breaking away from old paradigms—but God "is able to do immeasurably more than all we ask or imagine, according to his power that is at work within us" (Eph. 3:20).

Although my friend and I never learned the name of the nighttime stranger—we never even got a good look at his face—we did discover that he was well known to the monks in the hermitage, who held him in high regard as a spiritual director and lecturer. Thanks to our brief conversation with him, I could have easily ended this phase of my spiritual growth at the point where my imagination was no longer the gatekeeper of my soul. But a few days later the thought occurred to me that I should not limit my experience of God to my *conscious experience*. What I mean is this: God can perform a work while I may not even be aware of it. I may be asking him to do one thing, but he may choose to do another thing that I cannot "feel" in any conscious or sensory way. In fact, I am not even sure I can *feel* my own spirit. So now, because I want to surrender to the hands of the Potter, to all that he is doing in me, I acknowledge him at work at levels I cannot know, and it is at that precise moment that I sometimes—many times—feel his smile.

9

Are Christians the Morality Police?

The Place for Love and Acceptance

M

Elissa and I were stoked! Her parents had called to tell us they had come into some extra money and wanted to buy a rental property in Hawaii. This would mean we would have a place of our own, more or less. We found a good deal on a condo, walked it through escrow, and made the move.

Like most buildings in Kona, our complex was built on a terraced hill, with a main highway running along the lower end. At the upper end was the parking lot of the University of the Nations, where we both worked. A window in our corner unit was clearly visible from the campus, and our friends

141

often looked in and waved to us as they walked by. If we were sitting on our futon next to the window, we would smile and wave as people compulsively glanced in the window to see if we were there.

Not long after we settled into our unit, a close friend of mine from New York called and said he wanted to come and visit. You have to appreciate the fact that New Yorkers rarely leave the city, even for a place like Hawaii, and I had not seen Bret for a long time, so I was excited to compare calendars and set a date. I noticed that he kept saying "we," not "I," but I did not give it much thought. Later that week I found him an excellent airfare and called to give him my travel agent's phone number. When I received an email confirming his arrival time, I noticed there were two names: Bret's, of course, but also the name of a woman. Hmmm. How was I going to call and find out what was up without sounding like a complete idiot. Long story short, the next time we spoke, he told me he was bringing his girlfriend and that they had been living together for two years. *Awesome*, I thought. *Elissa and I will have a chance to meet Bret's girlfriend and get to know her.*

Once all of the arrangements were finalized and they would soon be arriving, it struck me, and I had a terrible feeling of impending disaster. My mind was struggling to work out the logistics in our small condo. *Okay, let's see . . . we have two bedrooms, so that works. Lis and I have our room and they can use the other one. They? But "they" aren't married! And this island is so romantic. I can imagine long walks on the beach, followed by a mai tai or a table for two at a seaside restaurant and then back to the hotel. Wait! They aren't staying in a hotel. They're staying at my place! Which means they will probably do . . . do . . . IT! What the heck am I going to do?*

When Elissa and I were at the airport with smiles and leis, I was feeling really miserable. *What are my Christian friends and co-workers going to think when they drop by to meet my friends?* I could already hear the conversation in my mind:
So, how long have you been married?
Oh, we're not married.
Really? [awkward silence]

How do you like Kona? Really? That's nice. What hotel did you choose?

Hotel? Matt and Elissa were nice enough to let us stay with them.

Really? as they glance around the room and notice the queen-size futon.

Oh man, I thought, *this is going to totally stink.* I felt like I was doing something terribly wrong. What should I say? Bret and his girlfriend had no idea that our values and those of our friends were strongly opposed to live-in relationships. Good grief! Both Bret's parents and her parents had suggested that they try living together before getting married. What was my "duty" as a believer in a situation like this? What kind of moral standard would I demonstrate if I said nothing to them about our beliefs? I tried to imagine the headlines in our school paper:

**MATT WHITLOCK, A TEACHER IN OUR
DISCIPLESHIP SCHOOL, GIVES ROOM AND BOARD
TO A COUPLE WHO ARE LIVING IN SIN.**

My brain was working overtime composing the smooth lines I would use to keep my friends away from my house that entire week.

Did I mention that Bret is a big guy, about six and a half feet tall? Which means he needs a big bed. Well, there was no way the bed in our guest room was going to work, but the queen-size futon in the living room was ideal. Of course, that meant they would be sleeping in perfect view through the window by the parking lot in our corner unit!

We had been home from the airport less than two hours when people were already asking questions. About five days into their visit, we were returning from the beach in the morning, and I decided that on the way back home I could grab my mail from my campus mailbox. Since we were near the condo, I told Bret and Judy they could walk back and start getting ready for lunch.

Why did it not immediately register that they would be taking the most trafficked walkway on campus? Why did I not remember that it was noon, and the walkway Bret and his girlfriend would use was the most direct route from the classrooms to the food line? Why did it not occur to me that Bret was not wearing a shirt and his girlfriend was still in her bikini? As soon as I let them out of the jeep, I saw the door to our adult education school open, and students began to spill out of their classroom where they had enjoyed a stimulating "Spirit-filled," "God-glorifying" lecture and worship time. I decided to run! Let *them* deal with her bikini and his shirtless tall frame. I had almost made my escape when my "pagan" friends crossed paths with the "righteous" students, and Bret's girlfriend pulled a cigarette out of her beach bag and lit it. Oh, the expressions on those missionary faces. People were so shocked, they could not take their eyes off my friends, watching them walk all the way to *Matt and Elissa Whitlock's place*. Let me just say, as far as I was concerned, that would have been a good time for Jesus to return and bring the world to an end.

Now when we look back on that harrowing week, we laugh. It was hilarious. I wish I could have told you the story in person, because I can duplicate all the facial expressions from the traumatic moment when the cigarette appeared. Better yet, I wish you could see a videotape of the whole episode. As I look back, several questions come to mind. Why was I so torn about having them stay in my house? Why did I feel pressured, as though it were my job to boss or police them? Why did my Christian friends look at them with raised eyebrows? Or did they? Was it my imagination that other people were critical of them (and me)? Why do I feel like I have to make all my non-Christian friends adopt moral values that apply to Christians?

Yes, Jesus spent a lot of time with sinners—and was criticized for doing so. But how bad were these sinners, really? Did Jesus ever give them the impression he did not like them, or did he constantly nag them? What was Jesus's first concern when associating and eating with sinners? The parents of some of my childhood friends from church did not allow them to hang out with anyone who was not a Christian. I wonder how that prepared them to relate to people who need what Christianity has to offer? How much time are you allowed to spend with a sinner before another believer will accuse you of being too tolerant or compromising?

What is my responsibility in situations like the one I faced with Bret and his girlfriend? Do I provide the plumb line for their moral obligations? If so, how do I assume that role when in their minds living together was not in the least bit wrong? They felt they were honoring their relationship and each other by putting off marriage until they were completely ready, financially, psychologically, and relationally. They took marriage very seriously. In their own way they were making certain that they belonged together so that once married, neither one would break their commitment to the other.

Now they are happily married. Recently Elissa and I were able to visit them, and we talked about their visit and how awkward it was for us at the time. They were very curious about our beliefs and the culture of our Christian community. Life for them, as with all of us, is a journey. They may have a long way to go, but they do love God at this point in their lives. Was it my job to interfere with the process through which God was taking them or to cooperate with him by showing them acceptance and love for who they were in that moment? When Jesus told the Samaritan woman, "You have had five husbands," did he also tell her, "And that is a very bad thing. You should not be living with a man who is not your husband"? Or did he state the facts in such a way that she knew whatever he had to give, it was available to her—yes, a woman like her (see John 4:7–26). Did he come into the world to condemn it? If Jesus were in your city tonight, would he be in all the Christian hangouts, or would he be among sinners? Would we recognize him? Would we tell him, "You have no business spending time with those people! That is not acceptable behavior for members of our church"?

Condemning the World

Matt has introduced an issue that requires some serious thinking and in the meantime is likely to create a bit of discomfort, if not ruffle more than a few feathers. Can we expect non-Christians to adopt Christian values? If they do not, are we justified in judging them for violating a standard that, for instance, Jesus gave to his *disciples*? Do we need to either dissociate ourselves from people who do not share our values or constantly let them know they are breaking God's commandments?

One place to begin sorting through this issue is with semantics—the *feeling* evoked by specific terms. Look at the following words and quickly rate your emotional response. "Hot" means the word has positive connotations, and "cold" refers to negative connotations. Ready? Go.

Pious	Hot	Cold
Judge	Hot	Cold
Preach	Hot	Cold
Convert	Hot	Cold
Crusader	Hot	Cold
Moralize	Hot	Cold
Proselytize	Hot	Cold
Missionary	Hot	Cold
Indoctrinate	Hot	Cold

If you responded with "hot" to all these words, you are probably a strong Christian or have a generous attitude toward Christian culture. However, you are light-years away from popular culture and the next generation of believers. For example, people outside the church use the word *preach* in a negative way to mean a demeaning and unwanted lecture. In the 1980s Madonna sang, "Papa, don't preach; I'm in trouble," which is to say that preaching does nothing for people in trouble. What they need is *real* help.

Dictionary definitions do not always help us understand the way people actually use words or capture the current meanings attached to them. What do people in popular culture *feel* when they hear these words?

Pious: self-righteous, prudish; proud of one's own moral goodness.

Judge: to determine that someone else is not as good or right as you are; to point out the faults in someone else while ignoring your own.

Preach: to talk down to people, telling them what they ought to do.

Convert: to pressure someone to adopt your way of thinking, believing, or living.

Crusader: someone who forces with threat of violence someone else to accept his faith.

Moralize: to pronounce judgments on other people's actions, to preach our own moral opinion.

Proselytize: to constantly attempt to either coerce or seduce others into our religion.

Missionary: someone who tries to destroy indigenous cultures in the attempt to Christianize or civilize those cultures.

Indoctrinate: to brainwash other people into a belief system.

One reason the Moral Majority failed to have a lasting influence in U.S. politics is because the true majority of North Americans felt the leaders of the Moral Majority exemplified all or most of the characteristics in the above list. Many people were terrified that if the Moral Majority succeeded in all of its goals, television preachers like Jerry Falwell or Pat Robertson would attempt to pass laws enforcing their moral convictions on the whole nation. To Americans, conservative as well as liberal, moralizing political leadership is to our country what the Taliban was to Afghanistan.

Old-school Christianity feels a responsibility to be the moral conscience of the whole world. If we have the light of Scripture, certainly we are obligated to tell everyone else how they are offending and disobeying God. This attitude is sometimes referred to as *imperialistic* and was characteristic of a particular form of missionary work. Old-school Christians feel duty bound to point out every sin they see (or think they see). In politics they want to "turn the nation back to God." In personal relationships they are given to exhortation. They are uncomfortable spending time with non-Christians without criticizing their language, habits, behavior, values, and morals. In fact, there are Christians who are convinced they are personally compromising with sin if they fail to rebuke the sins they see in the lives of others. They feel guilty for not confronting family, friends, neighbors, and co-workers with their disobedience to God's Word.

Paul said, "Have nothing to do with the fruitless deeds of darkness, but rather expose them" (Eph. 5:11). But Paul did not tell the Christians in Ephesus to go into the marketplace and proclaim the sins of their city and God's coming judgment, like Jonah in Nineveh. If we read the whole passage closely, we see that Paul was instructing Christians how to live with other Christians. Whenever we jump to an interpretation, it makes it more difficult to discover what Paul was actually saying. Every Christian community has the responsibility to be self-monitoring. There is a way for mature and humble believers to approach other believers compassionately when they are in the wrong (see, for example, Gal. 6:1–5). Take another look at the question Paul posed to the Corinthians: "What business is it of mine to judge those outside the church? Are you not to judge those inside? God will judge those outside" (1 Cor. 5:12–13).

Too often old-school believers have pushed people farther away from Christ by fixating on some sin without demonstrating real love and affection for people. Judgments are made and pronounced without first establishing rapport and credibility through conversations and other interactions.

The New Testament states, "God did not send his Son into the world to condemn the world, but to save the world through him" (John 3:17). If that is so, why do we feel that it is our job to condemn the world? Perhaps it is because of the Puritan pattern of salvation that was stamped on the great revivals in England and the United States, in which a person would be driven to salvation by an intolerable sense of guilt. But not everyone who comes to Jesus is driven by guilt. Some come to him simply because his person and character are attractive; others come in response to his invitation, "Come to me, all you who are weary and burdened, and I will give you rest" (Matt. 11:28), and some come to him because they need his help with a physical problem. My guess is that if we did a better job of being followers of Jesus, we would feel less pressure to tell nonbelievers how wrong they are and what they need to do if they want to be like us.

The More Excellent Way

The church, configured to reveal God's salvation to popular culture, consists of broken and transparent people. Like patients in a hospital, they may be willing to describe their own injuries, infirmities, and illnesses, but they are in no position to tell others how to get well. They leave that for the Doctor. They are happy to belong to Jesus Christ, but they are honest in their assessment of their own condition and progress. Like Anne Lamott's qualified admission, "I'm a Christian . . . not a very good one,"[1] they admit that their grasp on the truth is not absolute, their track record is not perfect, and their chances of getting to heaven without ever committing another sin are nil.

The new-school paradigm implies the development of a whole new cadre of leaders. Old-school leaders constantly posed as experts with saintlike qualities. They stood on top of the mountain and announced to those below, "Follow my instructions and I will guide you to the spiritual summit where I now stand." New-school leaders, however, are on the trail with everyone else. Their advice is tempered with humility. They will likely say, "I think this is the way we're supposed to go. If anyone has a better idea, let me know now. Otherwise, I'll lead the way and see if it works. But let's make sure we stick together, keep our safety line tight, follow the guidebook, and watch out for each other."

The men and women who deserve most to take the torch from the last generation of Christian leaders are not fixated on the sins of the nation or the sins of anyone else. They know that Jesus forgave people *after* they came to him (or were brought to him). If Jesus told a person to go and sin no more, it was *after* an encounter with him, not before. Therefore the priority of the new school is to bring people to Jesus and not make unnecessary comments about the condition in which they come. If they are limping, tapping a white cane, dressed in rags, have alcohol on their breath, or dress provocatively, they will be welcomed and accepted as members of a loving, dysfunctional family. Their sinful condition will not make the slightest impression on those who feel that introducing another person to Jesus is all that matters (let the Lord tell them what and how they need to clean up). New schoolers understand that spiritual wanderers need to know they are loved rather than judged.

Oh, and about that torch. Old-school believers have a hard time letting go of the torch that has been in their clutches for so long. They want to pass it on only to those who will continue to use it to illuminate the same institutions they built and have occupied for the last forty or fifty years. They are skittish about handing it to young men and women who want to use the light to strike out into the unexplored darkness in search of God's long lost children. The old soldiers were the pioneers at one time, and they cannot imagine a frontier beyond the one they have colonized. For that reason, we see many old-school institutions heavily endowed (in some cases, shamefully so), while many new-school Christians, who are venturing new works for Christ, must live on survival rations.

Are Christians supposed to be the moral police of society the way the thought police constantly critique public speech? What are your feelings about the thought police and others who raise a fuss over every politically incorrect statement or word? Do you admire them, appreciate their service to society, and hope to hear more from them? Do you wish they would back off? How effective will Christians be if we try to assume the role of the moral police? Not nearly as effective as we would be if we lived in society as Jesus did, associating and eating with sinners.

10

Do Good People Go to Hell?

Acts of Service

Today I was driving to one of my favorite surfing spots, listening to the radio. Hawaii is not known for its radio stations. In fact, we host some of the worst, but there is one station that almost everyone plays, so you hear it from other cars, playing in barber shops, or wafting from homes. The locals like it because of the relatively small number of commercials. The programming is created in a small town in Idaho. And it is Christian.

So I was in my truck listening to the island's favorite radio station when they ran an ad for Jesus. The announcer was explaining that you, the listener, could not get to heaven by being good. He told a story about a person who was given an impossible task—something about having him walk across a tile floor in wet wool socks carrying a stack of dishes he was not supposed to drop, and when he accepted the challenge, a bull was released that charged him. The announcer explained that anyone who thought he was good enough to go to heaven was foolish, because our secret sins are the bull that makes the task impossible. The announcer seemed to be saying there was something bad about wanting to be good.

Interesting, I thought. *So, is this what I signed up for? I became a Christian to escape hell?*

During one period in my teenage years, my friends and I became what was known as "straightedge." A straightedge kid could be recognized by the letter *X* displayed in tattoos, permanent ink on the hands, or sewn into clothes, backpacks, or whatever else was eye-catching. The *X* identified those of us who followed the unwritten law of straightedge.

To be straightedge meant that you hated "the man"—people who by virtue of their success necessarily robbed and oppressed the poor and needy. As straightedgers, we were committed to abstinence from drugs, alcohol, or sex, because these distractions would have prevented us from making society a better place. We were devoted to the environment and politics. Some of our number were so driven, they adopted radical diets to keep their minds clear in their quest to effect societal changes. That glorious movement has dwindled in recent years, and what is left of it consists of music written for screaming little girls in large coliseums—the dreaded nightmare of the underground hardcore straightedge scene.

The young men and women in our straightedge group did a lot of good things, including raising awareness of AIDS and of the depletion of rain forests in the Amazon, helping old women carry their groceries, and anything else to make the world a better place. But they never attended church. The church was to them the worst institution because Christians talked about changing the world but never did anything. To be honest, I do not know of too many churches in my community that would have been happy to see my friends enter their sanctuary. Still, these kids did good deeds, educated themselves, and loved their neighbors. But they were definitely not Christians.

A few years after my straightedge phase, I had the opportunity to visit Thailand. This beautiful country is one of my favorite places on earth—"the land of smiles," where the hospitality is overwhelming. All of Thailand is Buddhist, so it is understood that to be Thai is to be Buddhist.

The first time I went to Thailand I was eighteen years old and traveled with a group of kids who were also about my age. For two of the weeks we were there, a Thai family opened their home to us, cooked our breakfast and dinner, and charged nothing. I will never forget how sacrificially they served us and took care of our needs. When I returned to their home four years later with Elissa, the mother immediately recognized me, hugged me so tight I could not breathe, and invited us in for dinner. She dropped whatever she had been doing and ran to get food from the local shops. She even remembered my favorite Thai dish.

We sat, ate, smiled, and laughed, though we could not speak Thai, and they could not speak English. Their daughter translated for us, but they did not need to use words to show us we were loved. We truly had a home in Thailand with this warm and generous Buddhist family. They were good, kind, giving, and hospitable, but they were not Christians.

I struggle with the idea that there are many wonderful people in the world, yet because they have not made a specific decision or said a particular prayer, they are headed for eternal damnation. Why were my straightedge friends "hopelessly lost," though they did many more good things than the kids in my church youth group? Why is a Buddhist family in a small poor village going to hell when they give more of themselves and their belongings than any Christian I know in America? If it is true that our own goodness is not good enough to find God's acceptance, why do we package this information in banal radio announcements, "selling" the idea of human sinfulness with silly analogies?

Should we continue to focus our attention on grace only as it applies to saving our butts from hell, or should we think about the way it changes our lives and transforms us into better people?

The message I hear from televangelists is that everyone in the audience is a sinner, a very bad person in God's eyes. But with one easy decision we can be placed instantly on the right side of the fence. To me that sounds a bit like a used car commercial. No wonder so many of my friends used to mock Christianity; they took one look at it and said, "What's so special about you? We do far more good on earth than you people. And you tell me that even though you do nothing to improve the world or the lives of others, you have a ticket to eternal life just because you said a one-minute prayer?" What am I to say to that?

What does it mean that God is a judge? Could it mean that I am free from the responsibility of judging and rejecting people, free instead to love and accept them, to seek to understand them and assist them in their spiritual journey? Are we missing something? Should we want to be good people, or is this unnecessary because we are forgiven? Do we feel we have no responsibility to others, because we are not "saved by works"? Should we wonder about Christians who seem concerned about their own salvation but unconcerned with saving anything else (like the environment, the inner city, and people from the AIDS epidemic)? What if we stopped making commercials about not being good enough to go to heaven and radically devoted ourselves to fervent prayer until God made a transformation in our hearts that everyone can see? Do we fully understand the limits (or limitlessness) of God's mercy? I once asked one of my students what he thought it would take to change the world. He said, "Acts of service." I asked why, and he answered, "Because people have heard us talk enough about what we think and believe; now they want to see it."

C Oversimplifying the Gospel

A favorite pastime for my friends who grew up in conservative Christian homes involves swapping stories about the naive view of sex and procreation they held or heard from their youth group days. For example, one woman when in high school believed she could get pregnant by lying next to her boyfriend, even if fully clothed. She had learned from the King James Version of the Bible that when David "lay" with Bathsheba, she "gave birth to a son" (2 Sam. 12:24). She did not realize that *lay* was a euphemism for a more physically intimate encounter.

Today's teenagers are street smart, if not more enlightened than those of the Truman era. Few high school students today want to be the last in their class to discover how babies are made. But imagine a young man who thinks that his girlfriend might become pregnant if he says, "I love you," to her. My example is ridiculous, of course, yet how many believers are convinced that a person can be "born again" into the kingdom of God merely by saying certain words? I have heard evangelists tell crowded auditoriums that all they have to do is say a prayer in which they ask Jesus to be their personal Lord and Savior, wash their sins away, come into their heart, and they will be born again.

How naive would we be if we assumed that Jesus intended people to enter the kingdom of God or experience the radical transformation of spiritual rebirth simply by repeating a scripted "sinner's prayer." Even if preachers and evangelists emphasize the importance of "saving faith," their pitch comes down to the recitation of a word formula that guarantees a place in heaven. At least Orthodox, Roman Catholic, and High Church institutions require a period of theological education—catechism—before receiving a person into their membership. Even so, few people who take Christianity seriously would assume that everyone who has answered the questions correctly for confirmation, received baptism, and recited the Nicene or Apostolic Creed is indeed everything Jesus had in mind when he said, "I tell you the truth, no one can see the kingdom of God unless he is born again" (John 3:3).

In the New Testament, the process of coming to faith in Christ consists of being and doing rather than saying or reciting. In the Gospels, people became disciples of Jesus by doing his will and the will of his Father and not merely saying to him, "Lord, Lord" (Matt. 7:21–23; Luke 6:46–49). The follower of Jesus, according to the Sermon on the Mount, was a person whose good deeds were beneficial in social and spiritual effects, while not necessarily receiving public acknowledgment (see Matt. 6:16–18). The first word in the messages of both John the Baptist and Jesus was "repent," which above all means *change*.

If Christians are going to vehemently defend the New Testament claim that no one can come to God except through Jesus Christ (see John 14:6), they should also insist that people come to God *the way Jesus taught*. We do not receive Jesus with words alone. Jesus does not become our "Lord and Savior" simply because we refer to him in those terms. The faith that Jesus revealed to the world had less to do with stating one's beliefs and more to do with trust, obedience, and most of all love (Luke 10:36–37; John 13:13–17, 34–35; 14:1, 23–24; 15:9–14). Christianity is a *lived experience*, and whatever spirituality we may think we have is "nothing" if we "have not love" or we love only "with words and tongue" rather than "with actions and in truth" (1 Cor. 13:1–3; James 2:14–18; 1 John 3:17–18).

My concern here is not to question whether people who claim to be Christians are true believers or whether Jesus Christ is the only way to God—as he claimed. What I want to call into question is the narrow way evangelicals have defined what it means to come to God through Jesus Christ. The tendency of the old school has been to place all the stress on people saying the right words, using a vocabulary that has been canonized over the last two hundred years, but was not always a litmus test and may even misrepresent the heart of God revealed in the New Testament and shut people out of the kingdom of God who wish to enter (see Matt. 23:13–14).

Do good people go to hell? For most evangelicals, the question is answered as soon as it is asked. First, there are no "good people," because the Bible says clearly that all are "under sin" and all "have sinned" (Rom. 3:9, 23). Second, there is no way to earn a place in heaven through good deeds (or works). Third, Jesus said plainly that no one can come to God except through him. Peter affirmed this truth later when he said that salvation is "found in no one else" and that there is no other name—other than Jesus—under heaven "by which we must be saved" (Acts 4:12). Need we go any further?

The heart of the message that evangelical Christians refer to as the gospel is that there is one way, and only one way, to find acceptance with God and that is through Jesus Christ. Further details of the gospel are laid out and developed in the writings of Paul. There are two potential destinies for all human beings: heaven, which is eternal joy in the presence of God, and hell, which is eternal torment and banishment from the presence of God. Only a personal relationship with Jesus Christ can guarantee heaven rather than hell.

The basic formula of evangelism is well known, because it has been preached repeatedly and published in countless tracts. The current form of this gospel message was shaped by revival-era evangelists who needed a condensed version of the Christian message for quick communication to large audiences and through mass media. All of the tricky details of the New Testament lie hidden in the background, because if becoming a Christian is really as easy as merely "accepting Jesus Christ as my personal Lord and Savior" or by saying the sinner's prayer, why complicate the process or create theological challenges for people? They can deal with the hard demands and biblical difficulties after they are safely added to the fold. In fact traveling evangelists became notorious for their "love them and leave them" style of ministry. They made wonderful promises to those who would say the prayer; then they left town. It was the local pastor who had to minister to the disillusioned, wounded, and jilted new convert.

The problem with simplifying the gospel for the masses is that we oversimplify and misrepresent the truth. Conservative theologians are now advising us to be more careful in our study of Scripture; to give greater attention to the historical, religious, and cultural realities that gave the biblical text its particular shape and meaning; and to listen to scholars who have devoted their lives to the study of the culture, history, literature, and theology of the New Testament. The unsettling result of returning to the Bible to see what it actually has to say about the gospel is that our conventional ideas have wandered away from the teaching of Jesus and Paul. In fact, in some cases we have made it so easy for a person to "become a Christian" that many people who have said the sinner's prayer and attend church may not be truly Christian in any meaningful sense of the word.

The entire Bible is clear on the issue of sin; it is contrary to the nature and will of God, and its offense is great enough to separate sinners from God. Sin, therefore, demands some kind of resolution, either punishment or a ritual act that both covers the sin and purifies the sinner. In the Old Testament, offerings were made to God in which sinful people laid their hands on sacrificial animals to transfer their guilt to the victim so the sinner could be restored to fellowship with God.

In the New Testament, sinners are covered by the death of Jesus. Since we all have sinned, there is no one who can hope to find forgiveness and restoration with God except through Jesus Christ. Evangelicals stress two complementary facts: there is no one who has not sinned, and there is no way to work off the subsequent guilt of our sin. Some evangelists so devalue human works that they are practically not worth mentioning, except to say that they are worthless (as in the radio commercial Matt mentioned). This does not mean evangelicals have loose standards for Christian behavior; in some places evangelicals have devised rules that are more rigid than Old Testament law. But evangelicals assume every believer will continue to sin and constantly need repentance and forgiveness.

The emphasis on Jesus's sacrificial death to remove sin and the denigration of human works have led to a firm belief that makes little sense when analyzed logically. I will describe a hypothetical situation, but sadly we have seen too many real-life examples to consider the following story a caricature or exaggeration. This story is based on a large number of actual cases and events I have observed during more than thirty years of ministry.

Bad News Christians

Imagine next-door neighbors. The man in one home is a Christian, and the woman in the other home is not. The Christian regularly sins. He remains emotionally distant from his wife, abuses his children, is unethical in his business dealings, underpays his employees, dissociates himself from his "pagan" neighbors, and so on. But every Sunday night he strolls down the aisle of his church, kneels before God, confesses his sins, and promises to do better. After all, he has asked Jesus Christ into his heart to be his Lord and Savior. As he drives home from church, we see the bumper sticker on his car: *Christians are not perfect, just forgiven.*

The non-Christian neighbor does not believe in Jesus Christ, has not asked him into her heart, does not go to church or engage in rituals of repentance. She stopped going to church and believing in Jesus when she was eight years old. At that time, the fundamentalist (or Roman Catholic) church her mother attended in the Midwest excommunicated them because her mother divorced her father (who had been beating her). The church had strict policies regarding divorce that were spelled out in their doctrinal statement. Looking back on that sad and horrific period in her life, she remembers a Sunday school teacher telling her that Jesus was angry with her mother because he hates divorce. The implication was that he also hated divorcees and their children and did not want them around his church.

Nevertheless, now that she is a mature woman, she lives an exemplary life. She is selfless in her devotion to her children, kind to everyone who crosses her path, and volunteers for many charitable services, including a homeless shelter. Her friends know her as a generous person, perhaps the kindest person they have ever met. She is so careful not to exploit people who work for her around her home or in her office that she is often cheated by others who see her as a patsy. When her Christian neighbor's wife was sick, this woman brought them a meal every night for a week. In every way imaginable she is a "good person."

According to the standard evangelical thinking, the unethical and sinful Christian is on his way to heaven because he asked Jesus into his heart and regularly repents of his sins, while his neighbor, who outshines him in every way, is on her way to hell. The immoral person who fulfills the minimal requirements of belief in Jesus is covered, while the moral person is hopelessly lost because she has never prayed to ask

Jesus into her heart. In other words, according to the generally accepted formula, you have good people going to hell,
while bad people are going to heaven because they believe
in Jesus.

Theoretically, Jesus makes bad people into good people,
but I have spent my entire life in churches and around Christians and have seen for myself that many people who are convinced they are heaven bound are mean-spirited, unfriendly,
greedy, consumed with pride, selfish, and unethical. I have
heard these church people slander other believers nonstop,
seen them treat others (clerks, flight attendants, servers) with
inexcusable rudeness, and witnessed their bitter and loveless
attacks on Christians who deviate from their doctrine to the
slightest degree. One cannot help but wonder whether these
people are embracing a false hope. And if they are wrong about
themselves, could they possibly be wrong about good people
who live and die outside the church? Can they be absolutely
certain that God accepts them because they call Jesus Lord
yet live as if he is not, while God rejects people whose lifestyle
reflects the ideals of the Sermon on the Mount because they
have never asked Jesus to come into their hearts?

Evangelical Rhetoric

Have we depended so much on the language of salvation—
the language current in the evangelical subculture—that we
are insisting people subscribe to word formulas that do not
appear in the New Testament? Find the place where the Bible
specifically says people need a "personal relationship with
Jesus Christ" to be saved. I am not opposed to this language,
but it is not the only way of expressing the idea of knowing
God in Jesus, and I am convinced that there is much more
to a relationship with Jesus than what is often suggested or
explained in that terminology. Bear in mind that when the
Bible talks about "knowing" God or Jesus Christ, it is not
necessarily referring to a private or subjective intimacy in the
romantic or sentimental way these words typically suggest.
In fact, with few exceptions, biblical faith is communal and
public rather than subjective and private. Look for the verse

that says we must ask Jesus to "come into our hearts as our personal Lord and Savior." I am not saying that you cannot find that inference in the New Testament, but what happens when you look for that exact phrase or evangelistic word formula? Have we been oversimplifying the Christian life so much that we have misrepresented the radical commitment to Jesus that Christianity actually entails—a commitment to goodness, hospitality, stewardship, forgiveness, love for enemies, mercy, and kindness?

What does it mean to be born again? Jesus was very clear that his reference to being born again was not to be taken literally (John 3:5–8). So if the term *born again* is a metaphor, what does it represent? Must we require people to use this metaphor ("I have been born again")? If there is a literal spiritual experience that is represented by the metaphor, is it not better to have the experience than to merely parrot the words? Do you think it is possible there are many people who claim to be born again who have not had the true spiritual experience? And do you think it is also possible that some people have had the experience, yet never use the language?

In another page or two I will explain how it is possible for some people to fulfill the will of Jesus Christ by not believing in Jesus. Yes, that sounds weird and impossible, but Paul indicated that the Corinthians should not put up with someone who "preaches a Jesus other than the Jesus we preached" (2 Cor. 11:4). If the only "Jesus" a person has ever heard of or seen represented is that "other Jesus," then is it not appropriate for her to refuse to believe in *that* Jesus? If she refuses to believe in the other Jesus, yet lives according to standards taught by the true Jesus, is she hopelessly lost because she never said the words, "I receive Jesus as my Lord and Savior"? What if the way she lives indicates that Jesus *is* her Lord and Savior, even if he is unknown to her?

"Born again" was not the only metaphor Jesus used to illustrate what had to happen to a person before entering the kingdom of God. In one place, he said adults must become like children; in another place, spiritual life was like "living water"; in yet another place, people had to eat his flesh and drink his blood—we can be happy this is not the metaphor evangelicals chose to use as the primary requirement for Christian initiation (though in Roman Catholic and Greek Orthodox churches, the blood of Jesus is referred to as the "elixir of immortality").

The old school is adamant that if people do not use the language, "Jesus is my Lord and Savior," they do not have any hope of heaven, no matter how good their heart, words, or actions. So there are some people who use the right words but do not do the will of God, and there are other people who have never learned the right words—or have never been able to trust the people who tried to shove the right words down their throat—yet do God's will in constantly showing love and kindness to others. Now it seems that we have become imprisoned in a doctrine that hovers over the New Testament rather than holding to the truth of the New Testament in which Jesus tells of a son who uses the right words but never does what his father wanted, while a second son uses the wrong words but comes around and does as his father wanted (Matt. 21:28–31). Furthermore, Jesus used this story to explain why "priests and elders" of Israel would enter the kingdom of God behind "the tax collectors and the prostitutes" (Matt. 21:23, 31–32).

Young believers tend to be more critical of the church and generous toward people who are on the outside. Whereas former generations seemed comfortable with the masks they wore and the facade of success and happiness that was plastered on their congregations, the new school is extremely sensitive to religious hypocrisy and finds the mask intolerable. If they cannot come to church, confess how they are really doing, find acceptance and assistance, why go only to pretend everything is fine? Why crawl into the emergency room of a hospital and tell the doctors you do not need their help? And what good is a hospital if it can't accept and heal people who are wounded and sick but insists that only the healthy enter their doors?

If the term *Christian* appears no more than three times in the New Testament (two of those three references are in the book of Acts), if neither Jesus nor Paul referred to believers as Christians, then we cannot argue from the New Testament that a person has to be a Christian (that is, they have to wear that label) to be eligible for heaven.

The Open Door

According to the New Testament, there have been people who did not know Jesus's name but whose sins were covered by Jesus nonetheless. Paul explained in Romans that God had "left the sins committed beforehand unpunished" so that he could demonstrate his righteousness made available through Jesus Christ (Rom. 3:25). Therefore, people living prior to Christ enjoyed the retroactive benefits of Jesus's death and resurrection, even though they did not know Jesus by name. They came to the Father through Jesus without knowing the name of Jesus.

And while we are on the topic the *name* of Jesus, theologians have been trying to explain to us laypeople that the biblical concept of a person's name is not the same as our understanding today. When Jesus told his disciples that the Father would give them whatever they asked in Jesus's name (John 16:23–24), he did not mean for them—or us—to use his name as an incantation at the end of our prayers, as we hear so often: "In Jesus' name. Amen." Rather, Jesus was saying that the disciples could offer their prayers to God *through Jesus himself* as mediator between them and God.

The word *Jesus*—whether spelled in Aramaic, Hebrew, or Greek characters—did not give potency to the disciples' prayers. It's the person of Jesus, acting as their bridge to God, who gives the power to prayer. Again, my aim is not to rant against the practice of closing prayers with the word formula "In Jesus' name"—though we never find a prayer in the New Testament closed in this way—or try to put an end to the practice. I want to help Christians understand there is more not less to our words than we realize.

When God revealed himself and his glory to Moses, he "proclaimed his name, the LORD. And he passed in front of Moses, proclaiming, 'The LORD, the LORD'" (Exod. 34:5–6, where "LORD" translates the personal name of God, rendered

Yahweh by most scholars). The German theologian, Walther Eichrodt, explained:

> The close relationship apparent here between the Name and the nature of God can only be understood from a knowledge of primitive beliefs about names. For primitive man the name is not merely a means of denoting a person, but is bound up in the closest possible way with that person's very existence, so that it can become in fact a kind of *alter ego*.[1]

Also Eichrodt said that in disclosing his name to Moses, God revealed himself as a person and "definable" over against "an abstract concept." By divulging his name, God "came forth from his secret place and offered himself in fellowship" to his people, to give them reassurance of his nearness and a means to call upon him in worship or in trouble.[2] God was somehow present to Israel in his name, so that in it they "encountered him in person and experienced his activity."[3]

When Jesus taught the disciples to pray "hallowed be your name" (Matt. 6:9), he was concerned for the way they thought about God, held him in honor, and remained conscious of his holiness, and not merely that they showed respect for a particular word. When he told his disciples to pray in his name (John 14:13–14; 15:16) or when the disciples healed and preached in the name of Jesus (Acts 3:6; 4:7–11), explained that salvation was to be found only in the name of Jesus (v. 12), or asked God to perform miracles through the name of Jesus (v. 30), they had in mind the rich meaning of a name as representation—or stand-in—for the fullness of Jesus in his person and activity. We too need to offer every prayer to God in this larger sense and not glibly say the name of Jesus as if it were magic or a good luck formula.

I have heard believers cheer Christian celebrities when they boldly say, "In Jesus' name. Amen," at the end of public prayers—unnecessarily risking offending people of other faiths, as if rubbing in their faces the fact that in a "Christian nation" we are free to pray in this manner. These believers rejoice because their hero did not back down from a biblical form of prayer when, in fact, there is a more profound way to pray in Jesus's name that does not require pronouncing his name. My heart grieves the fact that we have become so like the Pharisees and scribes who constantly found fault with Jesus's disregard for their traditions. Like them we are prone to honor God with our lips—insisting on saying "In Jesus' name" at the end of our prayers—while our hearts are far from him and from the real meaning of praying in his name (Matt. 15:1–8).

One sticky question that is often asked among Christians is whether there are people in the world today who have not heard Jesus's name yet are covered by his life, death, and resurrection. Notice that the possibility of this does not in any way contradict Jesus's claim that "no one comes to the Father except through me" (John 14:6), because people of the Old Testament *did* come to the Father through Jesus even though they did not know the name or person of Jesus. There are still cultures that have not been exposed to the name of Jesus and others where his name is suppressed so that people do not know about him. Could people living in those areas of the world today possibly be included in God's kingdom, even if they do not know the name of the King?

Another even stickier question is whether there are people who have heard of Jesus, but not the true Jesus, and they reject only the one they have heard preached. Paul mentioned to the Corinthians that there was "another Jesus" (2 Cor. 11:4), different from the Jesus he represented. We know that Jesus Christ has been grossly misrepresented and even lied about by Christians and by other religions. Is it possible that there could be a depiction of Jesus that you would reject? What if someone described a Jesus who endorsed domestic violence to keep wives and children in their place, who scared children at night with visions of hell so they would remember to brush their teeth, who gave preachers permission to take the pensions of elderly widows to enrich themselves? Would you say that is your Jesus—the New Testament Jesus—and that you were his disciple? There may be good reasons why some people reject the "Jesus" that has been presented to them. I reject that Jesus too.

David Dark has adopted a wise course of action when asked whether he is a Christian. He says, "To avoid the pain of being pigeonholed, I've found it helpful to respond with something along the lines of 'Describe what you mean by the word, and I'll tell you if you're describing me.'"[4] He has to answer this way because we are well aware of the misrepresentation of Christianity and Christ in our culture, so that we dare not admit to being a Christian if it means we are lumped together with maniacs who carry placards that say, "God hates fags."

Will God punish people if they reject a Jesus who is not the true Jesus? Isn't that the very thing Paul told the Corinthians and Galatians to do—to reject any other Jesus or any other "gospel" than the one he preached (2 Cor. 11:4; Gal. 1:6–9)? If that is so, imagine someone growing up and never hearing of any other Jesus than the one who sends children to hell for not picking up their toys or for being aborted or for having parents who were divorced or for masturbating—an angry and unforgiving Jesus. If they say, "I will not accept or follow a cruel and merciless Jesus that endorses racism, is more concerned with church buildings than human lives, or indiscriminately infects babies and hemophiliacs with the AIDS virus because he is trying to punish or annihilate homosexuals," will they be condemned for that decision? If you say, "No, they will be condemned for not accepting and obeying the true Jesus," then the next question is, "And what if they have never heard of or seen the true Jesus? What if the only Jesus they know is this gross caricature or something equally repugnant?"

New-school believers are asking if it is possible for people who do not know the true Jesus to still be covered by his redemptive work, because he (alone) knows their hearts. They want to know about the salvation of those whose theology is incomplete or imperfect (as in the case of Old Testament believers and Christians prior to the completion of the New Testament canon and all the councils that determined the orthodox beliefs of the church). They want to know how orthodox a person has to be, how perfectly correct their doctrines, to be saved, or whether it is possible that having all the information is not as important as their inner transformation. They want to know if it's possible for "heretics" who misunderstood the two natures of Jesus to enter heaven, because they were trying their best to follow Jesus Christ according to the light they had. And if for that same reason Bible-thumping preachers who are convinced that the angry Jesus is the true Jesus have just as much chance of entering heaven (provided their lives show real evidence of his work) as people who reject their misrepresentation of Jesus. You see, the church from the fourth century on had the authority to brand and excommunicate heretics, but it never had the power to exclude anyone from the kingdom of God.

New-school believers are following with keen interest the biblical and theological works of scholars like N. T. Wright, Stanley Grenz, Leonard Sweet, and Bruce Malina and are getting help for their spiritual journey from fellow travelers such as Frederica Mathewes-Green, Anne Lamott, Brian McLaren, and Donald Miller. To return to the New Testament with a deep concern to understand its message in the light of the first-century Mediterranean culture, religion, language, and politics is to critically assess and rework some of the religious jargon of evangelicalism that for too long has been detached from Scripture. What new-school believers are discovering is that evangelists have misled them by giving them the impression that the gospel is primarily a fire-insurance policy. They are also learning that important themes like salvation and redemption have application to this present life and not exclusively to the next. What this means is that redemption is a work God does within the world we now inhabit, and we have not even begun to appreciate the breadth of its application. God wants to redeem not just our eternal souls but every part of our thinking, speaking, doing, and being.

What Would You Say?

A young woman sits down with a church minister to discuss funeral arrangements for her mother. She tells the pastor, "My mother was not a religious person. I don't think she ever went to church, and she never read the Bible or spoke of Jesus, but she was the best person I have ever known. She raised us by herself, never complained, was always there for us, and met our needs. She was kind to all of my friends, never judged anyone else, never said anything bad about anyone else. Even though she rarely had enough money to buy something for herself, she frequently gave two or three dollars to homeless people on the street. I could go on and on."

The more the minister talks with people who knew the young woman's mother, the more he discovers that everyone has the same opinion of her. They cannot say enough about how wonderful she was and how she made the world a better place. Every person honors her. She was a woman whose life was marked by love, goodness, beauty, and generosity. The minister, in fact, wishes that there were more Christians in his church who lived the type of life exemplified by this woman.

After the memorial service, in which the woman was eulogized by seven or eight different people who had only excellent things to say, the young woman returns to the minister and asks him, "Is my mother in hell because she never asked Jesus into her heart?"

I have been put in this position a number of times. How do we answer this question? "Yes, I'm sorry, but this wonderful person who was your mother will burn in hell for all eternity, despite her kindness and love." Does this answer make sense? I'm not asking right now if it can be supported by a string of biblical texts, but is it logical that an all-good, all-wise, all-loving God, whose second greatest commandment is that we love one another, would take pleasure in allowing this person to suffer for all eternity? Is this the answer Jesus Christ would have given had he been asked this question in the Gospel of Mark? An "immoral woman" kissed Jesus's feet and washed them with her hair, and Jesus forgave her even though the woman did not ask Jesus for forgiveness. Would this same Jesus tell the young woman whose mother died that, even though her mother was a good person and lived much closer to his teaching than many of his followers, she would be tortured forever?

New-school believers (at least many people in the ranks of the new school) believe that Christianity has been so misrepresented in our culture that we must start all over again, *showing* the world what Christianity is all about rather than *talking* about it. That is why the much-quoted phrase attributed to St. Francis strikes such a deep chord in them: "Preach the gospel at all times; if necessary, use words." We have not lived up to our words or the words of Jesus, but now nothing less will convince our world that he and we his disciples are for real. In the meantime, we wonder whether the mercy and compassion of God will cover people who have only seen the "other" Jesus and never heard the truth.

11

Does the Bible Contradict Evolution?

The Perceived Threat

Elissa wanted the used yellow bicycle as soon as she saw it. "How much?" she asked, and thirty-five dollars later the bike was hers. Like many freshmen at the university, Elissa was poor and in need of transportation to get around campus. As soon as she saved up enough money, she upgraded to new tires and a more comfortable seat. Her secondhand bike had evolved into a college classic.

The university was an exciting new world for Elissa—an opportunity to become her own person and think her own thoughts. She saw her life there as a gift, a new start. Being a likeable person, she quickly made friends and easily adapted to campus culture. Frequently she was told she had her head in the stars, so she registered for an astronomy class. That first class she found the massive auditorium with stadium seating and noticed that the projection screen near the front wall was as big as the one in her local theater back home. Her professor sat on a stool behind a lectern, waiting patiently while the students filed in and got situated.

Then with eloquent words and scientific detail, the professor began his presentation in which he described the moment when the universe began. Elissa was wowed by his opening remarks and the breadth of his vocabulary. He spoke smoothly, gliding from detail to detail, as he projected illustrations on the huge screen. Elissa glanced around the room and could tell the other students were also enthralled with his lecture. *What a beautiful explanation of creation*, she thought. She smiled to herself and for the first time in her life felt as though she was where she belonged. Her astronomy class was a perfect fit.

Elissa had grown up in rural middle America. Her parents had been swept into a massive movement of spiritual renewal in the late 1960s known as the Jesus Movement. Wanting to dedicate their lives to Jesus to a radical degree, her parents joined with other young couples to form a commune in which they shared their possessions and the responsibility of caring for the property where they lived. They adopted a lifestyle that was biblically structured according to their reading of the book of Acts. They gathered daily for prayer and several times a week for Bible studies, and during those times they were reminded of the evils in society and the dangers of the pagan world outside.

For Elissa in this separatist environment, everything from clothing to entertainment was regulated. No one was supposed to mimic the fashion of the world. There was no "worldly" entertainment, which meant she could watch only G-rated movies, no television, and rock 'n' roll was out of the question. If she was isolated from children her age outside the commune, she at least enjoyed a nonconfrontational, non-threatening environment, where everyone shared the same beliefs. However, when Elissa began to attend a public high school, she developed friendships with all sorts of kids, most of whom were non-Christian (and "sinful" by the standards of her subculture). Embarrassed to bring school friends to her home, Elissa found herself caught in a double lifestyle, trying to be one person in the commune and another person at school.

Elissa did not disagree with her parents' beliefs but was frustrated that they never allowed her to question or discuss them. Since the commune imposed doctrine on children and did not encourage dialogue, Elissa was at a total loss when it came to explaining her commune's beliefs to her friends.

In the university, however, Elissa felt a freedom she had never known. She loved the way her professor's teaching made so much sense—completely rational and scientific. Her belief in God's creation of the universe was enhanced by the big bang theory astrophysicists used to explain its origin. She was comfortable in college, loved the learning experience, enjoyed her friendships, and was free to grow as an individual. There was only one twinge in her heart that disturbed her; her parents would never go for this new information.

The leaders in Elissa's commune were die-hard creationists, which means they believed that God created the world in six, consecutive, twenty-four-hour days somewhere between six thousand and ten thousand years ago. They bolstered their beliefs with subscriptions to creation literature, which also assisted them in debating with people who held contrary views. Elissa had heard of evolution but always in a negative context. She was taught that to concede any ground to evolution would eventually lead to the destruction of Christianity. The fear of secular assaults on their faith inspired Elissa's parents to defend their creationist beliefs and protect the minds of their children from the infiltration of "the lies of secular society."

For Elissa the important issues of her life had little to do with how the universe began, how old the earth was, or the origins of life. She was more concerned with whether she could build a life for herself outside the tiny world of her commune. She was interested in issues like friendship, belonging, and doing well in her studies and career. She wanted to continue enjoying her education and student activities without feeling guilty. Whether life evolved or was created was not important either to her or her friends. Few students in her class even cared about the origin of the universe; it was simply a nonissue. They were concerned only with fulfilling a credit requirement, getting a grade, and moving on. The "evolution" of Elissa's bike—from a junker to a cruiser—was far more important to her than any other evolution. Her bike is what took her places.

I have been trying to remember if there was ever a time when any of my friends raised the issue of evolution as an argument against the existence of God. If I ever had a conversation like that, I cannot recall any of the details, because most of the time there were other issues that seemed more pressing. But here is the problem as I see it: Christian preachers, teachers, evangelists, and apologists continue to treat evolution as if it were a great threat to belief in the God of the Bible. There is no doubt that in the early twentieth century, with the Scopes trial, the rise and popularity of outspoken atheists like Madalyn Murray O'Hair, and classroom teachers and professors who took potshots at the Bible, the struggle to defend the universe as God's creation was an important enterprise for Christians. Believers who are baby boom age and older can still remember those heated debates in schoolrooms and public forums. But a large percentage of my generation no longer faces the same struggle, nor do we expect science to tell us the truth about God.

Among my peers there are, first of all, a number of university students who are majoring in science or philosophy who are looking for ways to reconcile Christian faith to what they are learning about the universe. Few of these people find the old-school creationist position (like that of Elissa's commune) a defensible position. They find that the "intelligent design" scientists not only make sense but provide better answers to some of the questions than do the evolutionary proposals. These students tend to be well-read and fluent in subjects that baffle those of us without the same level of education in their specific fields.

Among my peers there are also those young believers who read books on creation and evolution written by Christians, because they have been told this is an important issue. They do not fully understand all of the facts or the arguments, but they become proficient enough to hold their own at parties or Internet chat rooms. The big problems with their approach to this issue include the following:

- They interpret the statement "I don't believe in God" as "evolution disproves God's existence" and therefore present arguments against evolution when the person's disbelief has nothing to do with science.
- When they talk to someone who *really* knows the subject, they fall silent and are dumbfounded.
- Much of what Christian authors have written against evolution is pseudoscience and propaganda.

The majority of people I know around the world who are my age do not see any tension between science and belief in God. They are aware of intelligent design, but unless they bring up the subject, it is seldom mentioned. If science poses a problem to Christian faith today, it has shifted from biology to physics and from biogenesis to pantheism. In other words, there are many physicists who have been driven to belief in God through quantum physics, but they do not acknowledge or recognize the personal God of the Bible. What my Christian peers see, however, is not a conflict but an open door. At least these people are talking about God, and that is a great place to begin a journey to faith. As far as nonbelievers are concerned, it is not science that has kept them from the Christian faith, but rather it is the way they have been treated by people who call themselves Christians.

The prevalence of evolution as an explanation for the existence of the universe has created a great opportunity for young believers that many older Christians have failed to recognize. If a generation has grown up in America and Europe that assumes evolution provides an accurate account of how life evolved, this generation may see itself as no more than a random accident, a pack of animals, dispensable carbon units. Members of this generation have lost their identity, and they are constantly asking, "Who am I?" The answer revealed in the Bible has a powerful effect on them when they begin to comprehend the dimensions implied by the idea that they were created in God's image. The believer who knows who she is and where she is going (her identity and destiny) has a strong influence on others simply by being present and willing to explain how she came to know God and then herself in God.

We may be able to serve nonbelievers better by allowing them the option of both/and rather than either/or; they can believe in both evolution and God (as the One who directs evolutionary processes). Is it necessary in all cases to insist that either people accept creationism exclusively or they cannot become Christians? What would we lose if we stopped making an issue over this? People outside the church will tell you there are much bigger issues that concern them than the age of the Earth or how it came into existence.

Perhaps you are thinking, *Matt, you've compromised the faith, watered down the truth, and undermined the foundation of the Bible.* I understand your concern but would like to ask you why you think this way. Is it because you have been told we *must* believe the Earth has existed no more than ten thousand years or else the authority of the whole Bible falls apart? Does that logic really hold together when the Bible is read closely? The authority of the Bible certainly did not break down for Christians in earlier periods of church history who believed God created the universe through enormous spans of time. I do not want to compromise my faith or the truth, but I do think it is sad that many young people are being outfitted to fight battles that are no longer being waged with weapons that are no longer effective.

Suppose a young man who was thoroughly trained in refuting evolution successfully won a heated argument in his high school biology class, proving the teacher wrong in front of the other students. There are Christians who think that moment would spark a great revival, that the teacher and students would be won to Christian belief if the errors of evolution were revealed to them. They assume that those "facts" would affect people more profoundly than this message: God is near you in your heartache and wants to draw you to himself.

In reality most people today are willing to bypass the evolution debate to embrace the "God is near you" message. Must we walk them back to the debate and insist they accept creationism before going on? What is the greater issue here? If we could imagine all scientists conforming their theories to church dogma, what have we gained? Well, in historical perspective, we still would believe the Earth was the center of the universe. When the early chapters of the Bible were written, did God mean for them to be read as science? Are we as the church encouraging young scientific minds among us or do we discourage them from seeking an education in scientific fields? Who will take a stand in the various scientific disciplines to show God's magnificence as revealed in his creation? If God created the universe fifteen billion years ago rather than ten thousand years ago, does that not make him seem even more awesome?

I have one other concern, and perhaps I recognize it in others because it has been so apparent in me. I'm talking about pride. Christians seem to argue intensely over evolution and creation, not for the glory of God but out of pride. They argue, not for the other person's spiritual benefit but to prove that they are right. We need to realize this attitude is contradictory to the teaching of the Lord Jesus we represent.

Unnecessary Tension

In his book *The Creationists* Ronald Numbers documents the history of scientific creationism, demonstrating how it began with a marginal Christian sect (Seventh Day Adventism) and developed into the "orthodox" position for fundamentalists and some evangelicals. Ellen G. White, who received "divine messages in trancelike visions and whose pronouncements Adventists placed on a par with the Bible,"[1] had a vested interest in making sure the days of creation in Genesis chapter 1 were literal twenty-four-hour days. That is due to the Adventist doctrine of Old Testament Sabbath keeping. White believed her practice would be undermined if the days of creation were symbolic references to longer stretches of time.

In the 1930s George McCready Price, a follower of Ellen White, single-handedly took on the scientific community. Geologists had produced evidence that the Earth was millions and possibly billions of years old. Price insisted that a literal reading of the Bible demanded that the planet be no more than six to ten thousand years old. Henry Morris read and adopted Price's interpretation of Genesis and popularized it among fundamentalist believers as the orthodox position. He argued that if Christians did not hold to a creation account that took place roughly ten thousand years ago in six days, each consisting of twenty-four hours, then we would have to *scrap the whole Bible*. Though his argument was based on weak exegesis (Bible interpretation) and poor logic and lacked theological depth, a lot of believers bought into it.

There are two important observations we should make at this point about old-school Christianity. First, throughout Christianity's long history, there was never a strong movement among theologians, biblical scholars, or the orthodox church to interpret the days of creation as literal days. Only after Darwinian evolution gained popularity as a scientific model do we find Christians digging in their heels and insisting that the narrative of the six-day creation in Genesis must be literally interpreted. Second, not all Christians were immediately opposed to evolution. The age of the Earth was an open issue for many theologians prior to the inception of modern geology, which indicated that the Earth had existed for a very long time. Early on—in the nineteenth century—most Christian theologians were willing to grant geology as much time as was required to produce the current configuration of the Earth. Unfortunately, the early fundamentalists who adopted McCready's pseudogeology refused to believe that anyone who disagreed with their point of view could really be a Christian. They invented a new test for orthodoxy. One must hold to the dogmatic belief in a young Earth that was covered with animal life and vegetation in the span of a week. Even to this day there are believers who insist that "theistic evolution" (God working through evolution) is a contradiction in terms.

Real science is often conducted in research labs and requires extensive education to fully comprehend. Those who popularized young-Earth creationism had an advantage over the sincere and devout believers who were actually engaged in scientific research. The creationists who flatly rejected old-Earth views and evolution found a receptive audience for their oversimplifications, common sense, and pious harangues against evolution among fundamentalist Christians. The *American Scientific Affiliation*, founded in 1941, allowed Christians who were educated in various scientific disciplines to publish a more reasoned view of Scripture and science.[2] The ASA probably offers the healthiest and most promising opportunities for Christian interaction with science today.

Meanwhile, there are old schoolers who still rant against any form of science (geology, astrophysics, biology) that suggests the universe is billions of years old, and they often demand equal time in public schools to present their case for creationism. Of course, one problem with scientific creationism and public education is that the creationist point of view is inexorably bound up with doctrinal issues that are relevant only to Bible believers. But even more serious is the dogmatic assumption that Christian students must be indoctrinated with the young-Earth, antievolution position and must be able to defend it against evolution. There are many problems with this position, including the fact that nonscientists trying to defend a firmly held belief on scientific grounds will collapse when confronting someone (like a professor) who is more educated in the specific area. Christian faith should never be put in the position where it is predicated on the best or winning argument.

One of the tragic by-products of the creationist position is that it creates an either/or impasse for students who encounter evolutionary teaching in the classroom. Either you believe the Bible and discount evolution, or you buy into evolution and can no longer be a Christian. The old school does not recognize any middle ground; there is no such thing as a Christian who believes the Bible and trusts God for salvation through Jesus Christ and at the same time accepts evolution as a scientific explanation for certain physical and biological events and phenomena.

This inability to find a middle road has pushed many honest scholars and students away from Christianity and Christianity's God. After all, if the preponderance of scientific evidence conflicts with a ten-thousand-year-old Earth, then the Bible *must* be wrong—if the creationist interpretation is correct. When science students are forced to make a choice, the logical choice is to side with the most compelling evidence.

One victim of the either/or mandate of old-school creationists is Robert Wright. In *Three Scientists and Their Gods* he makes the following observation about the famous sociobiologist E. O. Wilson: "Like E. O. Wilson, I was brought up a Southern Baptist. Like him, I encountered the theory of evolution as a teenager. Like him, I was bowled over by its power and beauty. Like his religious faith, mine did not survive this encounter with science in good shape."[3] What if their Southern Baptist Sunday school teachers, youth ministers, and pastors had been more open-minded regarding the issue of creation and evolution? What if someone had told them it was possible to believe in evolution and the God of the Bible, that there are a variety of ways Christians can interpret the first chapter of Genesis? Perhaps neither the journalist nor the scientist would have had to abandon his faith. But there are old schoolers who would prefer to let people walk away from Christianity than admit that their interpretation of Genesis is not the only game in town.

Some old-school Christians still use creationism as a litmus test. They are convinced that evolution is nothing more than an atheistic attempt to replace Christianity with a materialist philosophy. I would be the first to stand up for their right to these beliefs (indeed, they were my beliefs at one time), but the question is, who made these old schoolers the ultimate interpreters of Scripture or gave them the authority to pronounce the orthodox position? Who empowered them to denounce Christians who do not accept their teaching as absolute truth?

No doubt there are professions in which science poses real problems in regard to Christian faith. Certainly there are engineers, journalists, and molecular biologists (as well as a number of philosophers) who do not believe in the existence of God and look to science to find explanations for the existence of the universe. However, these people are not likely to be argued into belief by someone who has attended a weekend apologetics seminar or even a semester course on arguments for creationism from geology. Indeed, even the professors of apologetics courses would not be able to change their minds. Brilliant scientists with a long list of credits to their name frequently hold public debates with nonbelieving members of the scientific community and make no headway with them.

A Nonissue

I have been privileged to talk to a number of Christian university students who are majoring in science, including those seeking advanced degrees in chemistry and biology. When I ask them which scholars they rely on in the science/evolution controversy, in almost every instance they skirt the issue with a remark like, "Well, philosophical debates like that really do not enter into my studies and research," or "I have never been in a position where I had to defend belief in God, so it isn't necessary for me to enter that debate."

For most people—inside and outside the church—science and evolution do not pose any problems for Christian faith. In other words, if at one time Darwinian evolution seemed like an airtight argument against belief in God, it no longer has that kind of force. Yes, there are some websites where self-proclaimed infidels rant on and on about how science disproves religion, but they represent a small and mostly ignored lunatic fringe. In the meantime, few students in American high schools and colleges see any significant conflict between evolution and faith in God. The concern that some Christians had in the modern era, that if a person believed in evolution then he or she would automatically discount God and the Bible, is no longer valid. Therefore, new-school believers do not see the need for every Christian to wage war on the teaching of evolution in schools or argue against its use as a scientific model.

The new school knows there is still a need within popular culture for arguments for the existence of God that deal with scientific and philosophical issues. However, they also realize people conditioned to a fifteen-second attention span (the length of a television commercial) are not going to tolerate lengthy or highly technical explanations about God. In fact most people are not looking for *rational evidence* to believe in God. Instead, they are looking for a religion that satisfies the spiritual needs of its followers and changes them into better people. If Mormons appear to be friendlier, nicer, more compassionate than Baptists, then Mormons will win over more people. The need for rational answers often comes some time after a person has come to faith in Christ.

I was asked to guest lecture for a week at the University of the Nations in 2003 (it was during that week that Matt and I first met). Since I arrived on campus a day early, I was able to visit the classroom where I would be teaching and observe some of the students who, the week prior to my coming, had been drilled in creationism. Each student had to present several arguments for intelligent design based on information he or she had learned through lectures and books. All of the students were tested on how well they handled their material, and all of them were expected to cover each of the four arguments they had learned.

One argument had to do with life evolving from a random collection of amino acids. The short version goes like this: Life depends on amino acids forming chains. Amino acids in proteins are all "left-handed" and amino acids in sugars in DNA, RNA, and metabolic pathways are "right-handed." A random collection of amino acids would include both right-handed and left-handed amino acids, but even one wrong-handed amino acid would rule out the possibility of long chains or the stability of DNA.[4]

I felt the students who took turns presenting their arguments for the necessity of intelligent design did a good job and handled the material well. They were graded on their performance and how they managed the information. I suppose that afterward they were deemed ready to convince evolutionists that there must be a Creator (or at least they had their own need to know that the interpretation of the Bible they had been given was true to science).

The following day, during my first series of lectures, I asked the students, "Who can tell me what the heck a left-handed amino acid is?" Not one hand went up, but there were a lot of sheepish grins. Then I asked, "How many of you know someone who is not a Christian because of evolution?" Again, there was no response. Either they did not feel like answering my question or not even one person in the class could think of a single individual who felt conflicted over evolution and God.

Then I asked a third question, "Okay, then, how many of you know someone who fully believes in evolution but is open to talking about and believing in God?" This time the response was nearly unanimous. In fact, the class was momentarily disrupted as several of them began volunteering stories of friends who assumed evolution yet wanted to know about God.

Evolution is not the serious hindrance to faith that it was made out to be fifty or ninety years ago—at least not for most people in popular culture. The battlefield has shifted, and new-school believers are moving with it. There are plenty of old-school advocates who are trying to convince the next generations that they must fight the same battles, carry on the same campaigns, struggle to hold the same ground; but popular culture has moved on, and so has the new school. To continue to wave the same banner will only involve us in unnecessary arguments, alienate the scientific community, put people on the defensive, and distract us from the main themes of Christian living.

More and more new schoolers are realizing that they have joined in controversial debates only because old-school teachers told them they were important. They no longer want to fight someone else's war. They are not afraid to engage in their own debates, but they tend to be much friendlier than the old-school warriors who were often recognized by their red faces and the veins in their necks popping out as they angrily denounced evolution. The new school is committed to presenting Jesus to the world, not in the form of arguments but in lives that reflect the touch of Jesus. Of course, we need to be touched ourselves before we can live those lives.

12

Am I Supposed to Hate the World?

Our Hidden Agenda

M

A few years ago Elissa and I went to Kuala Lumpur, Malaysia, for an entrepreneurship seminar, designed especially for people who wanted to engage in international business. We felt privileged to join thirty other participants who had come to this wonderful city from all over the world for three weeks of intensive lectures and training.

Three young guys with whom we had instant rapport were from Pretoria, South Africa, and spoke English and Afrikaans. They were enjoying a reunion of sorts, because one of them, Chris, had moved from South Africa to Varanassi,

India, to begin a silk business with the intent of providing a base for ministry. The other two South Africans attended the church that sent and supported Chris and his family. For Elissa and me, spending time with the three of them was definitely the highlight of the seminar, and we filled our time with story swapping, Bible discussions, jokes, and laughter.

After finishing our sessions one afternoon, the five of us walked the two miles to our hotel for lunch. Our conversation swung to the topic of the emerging youth culture and how in Chris's opinion it defined ministry in India. At some point, our subject shifted from theoretical notions of ministry to real-life experience. Over lunch Chris told us that he had made friends with some Kashmiri people in his town who were among the best businessmen in his industry. The Kashmiri people, however, tend to be hostile toward Christianity, and many of them were supporters of the Taliban in neighboring Afghanistan. But Chris made friends with one Kashmiri whom God used to teach him an important lesson.

Chris would get up early every morning to spend time reading his Bible and praying for the people of India, Kashmir, and Pakistan before going to work. Each time he prayed, he listed the names of his Kashmiri friends, requesting that God would create opportunities for him to tell them about new life in Jesus Christ. After all, that was the whole reason he had come to India and developed these relationships.

He grew frustrated with the reality that after two years of being in India, he had not seen God use him to effect any changes in the people or their culture. During his devotional time one morning, Chris was arguing with God over the whole purpose of his being there and whether there was any hope for these people. As he struggled in prayer, he clearly heard God call his name. He told us that as he sat quietly, listening, God asked him, "If your friend never came to me for salvation, would you still keep loving him? Would he still be your friend?"

Telling us the story in the hotel restaurant, Chris began to cry. I mean, really cry. Not often but every once in a while you find yourself in a conversation that you realize is so critical to your life that you dare not miss a single word of it. Our conversation with Chris was like that for me. For all I know, I had a fork of rice suspended halfway to my mouth the whole time Chris told this story. He went on to tell us that God said he had asked him a question and needed an answer. Chris's answer was no. As soon as this word came out of his mouth, he prayed that God would help him love his Kashmiri friends authentically, with no agenda, but simply because they were made in God's image.

That one dialogue with God transformed Chris's understanding of his life and work in India. He also had a new understanding of what a Christian might look like in India. Afterward, when he went about his business, God began showing him what he loved about this foreign culture. Here in this poor and needy community far away from South Africa, in a world of non-Christian religion and injustice, God was present. Chris now had eyes to see God's character in the way the people cared for one another. He realized that in spite of their superficial differences, he and his Kashmiri friends were very much alike. They cared for their families, wanted safety and happiness, and worried about violence in the world. The culture he had come to convert was teaching him things about his own God. Then oddly enough, when God changed Chris's perspective, the hearts of Chris's friends began changing. They desired something greater than their current beliefs.

I tell this story as often as possible because we need to ask ourselves if we are friends with non-Christians just to be friends or if we have an agenda. If we have an agenda, does that not invalidate the "friendship"? Chris learned how to be a Christian. He and his family had given up everything they had in South Africa to live in an impoverished foreign country for the sake of other people. In the process of developing his ministry, God gave him a deeper understanding of what it means to be a Christian. When I look at my own journey, I see that it has taken me many years of traveling and learning about different cultures of the world to apply that same kind of viewpoint to my own culture.

Loving Our Culture

I was born and raised American, but what does that mean? When we meet someone in the States, we often ask about the national origin of his or her family, because we figure that hot dogs and springtime baseball, selling ten-cent lemonade in the summer, or making hot cider in the winter hardly constitute a culture. For many Christian youngsters, the whole idea of culture brings with it many negative connotations. They have been taught that American culture, whatever it is, offends God because it is sinful. They are told that people outside the church live for no one but themselves and are unloving, unkind, listen to the devil's music, and are constantly yielding to temptations and seductions. The church of my childhood told me I was supposed to despise this world, not participate in its sinful amusements, and try to keep my distance. The effect of this culture-rejecting attitude in my early church experience caused me to hate God for letting my non-Christian friends have all the fun and forcing me to sit through the sheer boredom of church and its incredibly lame children's activities.

Is it possible that most people in popular culture want the very same things we want? Is it possible they have the same longings and hopes? When I talk with my non-Christian friends, I find that even though they do not share all of my beliefs and values, they do share many of my hopes and dreams—and they still want to be my friends. They do not have an agenda for our friendship. They care about me as a person. Is it okay for me to be their friend in the same way that they are mine? A few weeks ago I was hanging out with some believers and one of them mentioned something about his "secular" friend. What is a secular friend? Why is a friend not simply a friend? Is converting a person the only Christian justification for being friends with people outside the church? Should I not get to know people unless I have an agenda for our relationship? Is God pleased if I hate this fallen world and all the people in it? Is it not true that God's grace alone stands between me and the crackhead or prostitute on the street?

I wonder if God has infiltrated popular culture the way he has other cultures in the world and if there are cultural events, expressions, and institutions that can deepen my understanding of God. It seems to me that God has sprinkled popular culture with clues about his existence, and it is possible for me to find those clues and then point them out to others in a loving way. If I learn to love my culture and the people in it, if I learn to see God's thumbprint here and there, am I not learning to see the world as Jesus did?

The Challenge of Culture

Certainly Christians know they are not supposed to hate the world outside their church, yet many believers are at the very least ambivalent about the world around them, and some believers definitely harbor a hostility that comes close to hatred. What Matt and I are trying to sort out in this chapter is the stance believers are supposed to take, according to the Bible, in regard to the world. Once again we will have to either innovate or reach back to a time prior to the last one hundred years of fundamentalism/evangelicalism to recover an attitude that resembles Jesus's attitude regarding the cultures of his world.

A place to begin this discussion is H. Richard Niebuhr's work *Christ and Culture.*[1] In this landmark book Niebuhr suggested that the way various Christian traditions interacted with the wider culture around them could be divided into five categories:

1. *Christ against culture:* Believers perceive human culture as "fallen" and therefore reject and withdraw from it.
2. *Christ of culture:* Believers dissolve potential conflicts with culture and accommodate their faith to the larger political and social worlds around them.
3. *Christ above culture:* Believers are in culture to appropriate and bring to actuality the good that God has placed within it.
4. *Christ and culture in paradox:* Believers are in culture to do God's will, but they find that institutions both

serve and subvert God's will. Furthermore, in their own lives, sin subverts God's will, while grace helps them serve it. This uneasy tension will continue until the "dying world" breathes its last breath and God's kingdom comes in its fullness.

5. *Christ the transformer of culture:* Believers are in culture to commandeer it, to convert it to Christianity.

Few theologians and historians still believe these categories are either sufficient or accurate, but some have attempted to reconfigure and rehabilitate his model, because it proved to be a useful tool—a fact that even his most outspoken critics admit. Nevertheless, it is possible that "his analysis in its present form could be near the end of its usefulness."[2]

Whether or not Niebuhr's model is still useful, the implication shared by all five categories he described is that there is *an inherent tension between Christianity and culture.* Even if Niebuhr's model is flawed, the implicit assumption is that "Christ" and "culture" belong to two different and incompatible "sets," leaving us with the task of defining the relationship between them. This obvious division between Christ and culture is at the heart of old-school thinking and, in the words of George Marsden, depends on a "theological dualism that will be unacceptable to many people today."[3] Old-school believers assume that Jesus Christ and popular culture are incompatible, that there is an inherent conflict between them, and that loyalty to Christ means a radical breach with culture. They find biblical justification for this view in the New Testament language of "church" and the "world."

I have been listening to sermons and Bible studies my entire life. For more than thirty years, I have been reading Bible commentaries, and those that I read early on in my ministry were mostly "devotional," written by such luminaries as Harry Ironside, G. Campbell Morgan, Andrew Murray, William Barclay, Alan Redpath, and F. B. Meyer. Some of these authors did a fair job of summing up the theme of a book or passage, but almost all of them would occasionally focus on a single verse or even just a word without sufficient regard for the context around it. Therefore, the application to a believer's life that followed from this myopic reading of isolated texts often consisted of moralizing diatribes that did not really capture the essence of the text itself (Barclay being a notable but imperfect exception).

The verse-by-verse method of biblical "exposition" that became popular in mid-twentieth century lends itself to a leap from text to application without doing justice to exegesis or a close reading of what the Bible actually says. Christians dutifully sit through Bible studies with the hope of expanding their biblical knowledge when in fact they are learning about the teacher's religious opinions and convictions or those of their tradition. If we try to go straight from a page in the Bible to our situation in the world today, we will be rewarded with a deformed spirituality. We must go underneath the pages of Scripture by paying attention not only to what they *say* but what they *mean*. For example, your friend says she is *starving*, when what she means is she is *hungry*. A literal response to her words will result in what looks to her like bizarre behavior, whereas if you interpret her meaning correctly, you know what she wants.

I have heard Bible teachers read a verse like 1 John 2:15— "Do not love the world or anything in the world. If anyone loves the world, the love of the Father is not in him"—and then without reference to John's background, first-century culture, other writings from that era, or original language, apply these words to popular culture. So the teacher makes it look like John was talking about dancing, rock 'n' roll, sports, fashion, movies, nice cars, expensive food, or whatever else one might choose to condemn. Often youth ministers have given high school students the impression that anything that popular culture values or promotes is necessarily evil. It is "in the world" and therefore off limits for the true believer.

Preachers who find it convenient to characterize all of society by the grosser sins within it usually do not differentiate between "culture" and "world." Somehow they miss the fact that *world* (in the King James Version) translates several different Greek words, which range in meaning from universe to planet Earth to inhabitants of the Earth to a time period or age. Identifying "world" with "culture" or popular culture is misleading and maybe even harmful. If we assume that popular culture is inherently evil and must be avoided, we will miss whatever good God is doing in culture and likely fail to see the evil going on within the church.

The old school warns Christians to keep their distance from popular culture, that "their every contact with the world must be as light as possible" (1 Cor. 7:31 Phillips). But the old school has not applied enough critical thinking to translating the New Testament term *world*. For this reason some Christians are confused when they read that "God so loved the world" and Christians are not to "love the world."

Is *culture* synonymous with *world* in the New Testament? Is it possible that John (who, tradition tells us, frequented bath houses, which were a quintessential symbol of Roman culture) was not talking about culture in general but specific pitfalls that lie within every culture (that is, "the cravings of sinful man, the lust of his eyes and the boasting of what he has and does")? For example, money is neither good nor evil, but "the *love* of money is a root of all kinds of evil" (1 Tim. 6:10, my emphasis). Not everything in culture is good, not everything evil, and not everything neutral, but there is nothing inherently wrong with engaging culture.

Perhaps you have heard preachers say, "The Bible says, 'Therefore come out from them and be separate, says the Lord'" (2 Cor. 6:17). They explain this to mean that believers are to keep their distance from specific activities, objects, or artifacts of popular culture. If it were true that the New Testament has nothing good to say about the world, and *world* means "culture," then engaging popular culture would be a huge mistake because "anyone who chooses to be a friend of the world becomes an enemy of God" (James 4:4). Having created this dualism between church and world, the old school provides believers with an easy way to distinguish "good guys" from "bad guys." The simplistic and concrete boundaries implied in this worldview are typically childish; adults know it is not always that easy to discern the good guys.

I am not interested in arguing with Christians who insist that 1 John 2:15 tells believers not to love popular culture or anything in it. Instead, I want to know if this interpretation of

John's statement is based on the best analysis of the biblical text, how it compares to John's other writings, and how it compares to the general teaching of the New Testament. If a preacher tells me, "Well, son, you just look at the words on the printed page, because they're in *plain English!*" then I would recommend to him my book *Epiphany* (and several better books), which point out that even the most simple act of reading is also an act of interpretation. We cannot know the meaning of an ancient text until we have penetrated its surface.

Every word in the New Testament is a "used" word in the sense that it enters the text with previous associations in other texts. The author and original readers would have been aware of those associations, which later readers would not be able to find in any dictionary. For example, if in a political rally an American shouts "Stars and stripes forever!" we will not find out what he means by looking up the words *stars* and then *stripes* in a dictionary. To properly interpret his slogan, we need to know something about the history of the American struggle for democracy and freedom and how that struggle is symbolized in its national flag. For the same reason, we must research a variety of subjects—literature, archaeology, social science, anthropology, grammar, theology, and so on—to get to the meaning of biblical words and phrases.

In the first three Gospels of the New Testament, as well as the writings of Paul, the tension we find with the "world" is horizontal, having to do with time. "This present evil age" stands in contrast and opposition to the coming kingdom of God. In John's Gospel and letters, we find a vertical tension between heaven and earth. For example, Jesus was "from above" and not "of this world," while his listeners were "from below" and "of this world" (John 8:23). When we hear that Christians are supposed to be *in* the world but not *of* it (17:13–19), it may not be clear that the alternative to not being *in* the world does not mean one should live in an isolated religious subculture or monastery. Rather, to not be in the world means to be gone from the world—through death into heaven (13:31–38; 14:1–3; 16:28; 17:11). If Jesus's disciples were given to him "out of the world" (17:6), they were not removed from culture or society. They were merely selected to be on his team out of all the other potential candidates. Not to be *of* the world means that the Christian life and worldview are not shaped by the evil that exists in all human communities.

The old-school lessons I learned in my youth warned me away from forming too close a relationship with non-Christians and the social spaces they inhabit. I do not remember hearing that Christians could promote good through engagement with others and popular culture but rather that they were likely to sustain damage by these contacts. But if we run from popular culture, what will happen to those cultural spaces we vacate? Perhaps they will be overrun by evil (and have we allowed this to happen in public corporations, schools, government, and the entertainment industry?) or, more likely, God will find someone else to give witness to him—someone unafraid of contact with people outside the evangelical bubble. God will send someone who, like his Son, is not afraid to have a reputation for being "a friend of sinners."

Old-School Illusions

One of the unfortunate effects of the old-school attitude about popular culture is that it created an illusion of holiness and loyalty to God based on *negative* values. We used to hear phrases from teenagers like, "I don't go to dances, movies, auto races, parties, and [fill in the blank] because I'm a Christian." It is difficult for me to figure out how people can believe spiritual purity is maintained by nonengagement and yet think they are authentic followers of Jesus, who said, "For out of the heart come evil thoughts, murder, adultery, sexual immorality, theft, false testimony, slander. These are what make a man 'unclean'; but eating with unwashed hands does not make him 'unclean'" (Matt. 15:19–20). If we worry about being defiled by popular culture, we should remember our hearts do a masterful job of generating their own impurities.

The moral and ethical concerns of the old school were focused on culture as culprit and church as fortress against evil. Without being clearly defined, the term *world* was used loosely for society at large as the source of temptation, disobedience, and sin. Old school found itself in a "culture war," automatically opposed to whatever society endorsed, in conflict with culture rather than with the evil that threatens all humans, "Christian" or otherwise. Evil is not localized in a person, race, institution, or culture but runs through every human and everything humans handle, invent, build, and organize. Church history and current scandals remind us of our lack of immunity. While old-school soldiers declared war on popular culture, the real battle was not "flesh and blood." The church's objective in the world is to labor with God in his mission in redeeming humans, their culture, and the natural world.

People who seek refuge from an immoral world in the church and among good Christian people are living in an illusion not supported by the New Testament. The distance between church attenders and nonattenders in regard to moral, ethical, and charitable behavior is not that great. Demographers, radio personalities, authors, and other religious leaders often whine over statistics that reveal little difference between the opinions and behavior of people who identify themselves as evangelicals and those who do not. However, this may not be such a terrible predicament, because possibly it can help us take an important leap in our thinking and break down barriers evangelicals raise between themselves and everyone else. We do not walk on water. We could do the world and the kingdom of God a favor by doing away with our self-righteousness and know-it-all attitudes that result in wholesale condemnation of popular culture and keep many people from church for fear they will become self-righteous, unloving, narrow-minded, judgmental, uptight, and hypocritical like those "born-againers."

Youth leaders reminded me in high school that "bad company corrupts good character" (1 Cor. 15:33). But in the same letter where Paul made that observation, he also said, "If some unbeliever invites you to a meal and you want to go, eat whatever is put before you without raising questions of conscience" (10:27). In fact, the "bad company" turns out to be other believers. Paul did not teach Christians to live in isolation from non-Christians or their culture; otherwise, we "would have to leave this world" (5:10). Nor was Paul naïve regarding the human imperfections of church members. He told Ephesian believers to "put off" lying and stealing (Eph. 4:25–28), Colossian believers to get rid of sexual immorality and greed (Col. 3:5–6), and Corinthian believers to "stop sinning" (1 Cor. 15:34).

Old school spoke comfortably of two categories, "us" and "them," driving a wedge into humanity that is not unlike the wall that separated Jews from Gentiles in the first century. But is there anyone so gullible or uninformed of current events to doubt that plenty of sinning is going on in even the most conservative churches? Will anyone deny that there are good, compassionate, and morally upright people outside the church? Can we believe Christians are incapable of evil and non-Christians incapable of good? Is the wall really as thick and high as we have been led to believe? Why would we even want to build another wall like this, since Jesus paid the ultimate price to tear down the first one (Eph. 2:11–18)?

At one time, old school placed a complete ban on movies. Then, after the rating system was established to provide age-appropriate criterion for movie viewing, the ban was partially lifted. I do not have a quarrel with the believer who says, "I choose not to put that trash in my head." God grants us sovereignty over what we allow to enter our minds. Of course what defines "trash" and whether the contents of a movie are trash or if redeeming elements can exist alongside trash elements, are matters for which "each one should be fully convinced in his own mind" (Rom. 14:5). Every movie I refuse to see is a movie I cannot comment on in conversations with other people who found in it a spiritual message. Nor can I see for myself traces of God's self-witness in cultural activities I avoid. I am assuming, of course, that you are a reasonable person and will not draw the conclusion that I would condone obscenity.

If God leaves his fingerprints on a particular film (and I am by no means alone in my observation that God places evidence of his presence in secular film, literature, music, visual art, poetry, and so on) and yet all believers abandon popular culture, who will represent Christian faith in public discussions regarding the spiritual message of that movie? God is at work in many places where old-school Christians never thought to look for him. Few of the old-school preachers I have known would have thought to "look carefully" at inscriptions on pagan objects of worship until finding an altar "To An Unknown God" (Acts 17:22–23). If Paul had turned his head from those shrines in the streets of Athens, disgusted with idolatry as he was, he would not have come across God's self-testimony (14:17), which was the keystone to his message on Mars Hill.

Another thing to keep in mind is that withdrawing from popular culture can prevent non-Christians from ever seeing a real Christian; thus the only images of Christians that are available to these folks come from the media. Are we comfortable with that?

Every Christian is at all times and in every place an advertisement for Jesus, not a salesperson or telemarketer but a reflection of Christ, the lover of humans. We belong in culture as salt and light. In fact, there is no place in popular culture where we should not want to have some kind of presence and influence for good.

Standing in Front of the Target

Today theologians sometimes refer to Western society as post-Christian, which means we live in a different world from that of the theologians and Reformers who gave the church its doctrines and practices. In certain respects our cultural situation parallels the first two centuries of church history rather than the years that fell between Constantine's holy empire and the Enlightenment. Just as paganism was Christianity's antithesis in the first centuries of the church, today the flip side of post-Christian is neo-pagan.

How do Christians recognize each other in this new context? In the modern era, old-school believers would interrogate people they met to test their beliefs and experience. "Do you believe the Bible is God's inerrant Word?" "Have you been born again?" A Christian was known by his doctrine, denominational affiliation, conversion, or baptism. If two old-school believers differed on a church doctrine or practice, each would try to argue the other to his point of view. If they both failed, then they would part company wondering if there was enough room in heaven for both of them. This old-school behavior gave rise to the following observation: when Christians get together, they talk more about their doctrinal disagreements than agreements.

If you belonged to an old-school church that preached against every other denomination, you had no guarantee that the members of your own congregation accepted you. Without warning, the church leadership could decide that you were not living up to their version of holiness or sound doctrine or the 100 percent commitment they preached. They could take the same mean, self-righteous, and unloving spirit with which they condemned other churches and turn it on you. And once your unfortunate back became the target of their knife, the wisest thing to do was make a fast getaway, because your chances of ever reconciling with the person who judged you or of recovering your reputation in the church were slim to none.

I know far too many ex-pastors (and pastors' children) who are embittered toward church (not only those that abused them but the whole notion of church), because of the ruthless treatment they endured at the hands of those who were less intelligent, less honest, and less godly than they. Ministers are often held hostage by members of their churches whose threats may include withdrawing their financial support (which can literally kill a small church), voting them out, creating a church split, reporting them to the denominational headquarters, and any number of humiliations, insults, and punishments. Pastors are expected to perform specific duties, preach on particular themes, have an altar call in every service (or never have an altar call), or else feel the wrath of the angry old-school member.

Of course the pastor is not the only target of extortionists who think they are doing God's will. They throw their emotional acid on other human hearts as well. I have come to the conclusion that Christians who persecute other believers are convinced it makes them more spiritual (at least in appearance). They are quick to judge, gossip, write letters, criticize, and vent their righteous indignation. If you do not vote for the political candidates they endorse, if you doubt the church's doctrinal position, if you form your own opinions on controversial issues, if you do not show up at meetings they think you should attend, if you do not hold completely to the party line, or if—heaven forbid—you should actually feel that your conscience compels you to fight the system, you will discover how evil, cruel, and devious people can be who profess to be followers of Jesus. Though written in a different context, Walter Brueggemann's comment about "the ultimate consumerism of consuming each other"[4] is a good commentary on Paul's warning to the Galatians: "But if you bite and devour one another, take care that you are not consumed by one another" (Gal. 5:15 NASB).

The criteria new-school believers use in finding strangers with whom they wish to partner in Christian mission and service are different from those of the old school. New schoolers look for people who are *doing* the things they feel led to do, the things Jesus cares about within a community and the world. In fact, their first question is not "Is this other person a Christian?" but "Is this other person doing what a Christian should be doing, and if so, can I join her?" They do not have the old-school reflex of immediately writing off any organization that does not publish a doctrinal statement identical to their own (many are now refusing to publish doctrinal statements). Nor do they make friends based on shared points of view. They take for granted the pluralistic nature of society, and rather than avoid or condemn it, they simply live within it as agents of transformation.

Critical Engagement

Is it possible that the majority of believers from New Testament times to the third or fourth centuries (except the disciples, apostles, and theologians whose names we know and who led extraordinary lives) were average men and women who were simply trying to survive? We could probably make a strong argument that believers of all time, from Abraham to the present, spent the better part of their lives trying to negotiate their way through life and had little concern for philosophical and theological abstractions. They wanted to know the truth about God so they could earn his favor and reap his blessing. I do not mean to minimize their spiritual longings and experience, but I suggest it is a gross exaggeration to think these believers led lives of pure and unbroken devotion to God.

Average believers in the first and second centuries had few spiritual resources and nowhere to hide from community and culture. Probably they did not give much thought to culture as such. They were well aware of the temptations and seductions that lay close at hand, but until the rise of monasticism, few Christians considered removing themselves from society as an option; slaves, of course, had no choice. Christians shared the life of their community as active participants in whatever role they occupied—servants, masters, prisoners, or magistrates.

An interesting window into Christian thinking in the fifth century is found in St. Augustine's *The City of God*, in which he describes world history as the unfolding story of two cities. The city of men is human government, law, commerce, and corruption. This is the city to which Cain, the firstborn son of Adam and Eve, belonged. The city of God is the spiritual community of all believers, stretching as far back as Abel, the first martyr. Though the two cities coexist, they are independent of each other and move toward different destinies.

If Augustine were a modern-era evangelical, he might have exhorted his readers to flee human society (because it produces only sin and misery) to create a separate society as the city of God on earth, based totally on Scripture. Instead, he refers to "the present intermingling and future separation of the good and the bad" in Jesus's parable of the good seed and the weeds as an illustration of the way the city of God and the city of men currently commingle (Matt. 13:24–30, 36–43). In fact, everything that happens in human society, whether a stunning military victory or a shattering defeat, such as Augustine witnessed in the fall of Rome, is nothing less than the hand of God as he advances his own city.

Augustine believed that living in the city of man, developing friendships, and being involved in its social structures and public events would necessarily lead to heartache. But such engagement was nevertheless inevitable, because God made humans to live in society under government and law. So the two cities are "mingled together from the beginning down to the end," and Christians are citizens of the heavenly city who for the present live and work in the earthly city. Only at the end of time and only by the hand of God would the two cities be separated. In other words, for Augustine there was no "Christ and culture" tension in the way that it was addressed by Niebuhr (though Niebuhr inserts Augustine into his fifth category).

Though new-school thinking may or may not be influenced by St. Augustine's two-city theology, it does share the conviction that Christian involvement in society is the normal way believers honor God and conform to his will. God's will is not served, says the new school, by believers whose attitude toward popular culture is characterized by hostility, a bunker mentality, or total rejection. The history of the twentieth century has proven that even under the most godless human governments, Christians who refused to hide and play it safe have lived with such authentic devotion that even their enemies and jailers acknowledged the power of their faith. New-school believers recognize the many moral, political, and environmental problems to address in the world, but the thought of society as hopelessly depraved is not in their worldview. They see hope in society, and for good reason.

New-school Christians make no attempt to defend everything that appears under the banners of art and entertainment, but they are convinced that the image of God in human creativity and imagination was not completely defaced by the fall. Therefore, they find traces of divine inspiration in a wide variety of artistic expressions—including the works of artists who ridicule the church and reject the faith. They know that poems often contain more meaning than the poet intended, that a painting can reflect a vision greater than the artist's imagination, that a song can evoke a spiritual feeling the musician and singer never experienced in their own souls. God's hand is everywhere busy and nowhere locked out.

Do new-school Christians stroll through popular culture, embracing everything, affirming everything, participating in everything, and criticizing nothing? No doubt there are some people with a new-school worldview who think it is either cool or godly to make themselves relevant to popular culture through uncritical acceptance of its symbols, artifacts, and behavior. Their simple-minded participation in culture, however, does not reflect the position of most new-school believers who know only too well how much violence, exploitation, and injustice have been tolerated in human societies.

The term that best describes the new school's concern regarding popular culture is *critical engagement.* This term implies that believers do not simply go to the movies, but they watch movies in a particular way; we could say they "study" the film as they view it. We can trace this attitude to a Greek word that appears frequently in the New Testament, *krino,* which originally meant to separate or select. Through usage and the addition of prefixes, *krino* developed other meanings like distinguish, discern, decide, examine, determine, and judge (either to evaluate or pass sentence). Our English word *critical* is derived from this same Greek word, so *critical engagement* means that new-school believers ask a lot of questions, interrogate popular culture, discern what God is doing, and determine where and how their participation will be most effective.

More Love Than Law

I mentioned earlier that, for old schoolers, the "hate the world" issue spilled over into the way Christians treated other Christians. Growing up in the church, I somehow got the impression that we alone were right—about the Bible, our doctrine, the Holy Spirit, and everything else. Perhaps people could be Baptist and go to heaven, but they were certain to burn if they were Roman Catholic. To accuse people of being ecumenical meant they were too weak to maintain a strong commitment to the truth, had compromised their beliefs, and sold out.

For some reason we felt it was perfectly Christian to pass judgment on other believers because their doctrine was "bad." They baptized babies, for example, or they did not hold to our view of creation. Heated arguments and debates (even to the point of losing one's temper) in defense of the truth against the heresies of other denominations were not only legitimate but righteous. I do not know why I was never told in Sunday school or youth groups that it was really important for me to love people in other churches, that Jesus prayed we would live in "complete unity," and that Jesus said we would be recognized as his disciples if we loved each other. Perhaps our teachers skipped these lessons because they were convinced people in other churches were not God's true disciples, so we did not have to love them.

New-school Christians feel complete freedom to sample the worship of any church, to read the theological works of every denomination, and to reject any attempt to label their beliefs as Reformed, charismatic, Anglican, or any other tradition. They do not believe God has called them to pass judgment on others and are therefore free to work alongside believers from other traditions and extend mercy to people who need some kind of link to God. New schoolers grieve the lack of love between Christians of different backgrounds, and rather than try to beat others into their point of view, they are more interested in learning what others have to say. Trusting God to guide their spiritual journey, staying close to the Scriptures, and resolving to love all of God's children, new schoolers keep an open heart and an open mind to the variety of Christian expressions that make up the rich tapestry of God's church.

New-school believers are going to change existing churches or plant new churches. They will form spiritual communities that are devoted to love and mercy as well as holiness and righteousness. Indeed, holiness and righteousness have more in common with love and mercy than they do with law and doctrine. For a community to qualify as "church" in the new-school context, there will have to be more love than law, more grace than guilt, more acceptance than axes to grind. If someone asks, "What about church discipline? Don't we need to preserve the purity of the community?" a possible answer might be: you do not need to worry about that until the situation presents itself, and because the church has erred so far and for so long in the other direction, it is okay if we make some errors on the side of mercy for a change. Also a healthy body has a strong immune system and resolves many of its own "infections" if given time. We have been too quick to amputate wounded limbs of Christ's body in the past and need to develop more skill in gently restoring the dislocated members (see Gal. 6:1–5).

13

Are There Gay Christians?

The Greater Sin

M

I was nineteen, had finished my first year of Bible college, and was fresh off the mission field after a six-month international discipleship program. A local youth pastor asked me to speak to his senior high youth group. Kids from the community were pouring into their group, which had a solid reputation in the community for high energy and moral depth. The youth pastor was well known and well liked all over the state; everything he touched turned to gold. So the invitation for me to address the group was a huge privilege.

205

I arrived fifteen minutes early, my mind engrossed in the real-life lessons I had recently learned. I was realizing how important it is for me to be honest with other people, to let them know that like everyone else I am someone who struggles, and to receive whatever wisdom they might have to offer. At the very least I was learning to let other people pray for me regarding real needs. During that time of my life, I do not think I could have spoken effectively on any other topic.

After some crazy games and a lot of yelling by the youth pastor and his staff, everyone was corralled and then I was introduced as the evening's guest speaker. I spoke, they listened, and everything went as I expected, except when I finished there was no response. I had hoped they would want to practice this new skill of transparency. When they didn't, I began dipping into the despair speakers experience when they are convinced they did a terrible job.

After the meeting ended, I hung around until all the kids had driven away or were picked up by their folks. When it was time to lock the doors, the youth pastor asked me if I had a few minutes to talk with him. *Oh no*, I thought, *here we go. He is going to tell me what a loser I am and that I should not give up my day job.*

We found an office downstairs where we could talk without being overheard or interrupted by the few people left in the building. Then the youth minister began to tell me that the message I gave was meant for him. He was engaged to be married, and the wedding was only a few months off, but he needed to deal with some issues before he walked down the aisle. The first step he needed to take was to make a confession.

"Matt," he said very seriously, "I did some wild things in college before I gave my life to the Lord. I was involved in drugs and alcohol. But I was also involved with some homosexual relationships. A couple of times I was so drunk that I blacked out and woke up realizing I had had a night of sex with another guy." I used every inner muscle in my body to prevent the horror I felt from showing in my face or through my body language. He continued to recount his college days and divulged more details, which resulted in further shock to my system.

If I had known then what I know now, I would have realized how inappropriate it was for him to be telling me these things, and I would have recommended that he tell an older Christian leader. But I did not have any counseling experience and was probably already denying that I was even hearing this story. He explained to me that the last time he had tried to tell someone about these encounters, that person never spoke to him again. *Hey,* I thought, *God can forgive anything.* I thanked him for his honesty and for taking my message seriously (though on the inside I wasn't so thankful). I let him know that I believed in his ministry with the youth, that God would forgive and help him, and then we prayed. I was only a kid and really did not know what else to do for him.

Over the next three years we stayed in touch and built a close friendship. He sent financial support to Youth With A Mission to assist Elissa and me in our international work. I assumed he had worked through his former problems, and our whole weird talk that forgettable evening made no impression on me—that is, not until a couple years later when I was sitting in an Internet café in Chiang Mai, Thailand.

Reading email in another country is a piece of heaven on earth. Elissa and I were two kids on Christmas morning whenever we sat in front of the monitors and clicked into our mailbox. I read each subject line as the messages loaded on the screen and noticed one from my mother, so I opened hers first. My heart became a block of ice as I read her message. She said that the youth pastor with the great reputation and generous heart was found hanging from a rope tied to a rafter in his garage. According to Mom's report, the whole community was in shock; no one knew why he would want to end his life.

I knew—immediately. I could not help but feel like I had let him down. But then again, how was I supposed to know what to do? No one had ever taught me how to respond to a minister struggling with homosexuality. Still, my mind was tormented: *What if I had been more sensitive to his torment?* These thoughts lingered and gnawed on my conscience for several weeks.

For the rest of our stay in Thailand, I dreaded opening my email. Almost every other day my mother gave me some fresh bit of painful information. To summarize a long, heartbreaking story, people in his church discovered that the youth pastor was involved in a romantic relationship with a young man in the youth group. The church was appalled and furious. The kid in the youth group chose to "come out of the closet" during a Sunday morning service and announced that he was gay. People in the church wondered how God could have used the youth pastor if he too was gay. There were also questions about his suicide: "If suicide is murder, did he go to heaven?"

To my way of thinking, sin is sin no matter what wrapper it wears. Yes, the youth pastor struggled with homosexuality. So what? Have you ever heard the stories of hotel managers who report that every time a pastors' conference is hosted in their facility, the purchase of in-room pornography increases? Is there a different severity of sin and consequence between the Christian who struggles with homosexuality and the Christian who struggles with pornography? "For all have sinned," right? Few people who knew the youth pastor doubt that God used him regardless of his sin. In light of the facts that this opinion is reflected in popular culture and that a homosexual bishop was recently ordained in the Episcopal Church, many are asking, Why not? Why would God not use a gay person in Christian service? Are there any limits—self-imposed or otherwise—to what an omnipotent and all-merciful Being can do?

There is, of course, the other question this story raises: What about suicide? Does God's mercy extend that far? In fact, one question leads to another and another. For example, What is wrong with our Christian culture if a person admits to being gay but cannot find anyone in the church who will lovingly walk with him or her through the process of working out what this all means? If we automatically shun gays, ask them to leave the church immediately, treat their sin as worse than our own, then where are they supposed to go when they want to find God? Was there a wise and compassionate Christian who could have made the effort to work with the youth pastor and perhaps save his life? If not, why not?

I have been wondering lately what would happen to churches in the United States if we experienced a Great Awakening similar to that in our early national history. Many Christians have prayed for years that this very thing would happen. But what would we do if same-sex couples turned to God and came to our church for worship, Bible study, and spiritual direction? Would we meet them at the door and say, "First of all, you must abandon your gay orientation before you can enter"? Is this what we tell everyone who visits our church for the first time? How prepared are we to serve gays and their adopted children? If we never talk about this issue, how are we going to know how to respond when it comes to our door?

Only One Answer

Reading Matt's account of his conversation with the youth minister is sad yet revealing in the words he uses to describe that episode: *honesty, receive, transparency, forgive, sensitive,* and *compassionate*. That evening Matt used the opportunity to speak openly and honestly of his own "struggles" and open his heart to whatever wisdom the group wished to share with him. I am convinced that it was precisely for these reasons— his caring, honest, and vulnerable demeanor reflected in his choice of words—that explains why the youth pastor took the risk of speaking to him. He recognized in Matt a kind heart that just might provide him the lifeline to hope in his own lonely struggle with his sexual orientation.

Matt's last question about the issue of homosexuality coming to our door conceals a possibility that only a few conservative Christians are willing to face: What if the gay person who arrives at our church comes by way of our own family? What if that homosexual is our son or daughter? There are two reasons why we might want to address the question in this way: First, for those of us who have children, this is a very real possibility. I have known many Christian parents who received the announcement from one of their children that he was gay (less often, lesbian). There is no consistent pattern in their family profiles that would explain the child's homosexuality. Some of the parents are fundamentalists, some serve in the ministry, some were very strict disciplinarians, and all of them are Bible believers. Not all of these parents have received or adjusted to the news with equal grace.

The second reason to think of the possibility of our own children being gay is that it becomes rather easy to dehumanize people when we refer to them only as "gays and lesbians." These are people who should mean more to us than what a label implies. If in our thinking we allow ourselves to dump human beings into a category and stereotype them, we will fail to see the *person* who struggles and for whom Christ died. I do not mean to condone a lifestyle but to look past the lifestyle to see a human person.

How have Christians addressed homosexuality in the past? For the last two hundred years or more, Christians were preoccupied with discovering *the one right answer*. When conservative Christians asked questions like, Where do we draw the line? and What are the moral and ethical absolutes? they wanted to know what the Bible had to say. Liberal Christians also wanted to know what the Bible said, but they asked questions like, How are we to interpret the Bible in the light of our modern scientific, medical, and psychological understanding of human behavior? So by the middle of the twentieth century there were at least two "right" answers to the question of homosexuality:

1. The Bible condemns homosexual behavior. People who engage in homosexual sex (basically all homosexuals) will go to hell. Homosexuals must be transformed into heterosexuals or be excluded from the church.
2. In most instances homosexuality is a deviant psychological condition that cannot be cured without medical, psychological, and pastoral help. The homosexual is not responsible for this condition and therefore should not be judged but should be treated with compassion.

We should keep in mind that during this earlier period, the actual practice of homosexuality was radically hidden in the church and mainstream culture. Few people other than professionals even talked about homosexuality, with the exception of insults and crass jokes. The topic was discussed *theoretically* because few people knew any homosexuals and even fewer admitted to being homosexual. In those days it was extremely risky for a gay man to confess to his pastor (or even his family) that he had romantic feelings toward other men. Such an admission could result in immediate excommunication, public humiliation, and social ostracism. There were many gay people in the church, involved in a variety of ministries, but they were not public about their sexual orientation.

For the remainder of the twentieth century, and especially during the sexual revolution of the sixties and seventies, "right" answers continued to arrive through pastoral counselors, medical researchers, and concerned theologians. As more and more homosexuals came out of the closet (to use a colloquialism of that time), people began to get a better understanding of the nature of homosexuality and to distinguish between *orientation* and *gay sex*. Eventually some young people in Christian churches began to acknowledge that they felt the temptation to same-sex relations—much to the shock, horror, and embarrassment of their parents and others.

In conservative churches, these young people felt trapped between a sexual orientation they had not chosen and could not control and an unyielding doctrine and subculture that viewed their "condition" as evil. Sadly, there are many stories of young men, like Matt's friend, who took their lives because they could not see any hope for people like them.

Other "right" answers that emerged include the following:

1. A new conservatism created more resources for the homosexual through spiritual conversion, counseling, reprogramming, long-term treatment in care facilities, and in some cases exorcism.
2. A new liberalism accepted homosexuality as a different "gift" than heterosexuality, treating gay and lesbian people as spiritual equals within the church, ignoring or reinterpreting biblical injunctions against homosexuality and going so far as to lobby for gay clergy.
3. A fanatical fringe has taken a shocking and vocal position that denounces homosexuals as utterly and eternally hopeless. They are not interested in seeing homosexuals integrated into the Christian faith through

any means, and they hope they all die of plagues and pestilence. They have endorsed open hatred toward gays and lesbians.

4. Some faith communities admit homosexuals into their number if they practice lifelong celibacy. The people who hold this position differentiate between orientation and sexual practice. If gays cannot change their sexual preference, their only option is celibacy.

5. A growing number of gays and lesbians claim to be born again, to have received Jesus into their hearts as Lord and Savior, and gather for worship and Bible study in small groups and at "gay affirming" churches around the country. Some of these people take a strong stand against sexual promiscuity and intend to have one (same-sex) partner for life.

Though these points of view are diverse, there is something they all have in common. Advocates, who believe they have found the one right answer, have formulated them. Therefore much of the debate has been between people with differing beliefs on the subject who are trying to get others to recognize that their answer is the only correct one. This then is the old-school thinking and position: there must be and could only be one right answer to the question, Are there gay Christians? The liberals had their right answer and the conservatives had theirs, but each considered the other's response to homosexuality to be wrong. Some people are still thinking there can be only one right answer to an issue that is as complex and diverse as the myriad personalities that find themselves confronted by this challenge.

Compassionate Conversationalists

In talking with Matt, his friends, and others in his generation, I find they are skeptical of religious people who profess to have all the right answers or try to force their views on them. But we should not assume they have a laissez-faire or relativistic attitude regarding moral issues. They are sincere when they ask me what I think of homosexuality, live-in relationships, marijuana, and so on. They want to know my opinion, but they want also to form their own. My ideas provide a backdrop or resource for their own conclusions. However, if I take a hard line, they automatically resist my views even if moments earlier they apparently had no strong convictions of their own. Their reaction is the essence of popular culture when confronted by religious dogma. In the spirit of tolerance and pluralism, they resist hardened opinions when there is still so much truth to discover and such a variety of options.

The first concern of new-school Christians is to understand the mind-set of people in popular culture regarding homosexuality and the contexts in which it can be freely discussed. Here is the important point that we must remember if we want others to listen to what we have to say: they do not care if we think we have the answer, but they are intent on knowing if we are capable of discussing the issue compassionately, intelligently, and with an open mind to other opinions. In effect, they are telling us, "You do not have to set me straight on this issue; just tell me what you believe and listen to me when I tell you what I believe."

There will be many people whose opinions are totally opposite your beliefs, and some of them will be aggressive or try to cram *their* dogma down your throat—the whole time trying to pressure you into believing that if you do not adopt a more liberal or conservative view, you are a bad or unloving person. But when the dust settles, the most lasting impression will not be your clever or convincing argument, but you—your attitude, willingness to listen, grace, and love. To the degree that God's love is truly reflected in your behavior, you will be considered a good person and your contribution to the conversation will be welcomed.

The challenge for us is not merely to present our case well (that is, to argue people over to our point of view) but to demonstrate that we care about all people, that our love is genuine, and that we hold out hope for everyone. Many Christians do not like to hear this, but in popular culture being *intolerant* of other people, their beliefs, and lifestyles is considered a greater moral failure than being gay. I have heard old-school believers react immediately, "Yeah? Well what about intolerance toward *Christians*? Everyone wants tolerance except when it comes to Christianity. Then intolerance is the rule." There are at least two problems with holding to this line of thinking.

First, there are many Christians who have earned the respect of nonbelievers. Nearly everyone who stands outside Christianity opposes not sincere and devout believers who demonstrate the love of Jesus but those whom they perceive as a threat, obnoxious, self-righteous, hypocritical, and judgmental. Unfortunately, there are enough Christians who fit this description to fuel distrust and dislike of Christianity for a long time. But there are not many sane people who seriously dislike Mother Teresa.

Second, we do not make the rules for engaging popular culture. Once we set foot on their turf, we have to respect their beliefs. We are "guests" in their house and should behave accordingly. If we appear intolerant, we will immediately be perceived as immoral. Why should they listen to an immoral person tell them about Jesus? You may argue, "But that's backwards! It's the adulterers and fornicators who are immoral." But you must realize that your views are of no consequence whatsoever *if you cannot communicate in a way that compels others to listen*. You might as well talk to a brick wall.

Is tolerance as terrible as some Christians make it out to be? Did Jesus immediately condemn the Samaritan woman (or any "sinner" for that matter) for having five husbands or living with a man who was not her husband? He did not condemn her for her lifestyle at all. He merely brought it up in conversation. Jesus showed remarkable tolerance for the variety of broken people who came across his path. Perhaps because he was loving and open to people, they were not offended when he told them, "Go your way, and sin no more."

I do not want to give you the impression that Christians are not allowed to have opinions, convictions, and firmly held beliefs. I am just saying that if we begin a conversation with "The Bible says . . . ," that's as far as we will get. People will immediately turn away, because it will sound to them as though we are speaking out of prejudice, that we do not sufficiently understand a complex subject, and that we are robotic and not speaking sincerely from our heart. We will sound like we do not *care*, and Christians, if anything, are supposed to care.

For new-school believers, when it comes to answering questions regarding sexual orientation, the first concern is not whether we have the one right answer but how well we represent Jesus Christ in our attitude, actions, and treatment of other human beings, regardless of sexual orientation. New schoolers recognize the importance of earning their right to be heard by demonstrating love, kindness, generosity, and respect for others. To be right is not always right. Can you have a civil conversation without trying to convince others they *must* come over to your viewpoint? Are you willing to listen, to plant seeds, to begin a relationship that can accommodate a running discourse? Can you be generous enough to agree to disagree? Being able to converse compassionately with someone on the topic of homosexuality is much more important and powerful today than walking in the door with all the answers.

Let me suggest that we can do other people a world of good if we choose to show up in their lives the way Matt described showing up at the youth group—humble, honest, struggling, sensitive, and compassionate. In other words, show up as Jesus did among the broken people of his world. Sometimes showing up in a conversation—full of grace and truth—is all you have to do to reflect the likeness of Jesus Christ. Sometimes that is all it takes to save a life.

14

Is It Wrong to Take a Job in a Bar?

A Job That Embodies the Sacred

M

Mike was one of the few friends I had growing up who attended a similar church and shared my beliefs. We enjoyed lots of laughs together and could tell many stories about pulling pranks on people and generally having a good time.

After high school Mike and I could have easily lost touch, but our faith in Christ had the effect of keeping us committed to each other. Still, we were different. I was impulsively drawn to adventure and jumped at every risk-taking opportunity to serve God that came my way. Give me a few bucks, an airplane ticket, my favorite jeans, and I was out of there.

On the other hand, Mike approached life methodically. He enrolled in college and earned a degree in education. I was always trying to recruit him into whatever escapade called me across the globe, and in my immaturity I assumed he was "selling out" for money and security rather than more important and eternal treasures. How wrong I was!

Elissa and I visited Mike not long after he had landed a job in a local high school. He began his teaching career in an inner-city school that suffered from a shortage of teachers. No one wanted to work there because the students were notorious for their bad behavior. But Mike took on the challenge. He soon figured out that he did a better job of winning their attention if he taught unconventionally. For example, one day he wore a suit to school. While teaching, he took off his shoes, revealing mismatched socks with holes in them. He unbuttoned his suit jacket, and his tie was cut in half. When he removed his jacket, the sleeves were ripped off his collared shirt and his arms were tattooed. His antics illustrated his lecture, while holding his class in rapt attention. Mike engaged the students like no other teacher.

Mike watched the students jostle each other in the halls and observed the way the students engaged each other in hip banter, which the students call "battling"—a competition between two poets who compete at rhyming lyrics, showing off their own while attacking the other's skill. Spectators judge their efforts with ongoing verbal responses. The poet can either create lyrics on the spot or recite memorized lines. While other teachers on their way to the lounge ignored the students, Mike stopped and listened. Soon Mike was battling with the best of them. His secret? He would rap old rhymes from back in the day. In 1993 Mike and I listened to a lot of rap, hip hop, and The Tribe Called Quest. Mike found a way to put this interest to work and earned the reputation of being the teacher who was "off the hook"—slang for outstanding.

Mike developed such a strong reputation that when other teachers could not get their class to settle down, they would page Mike. The students respected him because he respected them and took the time to be with them. He learned how to communicate in their language and eventually became the most sought-after teacher in his area.

On a number of occasions Mike has served as an unofficial campus pastor for the students. Being able to connect with them in nontraditional ways has given him the opportunity to talk to them about God. I always knew he was a pastor; he simply has the gift. Anyone who knows Mike will tell you that ministry is in his heart. He is working every day, aware of God's presence and help. He does not need to plaster Jesus bumper stickers all over his car. He reveals Christ in his daily life.

I have other friends like Mike. One man I know started and runs a company that employs thousands of people; his goal is to provide jobs to help others care for their families. Another friend refurbishes older communities around the country, maybe a community near you. Another uses his earned wealth to support orphans and feed refugees. But no matter how God is using them in their current careers, when these people mix with those who hold paid positions in Christian organizations, they sometimes have been made to feel like second-class citizens.

What does it mean to be salt and light (Matt. 5:13–16)? I once heard a world-renowned Christian leader say, "You are either a missionary or a mission field." I would say that you are either a minister or a ministry, no matter what your career. In fact, we are all probably both minister and ministry, missionary and mission field.

I would like to see more Christians plunge into life and work the way Mike has in his teaching career. Can you imagine the transformation in our nation if every believer set out to "redeem" work and their work space? We *need* Christians in the workforce—factory workers, machinists, dentists, copyeditors, photographers, and postal workers.

Our nation could use a whole lot more Christian bartenders. Think about it. The bar is a place where people from all walks of life gather. Some come right from work, loosen their tie, and have a drink to relax. Others come to celebrate an event or watch a game with friends. Then there are those who come in complete despair. Whatever drives people to a bar, the bartender is the only person there who interacts with all of them. The bartender is often the promise of acceptance, the hope of forgetfulness. What if that bartender were a Christian? How many times a day could he share his life with another person? How many open conversations would he have every day? How bright would his life shine in that darkness?

What do you think about Christian bartenders? Is it a good idea? Would it be better if the person behind the counter were an unbeliever, someone who was there just for the paycheck? Would you be appalled or pleased if someone stood up in your Bible study group and shared about how her week went in the local bar? If we meet a stranger who says she works in a bar, do we immediately assume she does not know Jesus or would not be interested in hearing about him?

Why are young Christians who demonstrate a deep love for God told they need to go into the ministry? Why do we send strong believers off to spend the rest of their lives with other strong believers? Why do we leave unbelievers in the hands of professional evangelists who generally make no attempt to build loving relationships with them, console them, or provide helpful counsel but instead preach down to them in a language only other believers can understand?

There was a time when Christians understood that every chore, duty, and profession embodied the sacred as long as people had the "eyes to see and ears to hear." Martin Luther taught that all the things our bodies do, all of its external and physical activities, including its work with "needle and thimble," constitute "spiritual behavior if God's word is added to it and it is done in faith." He also addressed himself to Christian husbands and fathers who complained about the "bitterness and drudgery of married life" because of the menial tasks it required. He explained that faith opens the father's eyes to see "all these insignificant, distasteful, and despised duties in the Spirit, and is aware that they are all adorned with divine approval as with the costliest gold and jewels." In this new light, he realizes all the things he has to do for his child—"rock the baby, wash its diapers, make its bed, smell its stench, stay up nights with it, take care of it when it cries, heal its rashes and sores, and on top of that care for my wife"—meets with God's "perfect pleasure," and in fact he is unworthy of these special tasks. "God, with all his angels and creatures, is smiling—not because a man is washing diapers, but because he is doing so in Christian faith."[1] Can we learn to take faith with us into every imaginable job to beautify it with God's grace?

Sins We Love to Hate

Faith communities hold a variety of opinions regarding work inside and outside of religious institutions. Some religious subcultures in North America are defined by the boundaries they create for their members that distinguish them from the larger culture in which they exist. Ethnic cultures are easy to identify by such things as language, food, and unique traditions brought to the United States from the old country. Religious subcultures are not as easy to identify, though in some cases, such as the Amish, retro fashion/technology/symbol systems are clear indicators of their difference.

Fundamentalists and, perhaps to a lesser extent, evangelical subcultures also set themselves apart from mainstream culture. The more a religious subculture wants to separate itself from the larger culture, the more rules it will invent (as was the case among New Testament Pharisees). While the intention is to help each member live a righteous life in a sinful world, the rules also help old-school believers determine who is in their group and who is not, which for some religious communities is the same as distinguishing between the saved and the damned.

Because these religious subcultures exist within a larger and secular culture, it is convenient for them to identify specific "sin industries" that are off-limits to their faithful members. No doubt some industries produce commodities that most believers would agree are sinful (for example, pornography, prostitution, illegal drugs, black market adoptions). To some Christians there are also marginal industries, including gambling (and lotteries), alcohol, and in some states tobacco. Some believers occasionally boycott specific corporations and their affiliates for endorsing lifestyles or selling products that violate their beliefs or values, and I hope all Christians agree on boycotting companies that use sweatshops, slave labor, or child labor.

Preaching that targets sin industries condemns any use or engagement with their products or entertainment, especially employment in one of these industries. Believers who shun sin industries are convinced that Christians who work within them are compromising their faith and relationship with God.

The old-school attitude was based on two foundational premises—an inherent secular/sacred dichotomy of human society and a spiritual hierarchy of professions. Believers who are influenced by old-school thinking tend to divide careers into categories that are either "worldly" or "Christian." In fact, I have met people who, because they work in secular environments, doubt that their skills or knowledge have any value to God. To them a career that qualifies as having spiritual significance is one that is connected to some kind of evangelical endeavor through a church, foreign mission, religious publication and broadcasting, or a nonprofit charitable organization.

Once career categories are divided between secular and sacred, it is a short step to attributing prestige to one career and dishonor to another. In many old-school subcultures, the missionary profession stands at the apex, just above evangelist, pastor, and priest. To work for a computer firm, however, is way down the list. But if a computer tech wants to improve his status in the subculture, he can teach Sunday school and thereby move up the ladder of spiritual vocations. Forget that his technical expertise has value in itself as an expression of the image of God. All that matters in the subculture is that he scores well in the secular versus sacred axis.

Needless to say, within this system a career that has anything to do with sin industries is on the bottom rung. Tell a staunch fundamentalist that you are dealing cards in Las Vegas, trying out for a star role in an HBO special, or representing a beer company at a trade show, and you will quickly discover how far out of bounds you have wandered. In their mind "Christian" jobs are at one end of society and "non-Christian" jobs are at the other.

Speaking Their Language

While I was guest lecturing in a Bible school a couple of years ago, a young woman posed a problem during class time. She explained that her sister had become a model in Hollywood and was doing really well. Though she was raised in a Christian home, she was not currently attending church and did not feel any urgency to do so. Every time their father spoke to her sister, he got upset and told her she was going to hell. Rather than giving in to his threats, she became angry and even more resistant to church. If that is what church people thought of professional models like herself and her friends, she had no use for them.

The young woman's story agitated the other students, though a few of them were torn between family obligations and the father's insensitivity to his daughter's dreams and success. I attempted to walk them through this conflict—between the devout father and the apparently carefree daughter. I asked the young woman what she thought motivated her father to tell her sister she was going to hell.

"Well, he really believes she *is* going to hell," she answered.

"Yes, but why does he tell her she is going to hell?" I asked.

"Because he doesn't want her to go there."

"Exactly! And why doesn't he want her to go there?"

"Well, I think it's because my dad loves my sister."

"I think so too," I said. "So your dad loves your sister. When he talks to her, does she feel as though he communicates love?"

"No."

"Perhaps telling her she is going to hell is the most loving thing he can think of saying to her, like 'Don't play in the street, you'll get hit by a car' or 'Don't go near the pool, you'll fall in and drown.' The problem is that he may think he is communicating love and concern, but she hears rejection."

The students were nodding. Everyone has experienced the frustration of being misunderstood, and many of us know what it is to have a dad who finds it difficult to express his real feelings toward his children. Christians have often thought they were communicating good news to other people, but what others heard was bad news.

"Suppose your dad went about this another way," I suggested. "Imagine him calling your sister and saying something like, 'Hi, sweetheart, how are you doing?'"

The young woman rolled her eyes at the thought of her dad being that charitable, but she stayed with me.

"Your sister decides to be honest and tells him about her last three shows and her recent photo shoot and the possibility of appearing as an extra in a sitcom. He listens to her and makes interested sounds, like 'Uh-huh,' 'Hmm,' 'That's nice.' Then when your sister finishes, he says to her, 'Well, I'm very proud of you, honey. You chose your own career path and you've done quite well. I want you to know that I love you and I am praying for you.'"

The student had tears in her eyes. "I think that would totally change my sister's attitude toward my dad."

"Why?"

"Because she would know that he really loves her and cares about her as his daughter."

"That is what he thinks he's telling her already."

"Yes, he thinks so, but he's not."

The father will probably not be able to bring himself to communicate the message I suggested to his daughter, because of his saturation in old-school thinking. As long as she is in Hollywood, as long as she is modeling, as long as she is not going to church, there is no way—in his mind—that God can use her or she can be right with God. He will use every parental ploy at his disposal to try to control her decisions, and he will most likely continue to alienate her from him and from church.

The father's attitude is exactly what Matt has called into question above. Why does the daughter have to leave modeling? Why can't she find a Christian mentor to help her avoid the dangers of her profession and at the same time learn how to influence other lives? Imagine what good she could do among models who struggle with self-image issues and are bombarded with the message that their worth as humans depends on their physical beauty. For old-school thinkers, this is absurd. As long as she is in the "devil's industry doing the devil's work," she falls in the category of the backslidden believer.

Young people today do not live to work, but they work to live. Your education or degree does not mean you will work in your field of study, nor does having a great position in your company mean you will be there the rest of your life, next year, or even next month. Young people do not feel they are defined by their work, nor do they feel their spiritual lives are conditioned by their employment.

New-school believers are looking for ways to work within industries that influence people, change society, feed the hungry, care for the sick, give them a feeling of significance, and get as many people as possible thinking about Jesus Christ. They are wondering about how many broken people they could spend time with if they were bartenders. They would like to work on the inside of companies that the old school has handed over to the devil. They believe that working in a motorcycle shop or raceway will give them a better connection with bikers than the street preacher with a megaphone shouting condemnation. They recognize the influence that multinational corporations have in every part of the world, and they would like to direct that influence toward people at risk. They want to be everywhere for the cause of Christ.

Among new-school believers there is a general affirmation of life, nature, and the role of one's physical body in the service of Christ. Therefore, the vocabulary of the sacred and of the secular takes on different meanings. Even menial work—like flipping hamburgers, making calls in a telemarketing boiler room, dog grooming—can be made sacred. Therefore, teaching a Bible study is not necessarily more spiritual than writing a screenplay.

No longer do the professions of minister and missionary carry the prestige they once enjoyed. Old-school and mega-church preachers look too slick for new-school Christians, to say nothing of priests convicted of child molestation, preachers who have stolen funds or been caught in affairs, and missionaries who have obliterated cultures while converting and civilizing them. Religious careers are not as compelling as they used to be, and the "sin industries" do not look as dangerous as they appeared to conservative Christians of an earlier era.

Take the movie industry, for example. For a long time the old-school attitude has been, "Hollywood? Can anything good come from there?" In the more strict religious traditions, men and women vowed never to enter a movie theater, and I have heard a minister or two refer to theaters as "dark, seamy places." Some Christians draw the line at R-rated movies, others at PG-13, and others see only G-rated movies. That is, until February 25, 2004. That is the day Mel Gibson's movie *The Passion of the Christ* was released. Many old-school believers, who had long ago consigned Hollywood to the flames, were shocked by the fact that a gospel story they had read and heard expounded many times could be portrayed so well in film. Perhaps if more Christians understood the power of film to tell a story to the whole world, there would be more believers entering and influencing the television and movie industries.

New-school believers, however, were not surprised in the least by the effect *The Passion of the Christ* had on the entertainment industry and popular culture. In fact, they were waiting for a movie to come along with just this effect. If anything, many of them had hoped to produce or be involved in the first movie to move people in a profoundly spiritual way, and there were several sincere yet unsuccessful previous attempts (*The Omega Code*, *Left Behind*, *Joshua*, and others). The new-school generation was aware of the buzz generated by movies like *Fight Club* and the *Matrix* and *Lord of the Rings* trilogies. They knew a movie could be made that would have a similar potential for spiritual impact. The *Passion* merely proved it was possible with one particular form. Other movies will follow—provided new-school Christians are able to go where they feel led to be.

New schoolers are not asking whether they should work in places like Las Vegas or Atlantic City but how they can "live

Jesus" in their career. They want to know if their own behavior as an employee is ethical and if it is possible to discover the sacredness of their work. They do not fear occupations that take them into the heart of popular culture but want to know what industries have the greatest need for Christian influence, what companies will enable them to do the most good for people in need, and how they can meet their financial needs and still do short-term work overseas. If Jesus was willing to die for them between two thieves—and win one of them to the kingdom of God while dying—then they can live for Jesus in any kind of environment to which they are called.

15

Where Is Your God?

Caring Enough to Listen

I love this island of Hawaii for many reasons, but one outstanding feature is the fact that we have not been overrun by urbanization. When there is a full moon in a cloudless sky, its brilliance is not diminished by street lights, security lights, parking lot lights, and so on. Surfing the gentle waves of Kona under a full moon in a cloudless sky is one of life's great pleasures. My friends and I work our schedules so we can all go together, wait on the shore until the moon reaches the highest point in its arc through the sky, and surf our brains out. It's a little spooky sometimes but still a blast, especially when you surf with your buddies.

230 Frequently Avoided Questions

A few months ago the moon was bright, surf was up, and we were ready. We planned to meet at our favorite nighttime surf spot at ten o'clock. Jay and I were running late, and by the time we made it down to the beach, a layer of clouds hung between us and the moon, making it difficult to see (there are a lot of rocks and coral where we surf). After walking down to the water, we decided to sit and watch our friends surf. They were out there hooting and hollering, and quite a few times running into each other. We sat on a log, waiting to see if the sky would clear. Something about being out in creation, late at night with a good friend, causes the human heart to open.

Jay had been working as an outreach coordinator for one of our discipleship programs. While traveling and leading teams to several different countries, he had met a cute Norwegian girl named Gunn. When they were dating, everyone who knew them thought they were the nicest couple in the world. Gunn's eyes and smile are kind. A few minutes after you meet Jay, you feel like you have been best friends for years. I know it's an old, corny cliché, but their relationship was a match made in heaven.

On one of their travels, Gunn became ill and the doctor she saw determined that she had picked up a parasite, which is very common in Southeast Asia. The illness is bad, but the effects of the medicine are even worse. She took the medicine, but before she was completely well, she began to manifest other symptoms. The problem with the parasite was worse than the doctor had anticipated.

Gunn was very sick, could eat only certain foods, and would quickly run out of energy. Those were sad times, because whenever we got together over a big meal, there was poor Gunn eating her yogurt or crackers while we stuffed our faces with gourmet dishes. Of course, you never would have known that she was missing out on anything, because she was always bright and happy. We prayed for Gunn constantly, and in some ways I suppose we avoided asking for a miracle, not knowing how God might want to work in her illness. But Jay was facing Gunn's illness differently than the rest of us. He was accepting the fact that dealing with her suffering would be a way of life for him, especially because the doctors remained baffled as to the cause of Gunn's disease or whatever it was.

While watching our friends surf, Jay started telling me about a time when they invited a group of people into their home to pray for Gunn. The evening progressed in a fairly predictable pattern, and everyone was convinced they had done their best to pound on heaven's door for Gunn's healing. I am not sure of the details, but within a day or two Gunn started feeling better. After an office visit, her doctor announced there was no longer any sign of the parasite. She was thrilled and could hardly wait to tell all those who had prayed for her that God had heard and answered those prayers. The joy was contagious and increased everyone's belief in God's faithfulness to heal people in response to prayers. Everyone was ready to announce this miracle to the whole world. I had not been present for the prayer meeting but soon heard all of the happy reports. The whole episode was definitely a faith booster. Or was it?

A couple of weeks later Gunn began to feel really sick again. The same symptoms returned, and they had no idea why. Should they rush back to the doctor? But if she had been healed, would that be a lack of faith? And how did they know this was not some other illness? But they decided they would rather be safe than sorry, so they called the doctor and made an appointment. While in his office, they found out that she had not been healed from the parasite, but her symptoms had gone into remission. Shocked and disheartened, they went in search of a specialist who could give her the help she needed. God had not healed her after all.

Jay and I had a very open conversation that night by the ocean. We discussed how it felt to think God had performed a miracle in answer to prayer, only to have it snatched away. We both felt the same way about prayers that backfire; it sinks your faith. Once you open the door to these issues, you have to face the other questions: is God, this biblical God to whom we had devoted our lives and futures, is he real? Jay and I both knew book and seminar answers to this question, we have studied the philosophical problem that pain and suffering pose, and we understand the tension between living in a fallen world while believing in a perfect God. But at the end of the day his fiancée was so sick she was not going to be able to live and work for God in the way she had always dreamed.

So what's up with this world where anything can happen at any time, a world where there are no guarantees? You wake up one morning and learn that thousands of people are dead because some guy decided he does not like America. The world that Jay and I were born into is one in which nothing can be taken for granted, the family paradigm is destabilized, a blood transfusion meant to save a life may instead deliver death, and within the next nanosecond you could receive news that will radically alter your universe. The old question returns in a new context: how can a good God exist when the world is so full of pain and suffering?

There is one big difference between the old context and the new context. The standard answers—and most of the time, the philosophical answers—no longer work. The young girl who was gang-raped is not going to be consoled to learn that dark shades are added to the canvas to perfect the painting, that evil is merely the absence of good, or that God does not want us to be robots so he gave us the choice between good and evil.

This world of ours is chaotic, incoherent, and constantly morphing like a cosmic kaleidoscope. How do we address the problem of pain? Why are we reluctant to admit that the answers handed to us by our Christian teachers do not really satisfy us? Why are we given the impression that if we question God, we are somehow losing our faith? Is it all right for us to say that life stinks, to say out loud that the church's answers are not the answers at all?

When Jay first began to open up, I started into my "God is sovereign" speech but almost immediately realized I was going nowhere. No matter what I *said*, Jay's circumstances did not change. The raw reality was that Gunn was sick, and I found it difficult to just say, "Life can really stink sometimes, huh?"

We finished our conversation without closure. We were helpless, because there was nothing we could do for Gunn. We hoped and prayed she would get well, that someone was smart enough to give her the proper medication, or that God would do a real miracle. We hoped her ordeal would soon be over and she would be okay.

The full-moon surf night we spent talking rather than riding waves triggered some serious thinking for me later on. I thought of all the classes and books, the how-tos of answering questions, and the scripted speeches, but I could not remember a book or lecture that taught how to listen, how to shut my mouth and hear what the other person is saying. I wondered why we devote so much of our energy on learning what to say, rather than learning how to care enough to listen.

Are Christians exempt from suffering or doubts? Many of our Christian families are as dysfunctional as many others. We all struggle. Why are we not taught that it is a good thing to let people rant sometimes about how God let them down and admit that there are days when we too wonder if he exists? What would happen if we put aside our pat answers to pain and just listened to others' stories of suffering. What if we simply admitted that life hurts, it's not always easy, and sometimes our misery brutally challenges our belief in God.

Do you suppose it is possible that many people in popular culture would love to discover that Christians hurt too, are willing to listen to others, and will be compassionate and not attempt to answer the unanswerable? Do you suppose there are many people who either know our answers already or do not care to know them but would be grateful to learn that being persons of faith does not mean we never doubt but that eventually we move beyond doubt? Do you suppose these same people would be thrilled if we sat with them, listened to them, and admitted that as much as we love God and believe in him, these sorts of experiences cause us also to ask the same questions about his existence? Could that kind of honesty build greater trust and give them more comfort than hearing little sermons on the benefit of grief and pain?

Real Life

When I got to my desk this morning, the first item on my "to do" list was to send Matt an email. We live five thousand miles apart, and since he and Elissa are three hours behind our time zone, I did not want to call. We were ready to write the last chapter of the book and needed to talk some things over. To be honest, we had run into a snag. In our previous two conversations, we discovered that neither one of us felt comfortable with the question we had chosen for the end of the book. So in my email I suggested that we drop that question and look instead at Where is your God? A couple of hours later Matt sent me the following message: "That is AWESOME! What a perfect idea. What a relief." We both got our second wind and were ready to complete the project.

But then . . .

I am sitting in my car as I write these paragraphs. I almost always write using my computer. Writing long hand is for me both laborious and a waste of time—not to mention I cannot read my own writing. Correcting and editing a page of text is quick and easy with a word processor. But here I am in the parking lot of Hoag Memorial Hospital in Newport Beach. A few minutes after I received Matt's email this morning, I heard my wife, Barbara, on the phone downstairs. She was sobbing, so I went to her, wondering what terrible news she had received. Six years ago she lost her mother, and two years ago her father had passed away. This morning, her brother-in-law, Ray Duran, suffered a massive heart attack that ended his life. He was only forty-eight years old. So Barbara is now inside the hospital with her sister, Bonnie, and I am here in my car looking at the question, Where is your God?

Ray has always been one of those great guys. He was often the calm center at family gatherings, smoothing over any difficulties and making sure everyone else was having a good time. He loved Bonnie and his children, made friends with everyone he met, walked with God, wanted to assist others in their spiritual growth, volunteered tirelessly for Christian service, and enjoyed worship. In fact, I do not think I have ever seen Ray more passionate or excited than when playing drums with the worship team that he drew together for his church. At this particular moment, I cannot imagine what life will be like without him. I realize now I had assumed Ray would always be nearby.

What is this deep emotional pain that rips our hearts to shreds when we suffer the irreversible loss of someone we love? Two weeks ago a friend who is grieving the loss of his wife asked me, "Why do you think God gave us the capacity to feel such deep pain?" He was asking one of those "why" questions that people raise when suffering overrides their rational ability to comprehend it. When our grief is unbearable, we ask "why" questions, not only because we are curious about God's wisdom but because we doubt it. This skepticism is at the heart of what may have been the greatest challenge Christians have faced in the last one hundred years when arguing for the existence of the biblical God.

Through the centuries philosophers and theologians have produced many arguments for and against the existence of God (or a god). Most of those arguments flew right over the heads of the general public without having a direct influence on their opinions or beliefs. But one argument that did not fly over their heads is rooted in a reality that every human must face sooner or later: the world God created is imperfect; it is disfigured by instances of moral evil (immorality) and natural evil (physical suffering). If God is all-good, then why/how does evil exist in the world he created? If God is all-loving, then why/how do pain and suffering exist? If God is all-wise, why could he not think of a way to achieve his objectives apart from evil and suffering? If God is all-powerful, why did he not create a different kind of universe?

The obvious contradiction between a God of love and the injustice, immorality, and suffering that are rampant in the world was addressed as early as Job (even earlier in other cultures) and finds expression in Israel's poems of complaint, which appear in the Psalms and prophetic writings. The book of Job does not provide a rational solution to the problem but seeks to satisfy (or dissolve) the question in the infinite greatness and sovereignty of God. Seeing that the Bible *presupposes* the existence and nature of God and credits him with everything that happens under his jurisdiction (which is to say, every historical event; see Isa. 45:7), the Bible's typical answer to the question of evil and suffering is:

Woe to the one who quarrels with his Maker—
An earthenware vessel among the vessels of earth!
Will the clay say to the potter, "What are you doing?"
Or the thing you are making say, "He has no hands"?
Woe to him who says to a father, "What are you
    begetting?"
Or to a woman, "To what are you giving birth?"

Isaiah 45:9–10 NASB

From the time that Christianity entered the Greek world (Hellenist culture), theologians were forced to return to the question of pain and evil with answers that were rational enough to satisfy the demands of logic. Irenaeus in the second century argued that the world was a "soul-making place," where evil was necessary for the moral development of humans. For Augustine in the fourth century, evil was the absence of good. The world as God created it was perfect, but evil entered as a result of the fall. Since that time others have argued that good and evil form a necessary organic unity; or that good (like the natural law of gravity) can result in evil; or that one form of evil is punishment to prevent a worse form; or evil results from the free will God gave humans because he wants us to choose the good.

In 1710 Gottfried Leibniz coined the term *theodicy* (*theo*, "God" and *dike*, "justice"), which became the standard philosophical word for arguments that attempt to *justify God* in the face of moral and natural evil. Theodicy is the attempt to reconcile the world as it is to a God who is omniscient, omnipotent, and omni-benevolent. More recently John Howard Yoder argued that theodicies are a form of idolatry, because if "God be God," then to whom does he have to justify himself? In an unpublished essay, Yoder asked three fundamental questions: where do you get the criteria by which you evaluate God and why are those criteria the right ones; why do you think you are qualified for the business of judging God; and if you think you are qualified for that business, how does your judgment proceed—what are the rules? Of course, this line of reasoning only works if someone already believes in God, which brings us back to where we started.

Perhaps the most famous argument to date against the existence of a good, wise, powerful God was J. L. Mackie's, which he presented in "Evil and Omnipotence."[1] His argument goes as follows:

1. God is omnipotent—there are no limits to what an omnipotent thing can do.
2. God is wholly good—a good thing always eliminates evil as far as it can. The exception is if there is a morally sufficient reason not to eliminate evil. An all-wise and all-powerful being would not have a morally sufficient reason to allow suffering.
3. A good, all-powerful thing eliminates evil completely.
4. There are instances of suffering and immorality in the world.

Mackie concludes that there is an inherent contradiction in the following three propositions: God is all-powerful, God is wholly good, and evil exists. Either God is not all-powerful and therefore cannot get rid of evil totally, or he is not wholly good—and in either case he would not be God—or we are wrong about there being instances of immorality and pain in the world. Though some religions deny the existence of pain and evil, that is not the nature of Christianity, nor is it true to human experience. The first two propositions, as Mackie states them, are contradicted by the third; therefore he concludes that God does not exist.

In *God and Other Minds*[2] Alvin Plantinga demonstrated that Mackie's premises are not logically conclusive, because they are poorly defined (for example, what is *omnipotence?*). But Plantinga's work, though highly regarded in the academic community, is lengthy and difficult to follow and, at any rate, has not received the same attention as Mackie's essay. How many Christians do you know who have heard Plantinga's argument? Yet all of us have heard people say they cannot believe in God because of the suffering and evil in the world. I am tempted to say that Mackie's essay was both the climax to the modern age and one of the signals that it was coming to a close. Where do humans go after they eliminate their Creator?

Simplistic Answers

Old-school believers are in plenty of debates about the pain and suffering problem. Perhaps people who grow up in the church and are taught about the fall, about Satan, and about Jesus's death for human sin have a more difficult time understanding the magnitude of this problem. Therefore some of the answers they give in the heat of an argument (or in a sermon or apologetics seminar where there are no opponents to object) fail to convince people outside the church that a loving God could have a legitimate reason to permit as much misery and oppression as we witness.

Here are some of the logical mistakes would-be defenders of the faith have made because they have not thought through the problem seriously enough:

1. They have used poor logic or a logical argument poorly (for example, an analogy).
2. They have presented a case that did not account for the magnitude of suffering that exists (for example, their argument did not prove why an animal would have to die a slow, painful death in the desert far from any human being).
3. They have failed to show how the good that follows from pain is worth it.
4. They have not taken into consideration the possibility that an all-wise God could come up with a better idea.
5. They have not established a strong connection between good and evil to prove that evil is a logical necessity.

These mistakes by themselves are not serious problems, because if a person is sincere, reasonable, and agreeable, then others can appreciate her efforts to address the issue or to make it possible for an unbeliever to believe. Unfortunately, the old school has not been known for its patience, kindness, or tolerance for skeptics, agnostics, and atheists. Regardless of their attitude, old-school answers to the problem of evil are not as effective today as they were forty or fifty years ago, especially when the answers come straight from the Bible, are cliché, are given in a heavy-handed manner, sidestep the issue, or treat the other person as though he has blasphemed God simply for asking the question.

Often old-school preachers and evangelists (and so also those who follow their teaching) have brushed off this difficult subject with simple dismissals like, "How God can be good and allow evil is a mystery we will never understand," "You cannot create a mountain without creating a valley," or "God's painting of the universe requires dark strokes as well as light." To treat this issue as if it could be so easily waved off is disrespectful to the person who asked the question, to people who suffer, and to God.

Believers who enjoy popularized apologetics need to realize it is much easier for our arguments to succeed when we are talking among ourselves and everyone present is in agreement. Christians who debate on blog sites or in chat rooms have a better idea of the sorts of objections people will raise to their answers, and they also discover the arguments that work and those that do not. But sadly, when believers despair of their ability to answer questions, they often resort to messages like, "You will burn in hell for disagreeing with God's Word!" Definitely old school.

Taking the Spiritual Journey Together

If someone is willing to listen to us explain why we believe God is justified in allowing pain and suffering, we might want to treat our conversation as a quest for truth, drop our dogmatism, and take seriously the other person's objections. Otherwise we are preaching, not conversing. The art of pleasantly ending a conversation is also helpful if the other person is belligerent or obviously interested in arguing only for argument's sake.

When dealing with the problem of evil, the most severe weakness of the old school has been its tendency to confront the apologetic challenge and fail to hear the voice of suffering behind the question, "Where is your God?" The unspoken assumption that often lies behind this question today has not so much to do with atheism as with the fact that it feels like we have been deserted. To not weep with the person who suffers but rather to offer platitudes, Bible verses, even excellent philosophical lectures is like sending greeting cards to people in a burning building. We need to listen to the *voice* and not merely the words. As Matt said, we need to listen to people and listen especially to the *way* they ask the question, "Where is your God?"

I do not know whether there will be a new-school apologetic. My suspicion is that Christians will become the apologetic. In other words, *you* are the new apologetic, which means the way you live is much more important than the words you speak, no matter how articulate, profound, and convincing your arguments. So working where there is human suffering (for instance, caring for AIDS babies in Africa) is a convincing theodicy, because it demonstrates to the world that God is doing something about human suffering; he is sending us into the heart of it to heal and redeem it.

I do not know if we will see a postmodern theodicy that will have the same influence in popular culture as Mackie's essay. However, there is an interesting possibility for a new way to think about the problem that I will mention in passing. Zachary Braiterman is well versed in the works of post-Holocaust Jewish theologians, whose thinking about God and Scripture has been altered by the effective means of modern technology in the extermination of Jews. In *(God) after Auschwitz*, Dr. Braiterman connects postmodernism with the revised Jewish theology (since the Holocaust), producing a new theological position that he has dubbed "antitheodicy." Conservative Christians who maintain that the whole Bible is a reliable authority regarding the revelation of God will not share his conclusions, but we may perhaps find some interesting possibilities for enabling people to transcend doubt because they cannot find a satisfactory, rational answer to this problem.

If a theodicy seeks to justify God in the face of his flawed universe, an antitheodicy "refuses to justify or explain" the relationship between God, evil, and pain or to find any redeeming value in catastrophic suffering. Antitheodicy is essentially complaint against God. If antitheodicy sometimes sounds like blasphemy (as Job's complaint sounded like blasphemy to his friends), it "does not constitute atheism; it might even express stubborn love that human persons have for God." In fact, the person who raises the complaint against God must not only believe in God but must also love him to be offended by his relationship to evil.[3]

In the musical *Fiddler on the Roof*, Moscow orders a political "demonstration" in the village of Anatevka, where Tevye lives. So during an engagement celebration for his oldest daughter, local authorities stage a raid. Music, dancing, and laughter are suddenly replaced by hoof beats, clanging swords, and destruction. Tevye stands in the middle of the square with remnants of the demolished decorations, food, and gifts strewn around the broken tables, looking up at God. With palms turned upwards, he lifts his shoulders and gestures with his hands as he mouths a soundless, "Why?" He does not reject God, but neither does he let God off the hook for the unnecessary and meaningless assault on their village.

The general attitude of Western society at the beginning of the twentieth century was almost comical in comparison to the way the twenty-first century started. The early 1900s were marked by heady optimism, whereas today the general attitude is disenchanted cynicism. The "power of positive thinking" still made sense in the 1950s because Westerners believed that anything they wanted, science would eventually give them. Now people do not want the world of unforeseen and unwanted by-products that science has given them. There is no denying the beauty of creation, but when we come on a beer can when hiking in the Sierras, we realize that everything humans have touched is spoiled.

So an antitheodicy might work for people who, no matter how hard they look at the dark clouds of human society, simply cannot find the silver lining. Perhaps there is a way through the problem of pain and evil that surrenders itself to the sovereignty of God at the same time it raises a constant cry of complaint until he finally turns back the tide of suffering and immorality. Braiterman concludes his first chapter with this tentative observation: "Perhaps after Auschwitz, to some degree or another, the act of loving God must remain unjustified."[4]

New-school Christians are not likely to attempt to produce a new philosophical answer to the problem of pain and evil. Rather, they struggle with the question along with everyone else. With their lives more so than with their words, they try to show others how God enters the places of dark suffering, redeems that which has been defaced by evil, and deals with it not as a theoretical challenge to be solved but as an empirical tragedy to be remedied. They seek to live as people who have been enlightened by Jesus Christ, who was both Victim of and Victor over evil and suffering.

Answer with Actions

We should not think new-school believers are afraid of difficult questions or hope to avoid having to address them. They realize the limitations of attempting long, complicated equations in a sound-bite culture. There is a place for academic argumentation and logical proofs, but it is not in the streets. There we must attend to evil, as a threat to righteousness, and suffering, as a threat to shalom.

If we are going to try to grasp the whole idea of injustice, suffering, and immorality; how these things relate to God and his creation; and how they affect a human being, we cannot find a better reference than the book of Job. The story of Job presents a soul that is wracked with grief and misery and tells about how Job calls every belief into question and moves through several stages in search of resolve. It also beautifully illustrates the shattering of comfortable religious worldviews that allegedly have God and his universe all figured out. We must not, however, give in to the modern temptation of chopping Job up into unrelated pieces of literature; otherwise, we miss the point that the wise people who really knew about suffering and sadness were trying to tell us. All the questions we have about why God allows pain and evil are resolved, not through philosophical speculation, but in a breathtaking encounter with God himself.

Our church is currently going through the book of Job in our weekend services. I am not teaching Job as a Bible study. I am turning my research of this mind-boggling book into something like a mini-novel and then reading the results of my own study in story form. Even without lengthy historical, theological, and literary explanations, people are hearing universal themes of suffering, doubt, prayer, debate, anger, frustration, and sorrow in ways that awaken the broken places in their own souls and give them hope. The value of this compelling and dramatic story does not lie in Job's restoration at the end but in everything that comes before that last episode.

One form that the new question of pain and evil takes is reflected in the following excerpt from an email sent to me by a university student in San Diego. He has expressed well the urgency of his concerns:

> Now, an all-seeing, all-knowing God such as that described by the Bible must surely have foreseen the results of Jesus' coming to Earth. As I understand the whole story, Jesus was "sent down" to cleanse the world of evil, to turn men back to "goodness" and away from evil. But look at the world in which we live today! There is nothing but lies and corruption and war. There is nothing but hopelessness and decay and pollution. We are killing our world and we are killing the souls and the spirits of the people that live upon it. OK, so things are pretty "happy" and content here in Southern California, but at what expense? We cover our lives with materialism and cosmetics and television, and all people seem to do is ignore the difficult questions about life and replace them with another bowl of ice cream! This world is in a terrible, terrible state. I read the newspaper every day and follow world events on the internet all the time. The state of the Middle East terrifies me, the rampant corruption inherent in practically every government brings me to despair and the religious hatred that runs deep in every race of the world gives me no hope for humanity. Where then, are the results of Jesus' work? I see no evidence that the world has become a better place than

it once was . . . so . . . what was the "point" of Jesus? (or, to put it bluntly surely Jesus "didn't work," and . . . God, as all-knowing, knew he wouldn't, so . . . why bother?)

When I replied to him, I began with a confession and an apology. If world conditions make it seem like Jesus "didn't work," it is the fault of his church in whose hands he left the mission of world transformation. I explained that Jesus's teachings have inspired some of the most beautiful acts of love and personal sacrifice in the last two thousand years, so his teachings have worked. Unfortunately, few Christians have risen to the level of virtue and love embodied by his life and lessons.

Even though this young man is attending a university, acquiring skills in critical thinking, and being exposed to philosophy and logic, he was not really asking me to produce an argument that was logically satisfying. He is frustrated not because he is working on a difficult riddle or math problem that he cannot solve but because he *feels* the weight of a world burdened by violence, oppression, greed, innocent suffering, and grief. As is the case for most people, it is not the pure logic of the problem that prevents him from reconciling the God of the Bible with the world of experience, but rather it is the tension he feels when trying to live with a belief that is contradicted by circumstances.

Many new-school believers are trying to rectify Christianity's poor record of world change. Matt and I can list dozens of believers from South America to Southeast Asia, from Russia to South Africa who are working with street children, AIDS babies, orphans in refugee camps, impoverished farm communities, and residents of war-torn countries. But there are too few Christians living the agenda of Jesus (Luke 4:18–21), and the church is simply not doing enough to produce more believers whose evangelism is the life they lead and who defend the faith with acts of charity. If every Christian in the world, in a community, or even in one church would do one thing once a week to improve the life of another person, we could point to something significant and convincing when people ask, "Where is your God?"

Postscript

C

Matt and I are not rebels, prophets, or troublemakers. We want believers to hear the questions that are being asked outside the bubble of evangelicalism—and among evangelical young people when their parents are not around. We suspect that many of our readers are already aware of these questions and approach them in ways similar to what you have read in this book. We hope to get people thinking out loud, testing the boundaries and legitimacy of their traditions, and expanding their worldview. We also hope to generate more conversations regarding these issues and more action that will lead to positive change.

We are not interested in rebellion, because rebellion is about being *against* something. We would like to see a revolution, however, which is about producing major change. What happened in the Garden of Eden was a rebellion, not a revolution. Even though our careers have us (for the time being) embedded in specific religious organizations, our experience of church is broad. We love the whole community of Christian believers; we love God's church. We simply want to see Christians think through new paradigms that will enable them to live more joyfully with God and more effectively for him.

The questions in this book are only a small handful of the countless quandaries put to Christian young people every day. Some of the questions we thought about but did not include are, Should *Left Behind* be left behind? Do I have to join a political party? If this is the "abundant life," why did it get so difficult? If God is so awesome, why is church so boring? If Christianity is everything the New Testament says, why doesn't it transform more Christians? If you have an important question that we have missed, we would love to hear from you and add your questions to our list.[1]

M

The revolution, as Chuck said, begins in our hearts and minds. A professor at the University of the Nations has recently felt compelled to remind his students constantly of the truth embodied in Richard Weaver's book *Ideas Have Consequences*. Every one of the billions of people on this planet is a complex and intricately designed being. Potentially any one of us could produce an idea that would have huge consequences in our culture. The fact of knowing God increases the possibility of our articulating a concept that reconfigures society. If God were to grace us with a prophetic imagination, we could participate in his (re)creation of society.

Only a few weeks ago I witnessed the power of (re)creation while experimenting with new ideas. The last time Chuck was in Kona, he wanted to catch one of marketing strategist Gordon Pennington's lectures, so we slipped into the classroom and listened to Gordon talk about revolutions. Both Martin Luther and Hitler set off revolutions by generating and communicating ideas that had consequences for millions of lives in multiple generations. Gordon asked the class if it was possible to set loose some ideas on campus that might provoke a revolution of love. He had us separate into teams according to our abilities and interests—creative writers, graphic artists, computer geeks, and so on. Each group sought inspiration from God, the ultimate creative mind, then we combined our brainpower in the quest of generative ideas.

The process and results were amazing. After a few minutes of discussion, the depth and brilliance of the ideas that were flying around blew me away. It was a wild and exhilarating morning as I watched the blue ideas meet the yellow ideas, which created green ideas. Students volunteered their thoughts, fed off the thoughts of others, stimulated even more ideas, producing even more original combinations. It was crazy. We dreamed up a marketing campaign, developed communication tools (in multiple languages—the revolution was suddenly global!), and put our artists to work on T-shirt designs and campus signs.

What if Christians engaged in this sort of exercise all the time? What if we were committed to the synergy Paul and John mentioned in the New Testament ("fellow workers" in 1 Corinthians 3:9 and "work together" in 3 John 8, which translate to a concept we would call today "synergy")? What if we dedicated a time together—on living room floors, in coffee shops, around a park bench—intending to start a revolution in the world, with God leading the creative process? What if we were not all waiting for one person to come up with the next great idea, but set thousands of young people free to collaborate and create new ideas?

How far could the revolution go? What if we created new systems and structures to effectively accommodate a biblical faith and reveal Jesus Christ to popular culture? What if we created new models, wrote new laws, created new businesses, set our sights on leading the nation, producing cures for AIDS and cancer, and producing a better means of supplying food, clothing, and shelter to the world's poor and starving? What if our lives became more than just a career and developed instead into an irrefutable demonstration of God at work on earth? What if we got deep into all sorts of new ideas and discovered the pleasure and happiness for which we have always yearned, but never found, because joy is found in living for others rather than for ourselves?

This is doable! We begin with questions, and the first one is, "If God is for us, who can be against us?" (Rom. 8:31). Until we are imprisoned for our faith, persecuted from the face of the earth, or breathe our last breath, we can be innovators and sculptors and have a hand in shaping the remainder of this century. This short life is my chance, it is your chance, it is our chance to launch the revolution.

Notes

Chapter 2 Why the Bible?

1. N. T. Wright, *The New Testament and the People of God* (Minneapolis: Fortress, 1992), 385.

2. If you are interested in a brief overview, see Nancey Murphy, *Beyond Liberalism and Fundamentalism* (Harrisburg, PA: Trinity Press, 1996), especially pp. 1–35. For a more detailed study, see Stanley Grenz and Roger Olson, *Twentieth-Century Theology* (Downers Grove, IL: InterVarsity, 1992).

3. Francis Schaeffer, *The Church at the End of the Twentieth Century* (Downers Grove, IL: InterVarsity, 1971), 72–73, 134, 141.

4. Wright, *New Testament and the People of God*, 5.

5. Kathleen Boone, *The Bible Tells Them So: The Discourse of Protestant Fundamentalism* (London: SCM, 1990), 83–84. In my opinion, this is a book every thinking Christian should read.

6. Augustine, *On Christian Doctrine* (ii. 60–61). *The Nicene and Post-Nicene Fathers*, vol. 2 (Grand Rapids: Eerdmans, 1979), 554–55. He begins chapter 60: "Moreover, if those who are called philosophers, and especially the Platonists, have said aught that is true and in harmony with our faith, we are not only not to shrink from it, but to claim it for our own use from those who have unlawful possession of it." *The Confessions of Augustine* (vii. 9) *The Nicene and Post-Nicene Fathers*, vol. 1 (Grand Rapids: Eerdmans, 1979), 109.

7. Justin Martyr, *The Second Apology of Justin Martyr*, vol. 1 of *The Ante-Nicene Fathers* (Grand Rapids: Eerdmans,1979), 193.

8. John Calvin, *Institutes of the Christian Religion* (ii. 2.15–16), vol. 20 of *Library of Christian Classics* (Philadelphia: Westminster Press, 1960), 273–75.

Chapter 3 Do I Have to Go to Church?

1. Pete Ward, *Liquid Church* (Peabody, MA: Hendrickson, 2003), 18.
2. Jonas Ridderstrale and Kjell Nordström, *Funky Business* (London: BookHouse, 2000), 57.
3. Jeanne Halgren Kilde, *When Church Became Theatre: The Transformation of Evangelical Architecture and Worship in Nineteenth-Century America* (New York: Oxford University Press, 2002).
4. Ridderstrale and Nordström, *Funky Business*, 57.

Chapter 4 Do I Have to Sell God?

1. N. T. Wright, *What Saint Paul Really Said* (Grand Rapids: Eerdmans, 1997), 41.

Chapter 5 Can Christianity Be Reduced to Steps or Stages?

1. Bill Bright, *Have You Heard of the Four Spiritual Laws?* (Orlando: Campus Crusade for Christ International, 1965).
2. Mike Yaconelli, *Messy Spirituality* (Grand Rapids: Zondervan, 2002).
3. Rick Warren, *The Purpose-Driven Life* (Grand Rapids: Zondervan, 2002).
4. http://www.radicalcongruency.com/20040327-the-angst-driven-life.
5. George Ellis, "Intimations of Transcendence: Relations of the Mind and God" in *Neuroscience and the Person: Scientific Perspectives on Divine Action*, eds. Robert John Russell, Nancey Murphy, Theo C. Meyering, and Michael A. Arbib (Berkeley, CA: Center for Theology and the Natural Sciences, 2002), 451.
6. Walter Brueggemann, *Finally Comes the Poet* (Minneapolis: Fortress, 1989), 109–10.
7. Ibid.
8. Wright, *The New Testament and the People of God*, 40, 67–74.
9. Walter Brueggemann, *Texts under Negotiation* (Minneapolis: Fortress, 1993), 25. See pp. 21–25 as well as his comments in *Cadences of Home* (Louisville, KY: Westminster John Knox Press, 1997), 25.
10. Ibid., 34–36.

Chapter 6 Does God Speak outside the Bible?

1. David Dark, *Everyday Apocalypse* (Grand Rapids: Brazos Press, 2002).
2. Ibid.,19.

Chapter 7 Is Forgiveness Real?

1. Vincent Brümmer, *The Model of Love* (London: Cambridge University Press, 1993), 185.

Chapter 8 What Makes the Christian Experience Unique?

1. Ronald H. Bainton, *Here I Stand: A Life of Martin Luther* (New York: Penguin, 1995), 144.

2. Calvin, *Institutes of the Christian Religion* (ii. 2.12, 17; i. 7.4; i. 8), 270, 276.

3. Charles Hodge, *Systematic Theology* (Grand Rapids: Eerdmans, 1977), 2.

4. Ibid., 178.

5. B. B. Warfield, "Apologetics" in *The New Schaff-Herzog Encyclopedia of Religious Knowledge,* ed. Samuel Jackson, vol. 1 (Grand Rapids: Baker, 1977), 237.

6. B. B. Warfield, "Editorial Notes," *Bible Student,* n.s. (Jan. 1901): 1–5.

7. If you are unfamiliar with the meaning of *postmodern,* please see Chuck Smith Jr., *There Is a Season: Authentic, Innovative Ministry in Popular Culture* (Colorado Springs: WaterBrook Press, 2005).

8. Calvin, *Institutes of the Christian Religion* (i.7.5), 80. Beginning with Calvin's internal witness of the Holy Spirit, Bernard Ramm developed this "experiential" theme in both theological and personal dimensions in *The Witness of the Spirit* (Grand Rapids: Eerdmans, 1960).

9. See, for instance, Morton Marks, "Uncovering Ritual Structures in Afro-American Music"; Erika Bourguignon, "Cross-Cultural Perspectives on the Religious Uses of Altered States of Consciousness"; and Felicitas Goodman, "Trognosis: A New Religion?" in *Religious Movements in Contemporary America,* eds. Irving Zaretsky and Mark Leone (Princeton, NJ: Princeton University Press, 1974).

Chapter 9 Are Christians the Morality Police?

1. Author Anne Lamott made this statement during an interview with Chris Seay at a writers' conference at Baylor University.

Chapter 10 Do Good People Go to Hell?

1. Walther Eichrodt, *Theology of the Old Testament* (Philadelphia, PA: Westminster Press, 1961), 207.

2. Ibid., 206.

3. Ibid., 208.

4. Dark, *Everyday Apocalypse,* 18.

Chapter 11 Does the Bible Contradict Evolution?

1. Ronald Numbers, *The Creationists: The Evolution of Scientific Creationism* (Los Angeles: University of California Press, 1993), 73–74.

2. See http://cesc.montreat.edu/ceo/ASA.

3. Robert Wright, *Three Scientists and Their Gods* (New York: Perennial Library, 1989), 191.

4. For a better scientific explanation from someone who knows what he is talking about, see Dr. John Sarfati's article, "Origins of Life: The Chirality Problem" at http://www.answersingenesis.org/docs/3991.asp.

Chapter 12 Am I Supposed to Hate the World?

1. H. Richard Niebuhr, *Christ and Culture* (New York: Harper and Row, 1951), 3.

2. George Marsden, "Christianity and Cultures: Transforming Niebuhr's Categories," *Christian Ethics Today* (Dec. 2000), 18–24.

3. Ibid. What Marsden means by *dualism* is the implication that "Christ" and "culture" belong to two different sorts of reality.

4. Walter Brueggemann, *The Prophetic Imagination* (Minneapolis: Fortress, 1978), 50.

Chapter 14 Is It Wrong to Take a Job in a Bar?

1. From Martin Luther's "Treatise on the Estate of Marriage," quoted in Paul Marshall and Lela Gilbert, *Heaven Is Not My Home: Learning to Live in God's Creation* (Nashville: Word, 1998), 77–78.

Chapter 15 Where Is Your God?

1. J. L. Mackie, "Evil and Omnipotence" in *Reason and Responsibility: Readings in Some Basic Problems of Philosophy*, ed. Joel Feinberg (Belmont, CA: Wadsworth, 1981), 70–77.

2. Alvin Plantinga, *God and Other Minds: A Study of the Rational Justification of Belief in God* (Ithaca, NY: Cornell University Press, 1975).

3. Zachary Braiterman, *(God) after Auschwitz: Tradition and Change in Post-Holocaust Jewish Thought* (Princeton, NJ: Princeton University Press, 1998), 4.

4. Ibid.

Postscript

1. Come and dialogue with us at www.godrisk.com.

Chuck Smith Jr. started Capo Beach Calvary in Capistrano Beach, California, and has served as its pastor for thirty years. His current passion is the journey to a spiritual life in God that he calls the "real deal" and helping others understand the importance of receivng the spirit of wisdom and revelation to know God. Chuck is a popular speaker and author of several books. He and his wife, Barbara, live in Dara Point, California.

Matt Whitlock works for Youth With A Mission (YWAM) at their training location in Kona, Hawaii, known as University of the Nations. There he teaches, is involved with leadership, and is a consultant to leadership groups. He and his wife, Elissa, have traveled with YWAM around the world.